Disability and Child
Sexual Abuse

Disability and Child Sexual Abuse

Lessons from Survivors' Narratives for Effective Protection, Prevention and Treatment

Martina Higgins and John Swain

Jessica Kingsley Publishers
London and Philadelphia

First published in 2010
by Jessica Kingsley Publishers
116 Pentonville Road
London N1 9JB, UK
and
400 Market Street, Suite 400
Philadelphia, PA 19106, USA

www.jkp.com

Library of Congress Cataloging in Publication Data
Higgins, Martina.
    Disability and child sexual abuse : lessons from survivors' narratives for effective protection, prevention and treatment / Martina Higgins and John Swain.
      p. cm.
    Includes bibliographical references and index.
    ISBN 978-1-84310-563-3 (pb : alk. paper) 1. Child sexual abuse--Case studies.
2. Children with disabilities--Case studies. I. Swain, John. II. Title.
    HV6570.H54 2009
    362.4083--dc22
                                                    2009017113

British Library Cataloguing in Publication Data
A CIP catalogue record for this book is available from the British Library

ISBN 978 1 84310 563 3

Printed and bound in Great Britain by
Athenaeum Press, Gateshead, Tyne and Wear

Dedication

To our children:
Holly, Anna, Daniel, Sam and Tamsin

Acknowledgements

Our thanks go to the people whose stories are the foundation stones for this book – Lyn, Josh, Jean, May, Thomas, Chloe and Lizzie. Without their resilience and determination to tell their stories we could not have written this book.

Contents

Introduction

To address the sexual abuse of children is to step across the gulf between the private and personal, and the public and societal. Child sexual abuse is a violence, which violates lives. It turns the connectedness between human beings, the sharing of warmth and tenderness, into destruction, isolation and fear; humanity turned into inhumanity. Child sexual abuse, then, is not simply an arena for expert knowledge, but is an aspect of human existence that touches all our lives and challenges our values and beliefs about the society in which we live.

The power of this book lies in the detailed narratives of a group of disabled survivors whose circumstances, age and impairments differ markedly. Their stories reflect the experiences of those who have been silenced, in the first instance, by child sexual abuse, and then silenced once again by a society that is not motivated enough to hear what they have to say. As a result of the clear articulation of their ever-evolving life story account, their narrative offers unique perspectives that extend an existing, but limited, knowledge base. Furthermore, their stories ask professionals to examine their belief systems and professional practice, asking others to consider the implications of these narratives for therapeutic intervention. This book, therefore, is intended for both survivors of child sexual abuse and practitioners alike. It offers hope to those who are coming to terms with their past, and provides insights for childcare practitioners working both in the field and within different therapeutic settings.

It is grounded in and generated by a research project conducted by Martina for her doctorate (Higgins 2006) and supervised by John. Seven stories, or narratives, are the backbone of this book, told by disabled people who have experienced sexual abuse. They talk of their experiences, the support that they did or did not receive, their personal relationships and, at heart, the violence that shaped themselves and their lives.

In childhood, the barriers to disclosing sexual abuse are numerous and well documented. Disabled children, who are at increased risk of child sexual abuse, may face extra deterrents when trying to tell their story. These deterrents are both impairment related and attitudinal. The complex patterns of service delivery, designed to support and assist disabled children and their families, can create situations of increased risk. Children placed in segregated educational settings, for example, can encounter ad hoc placement reviewing procedures (Morris, Abbott and Ward 2002), and are often isolated from their friends and family; people who might potentially pick up on the signs of their distress (Kennedy 1996; Williams and Morris 2003). The experience of multiple carers, at home or within institutions, means that disabled children are more likely to encounter abusive adults. Limited access to appropriate communication tools, for children with speech and language impairments, cuts off avenues for disclosure (Kennedy 1996; 2002).

These factors are all in addition to the general wearing away of disabled children's self-confidence, by the prejudices they encounter in their daily lives and in different private and public settings. On a more general level, there is a belief by society that sexual abuse does not happen to disabled children (Kennedy 2002), an opinion which has hindered the development of thinking in this area. Similar to non-disabled survivors, disabled survivors are often only able to disclose their abuse, and attempt to piece together their personal life history, in later life and in the context of a trusting relationship. This book aims to expose readers to the stark reality of some disabled children's lives. It examines, in detail, the ways in which disabled children are disempowered and discounted in their encounters with others. Equally, it illustrates the capacity of disabled individuals to resist the devastating impact of their abuse and ultimately succeed in life.

MAKING SENSE OF TERMINOLOGY

Certain key terms frequently used within this book may have different meanings for different readers. This section of the introduction intends to pull apart some of this terminology and offer further explanation. Particular terms such as disability, for example, offer a perspective which requires the reader to look at the subject matter in a particular way. Its political energy weaves its way throughout the content of the book and asks the reader to link causality with the ways in which disabled people are treated by our society, rather than within the individual disabled child. Similarly, the less controversial definitions of child abuse and narrative are elaborated upon in order to establish the meaning that is intended.

Disability

Disability is understood in this book by applying a 'social model' perspective. The social model of disability makes a clear distinction between impairment, which is an individual's bio-physical condition, and disability, which describes the numerous ways in which disabled people are excluded by society (Barnes 1996). Exclusion can take many forms, ranging from the inaccessible built environment that disabled children have to deal with, to the prejudicial attitudes that they encounter daily. Disability theorists therefore define disability as a form of social oppression. The social model of disability stands in opposition to the more traditional and commonplace medical/tragedy model of disability (Swain and French 2000; Swain and French 2008). Whilst the social model positively affirms the presence of disabled people within society, the medical/tragedy model of disability focuses on bodily deficits and the necessity to achieve an ill-perceived normality.

Disability and impairment

Disability is a form of social oppression involving the social imposition of restriction of activity on people with impairments and the socially engendered undermining of their psycho-emotional well-being.

Thomas (1999, p.60)

Impairment is a characteristic, feature or attribute within an individual which is long-term and may, or may not, be the result of disease, genetics or injury.

Thomas, Gradwell and Markham (1997)

The medical model has traditionally dominated service provision for disabled people, where a charitable and individualizing essence has permeated service delivery. State responses to impairment have been focused on 'care', 'cure' and 'rehabilitation' (Priestley 1999) with a paradoxical aim to master impairment. Service delivery, however, continues to reinforce dependency and highlight a sense of inadequacy. The social model, by contrast, has been a liberating force in many disabled people's lives, both at an individual level, when trying to understand our own internalized oppression (Reeve 2002), and collectively, when groups of disabled people are motivated and inspired to take political action. It has formed the foundations of a developing disability culture, which celebrates difference and diversity, and identifies the positive psychological features of being able to opt out of a competitive mainstream culture (Swain and French 2000). One of the participants stated:

> There was no space for me in the world; there was nothing for me to do with my skills. There are things that I thought were bad points, that I now know are skills, things that you reclaim as a disabled person. That's what disabled people are supposed to be doing. We fight back, we fucking fight back, and if it takes me the rest of my life then I'll do everything I can to keep fighting back. (Chloe)

The social model has been criticized by a number of disabled feminists as marginalizing disabled people's personal reality, including that of impairment (Crow 1996; Morris 1991). The task in hand, however, must be to recognize the importance of both disability *and* impairment (Burke 2008; Thomas 2004), with recognition that impairment facilitated the subsequent theorization of disability (Thomas 2004). In addition to acknowledging the very real socioeconomic disadvantage that disabled people face within society, this book concerns itself ostensibly with the impaired body and its relationship with prejudice. The many manifestations of prejudice will be explored further in Chapter 3, but essentially prejudice marks a significant percentage of disabled and non-disabled people's interpersonal relationships. It contributes to disabled people's objectification (Shakespeare 1997) or dehumanization; a process referred to as 'othering' in feminist literature (Kitzinger and Wilkinson 1996). This prejudice has the potential to severely impact upon disabled people's emotional well-being and sense of who they are (Thomas 1999). For some, it can create self-imposed, self-limiting attitudes that the disabled person themselves are oblivious to (Marks 1999b).

The effect of understanding the sexual abuse of disabled children from a social model perspective, asks the reader to understand child sexual abuse from a standpoint of indifference (Calderbank 2000). Indifference means that as a society we are happy to collude in the creation of systems that segregate disabled children from the rest of society. As a result of indifference we are happy to place disabled children in situations of unacceptable risk.

Child abuse

> Children are the most vulnerable major subgroup of the human family; they are least capable of assuring their own welfare and most negatively affected by mistreatment. They are also the developing substance of the future of humanity. (Hart 1991, p.53)

It can be argued that the historical origins of abusive and devaluing childcare practices rest with the notion of 'children as property' (Hart 1991). By pointing to the work of others, Hart suggests that in the early histories of childhood, parents had unquestioned autonomy when raising their children, including the right to abandon, abuse or sell them. Over time, children have moved 'from property to person status' (p.55). This has resulted in the accumulation of particular rights, including a right to protection from harm, which might include harm perpetrated by a parent. Britain's continued ambivalence towards the issue of child protection and child abuse, however, can be most clearly observed in the continuing debate surrounding the use of 'reasonable physical chastisement'. Despite criticism from the European Court on Human Rights, Britain continues to withhold its position on a parent's right to physically chastise their children, but makes concessions by banning 'inhumane and degrading punishments' (Freeman 1999, p.131). Freeman (2000), who argues principally from a children's rights perspective, proposes that the outlawing of physical chastisement would mark a clear commitment by society to a child's protection rights. Without it, children will remain vulnerable and de-valued citizens.

Similarly, an ambivalent relationship towards child sexual abuse can be demonstrated. Attitudes have varied across history ranging from acknowledgement of its acceptability in early Christianity, to its later denial and reinterpretation as childhood fantasy (Armstrong 2000). Currently, whilst there is overt social condemnation of child sexual abuse, the reality is that the legal system works in ways that present many obstacles to the prosecution of paedophiles, and prevalence data illustrates that child sexual abuse continues to be a significant global problem (Hamer 2002). Feminist writers have drawn a direct link between male privilege and violence towards women and children, arguing that it is 'endemic to all patriarchal societies that prioritize the needs of men in public as well as private settings' (Reavey and Warner 2003, p.3). It can also be argued that child sexual abuse is sanctioned in more covert ways by the use of pseudo-sexual portrayals of children in advertizing. Increasingly, parents express their concern about the trend within western society towards early child sexualization.

Arriving at a definition of child sexual abuse, although seemingly straightforward, has presented a number of challenges for practitioners working in the field. Definitions range from broad based constructs employed by clinicians to narrower prescriptive definitions used by the legal profession (Haugaard 2000). Haugaard suggests that the process of arriving at a consensus of opinion is hampered by society's difficulties in agreeing where the dividing line stands between behaviours that are non-abusive and others that are more clearly sexually abusive. As Haugaard points out, the process is further complicated by the fact that differing contexts and combinations of characteristics skew interpretations of the adult's behaviour. For the purpose of this book, a broad based definition of child sexual abuse is used, which is a conflation of both the work of Berliner and Elliott (2002, p.55) and Department of Health Guidelines (1999, p.6).

Definition of child sexual abuse

Sexual abuse involves any sexual activity with a child where consent is not or cannot be given. This includes sexual contact that is accomplished by force or threat of force, regardless of the age of the participants, and all sexual contact between adult and child, regardless of whether there is deception, or the child understands the sexual nature of the activity. Sexual contact between an older and a younger child can also be abusive if there is a significant disparity in age, development, or size, rendering the younger child incapable of giving informed consent. The activities may involve physical contact, including penetrative or non-penetrative acts. They may include non-contact activities, such as involving children in looking at, or in the production of, pornographic material or watching sexual activities, or encouraging children to behave in sexually inappropriate ways.

Other forms of child abuse, such as physical abuse, are shown to accompany sexual abuse. Emotional abuse is implicit when trying to gain understanding of both the short-term and long-term consequences of child sexual abuse. Glaser (2002, pp.703–704) describes a number of conceptual frameworks for understanding emotional abuse and neglect. Two of these frameworks describe parental behaviour, one of whose categorizations are clearly linked with the child sexual abuse experience:

- Emotional unavailability, unresponsiveness, and neglect.

- Negative attributions and misattributions to the child.

- Developmentally inappropriate or inconsistent interactions with the child.

- Failure to recognize or acknowledge the child's individuality and psychological boundary.

- Failure to promote the child's social adaptation.

Additionally, disabled children may experience childcare practices, which some might deem insignificant, but others see as abusive and a clear breach of their human rights. Drawing from a study investigating the abuse of disabled children between the years of 1989 and 1992, Kennedy (1996) identifies some of the controversial practices that disabled children are frequently exposed to. Similar to some of the findings of an investigation looking at the abuse of people with learning difficulties in Cornwall (Healthcare Commission 2006), she questions the routine use of force-feeding, physical restraint, the misuse of medications and the photographing of children's impairments (by medics) in intrusive ways; seeing them all as differing forms of abuse.

Equally, this book also refers to a range of practices that are recognized by disabled people themselves as being a misuse of power, and where disabled children's treatment is considered 'less than humane'. In this respect, the book in some ways deals with child abuse more comprehensively than the book title might first suggest.

We also frequently refer to psychological processes that were used in childhood to survive the sexual abuse experience. This is both at the time of its occurrence, where an 'out of body' experience is described, and later when trying to psychologically accommodate the abuse. These psychological processes are seen to be dissociative, and generally involve the child turning on their damaged body in a self-destructive manner (Young 1992). Van der Kolk, van der Hart and Marmar (1996) describe dissociation in the following way:

> Many children and adults, when confronted with overwhelming threat, are unable to integrate the totality of what is happening into consciousness. Sensory and emotional elements of the event may not be integrated into personal memory and identity, and remain isolated from ordinary consciousness...
> (p.307)

In some situations, the protection of the 'self system' by the reduction of an individual's consciousness can evolve into complete forgetting, otherwise known as dissociative amnesia. Research indicates that forgetting is common when trauma happens in early childhood, particularly when under the age of two (Courtois 1999). The emergence of a forgotten memory in later life is sometimes referred to as a 'recovered memory'. The complexity and controversy surrounding recovered memory will be discussed in some detail in Chapter 9, but needless to say the ways in which trauma can later show itself hinders the ability to integrate the experience into the personal narrative, and story the self in an acceptable way to the individual.

Narrative

Definition of narrative

A story or a narrative is eloquently described by Polkinghorne in the following way:

> The products of our narrative schemes are ubiquitous in our lives: they fill our cultural and social environment. We create narrative descriptions for ourselves and for others about our own past actions, and we develop storied accounts that give sense to the behaviour of others. We also use the narrative scheme to inform our decisions by constructing imaginative 'what if' scenarios. On the receiving end, we are constantly confronted with stories during our conversations and encounters with the written and visual media. We are told fairy tales as children, and read and discuss stories in school.

(Polkinghorne 1988, p.14)

As Polkinghorne describes, storytelling is a regular feature of our human existence and as a subject area it is highlighted in many ways throughout this book. Some disabled children are deprived of an ability to tell a story (particularly stories of abuse) because of the attitudes and practices of others who fail to consider alternative methods for assisting their communication. The ability to put experience into a narrative format is interrupted by sexual abuse, and later storytelling becomes instrumental in relaying the abuse story to others; acting as a catalyst for personal healing.

STRUCTURE OF THE BOOK

Chapter 1 'Seven Disabled People with Telling Stories' introduces the survivors whose narrative appears throughout this book. It discusses how these survivors were identified and the basis for the research agreement. Within this, there is discussion of the emancipatory disability research imperative, the contribution of feminist theory and the ethical context of the research. The chapter concludes with descriptive summaries of the participants involved in the research project.

Chapter 2 'Narrative and Enabling Stories of Child Sexual Abuse' explores the concept of narrative, its psychological function for the individual, and its role in terms of identity formation. The chapter looks at the issue of first time disclosure, which invariably happens in adulthood where some distance has been achieved from the original abuse. It later considers the telling of the story in the research context, including factors that were assistive in the research process and the dilemmas that the researcher faced.

Chapter 3 'An Abusive Society?' begins by examining some of the cultural and societal assumptions that surround the concept of impairment, and which contribute to the creation of prejudice and discrimination within our society. We argue that these assumptions underpin the demotion of the subject of the abuse of disabled children in both research terms and in professional practice.

Chapter 4 'The Double Whammy Effect' looks at the impact of prejudice on the quality of parenting that some disabled children receive. A compromised parental relationship can be seen to adversely influence the child's self-esteem, act as a barrier to disclosure of sexual abuse and put disabled children at further risk of abuse outside the family.

Chapter 5 'Expressions and Survival of Pain' examines the way in which disabled children have to employ a number of self-protective mechanisms to secure their survival. Sexual abuse and a disabling parental experience can compound a 'bad body' identity heightening a need for dissociation. Dissociation can involve inwardly directed self-destructive behaviours. Coping can also involve aggressive behaviours that are directed at others. For children who experience abuse within the family home, their situation may be further compromised by their perceptions of the non-abusive parent.

Chapter 6 'Organizational Abuse' argues that the key organizations that disabled children and their families engage with can mirror some of the same objectifying attitudes present in society at large. These attitudes can be so ingrained in the fabric of professional practice that their presence can go unheeded. This chapter gives consideration to hospital care, past and present, and the workings of educational systems, mainstream and segregated. Without critical analysis and objective appraisal this chapter illustrates how easily abusive environments can evolve.

Chapter 7 'Who Abuses and Why?' has as its main focus perpetrator behaviour. It compares and contrasts some of the major psychological and sociological perspectives when trying to understand a perpetrator's motivation to abuse, and considers what strategies they might employ to achieve this end. It then considers how this information might relate to the sexual abuse of disabled children. The chapter illustrates that paedophiles have many more opportunities for gaining access to the disabled child.

Chapter 8 'Collective Identities' explores the impact of child sexual abuse on the development of adult identities; more specifically the survivor identity, disability identity and sexual identity. The acquisition of any of these identities is not a straightforward process and this chapter endeavours to illustrate the complexities involved for the individual.

Chapter 9 'Narratives of the Narrative' illustrates how child sexual abuse can undermine the development of the personal narrative. It considers how, when defence mechanisms are less necessary, or circumstances dictate, the sexual abuse narrative re-emerges and becomes a more dominant force in the individual's life. The chapter begins by looking at the healing process; the need to re-attribute responsibility, and to address parts of the narrative that have been adversely affected by abuse. The chapter concludes by exploring the individual's concern about the validity of their abuse narrative for others, particularly if the narrative is recovered after a period of forgetting.

Conclusion 'Towards a Non-Abusive Society' draws together and summarizes the individuals' narratives illustrating the complexities faced by disabled children who are sexually abused; the double whammy. The conclusion also considers the implication of sexual abuse for policy and professional practice.

CHAPTER 1

Seven Disabled People with Telling Stories

INTRODUCTION

The stories or narrative of seven disabled people who have experienced child abuse lie at the heart of this book. Who are they and how did they become involved? This chapter is about introductions. First there are complex questions about how they were introduced to the project. How could disabled people who wanted to tell their stories be approached? Why should they become involved and what would their involvement be? In the latter stages of this chapter we shall introduce you to the participants – the seven disabled people who chose to tell their stories using a variety of methods and whose voices then appear throughout this book. Finally we shall introduce ourselves. This whole project was collaborative, and the narratives themselves were, for us, collaborative. Thus we place ourselves within the project, rather than being neutral, outside commentators.

HOW THE RESEARCH PARTICIPANTS WERE IDENTIFIED

The idea of involving disabled people who had experienced sexual abuse in telling their stories was, from the outset, problematic and challenging. How were possible participants to be approached? How would they tell their stories (by email, verbally, etc.)? What would be the relationship between Martina (and the whole team, including John) and the participants? What were the dangers in tackling this highly emotional topic, for all concerned? But also, what were the possible benefits for all concerned?

All the seven participants became involved through a process of self-selection. Disch (2001) draws attention to the importance of research participants being able to freely volunteer themselves for involvement in research. Although this recruitment method would probably not produce a representative cross-section of the disabled population, this bias was felt permissible as it cut down on the difficulty created when a third party attempts to explain one's work (Booth and Booth 1997). This self-selecting method also meant that the people who responded to advertizements would probably have reached a significant stage in their own personal healing process, enabling them to feel confident and robust enough to 'speak out' and share their realities.

Details of the research were publicized using a box advertizement placed in a number of national disability magazines, and the newsletters and websites of different regional and national disability organizations. The advertizement also appeared at the end of an article written for a national disability magazine, discussing disability and child sexual abuse and describing some of the factors that increase a disabled child's vulnerability. The advertizement spoke of the need for participants to have already spoken to somebody about their abuse. This requirement reduced the chances of receiving previously undisclosed sexual abuse narratives, which might pose an ongoing threat to children presently in contact with the perpetrator (Swain, Heyman and Gillman 1998). It also increased the likelihood that the disabled survivor had adequate support systems in place; friends and family who might in theory provide support throughout the research process.

It was felt particularly important to gain access to the experiences of people with learning difficulties because, in research terms, these individuals are recognized as being a marginalized subgroup of the disabled population (Walmsley 2001). In reality, they have been shown to be particularly at risk of child sexual abuse (Sobsey and Doe 1991, Sullivan and Knutson 2000). Consequently, a period of time was spent working with a People First group, preparing an accessible article for one of their magazines and discussing broader issues relating to sex and sexuality. Although unproductive as a means of generating volunteers, it did act as a catalyst for discussion about involvement in physically and sexually oppressive relationships. This was often, with other adults with learning difficulties, a factor that appears in others' research (Brown, Stein and Turk 1995).

In total, advertizing (and more direct methods of participant recruitment) produced eight suitable volunteers, one who later withdrew because of their possible involvement in a non-related but relevant court case. Five of these respondents were female and two male. Their ages ranged from mid-20s to mid-50s and, with the exception of one person, they were evenly spread across the UK in terms of their place of residence. Most identified as white British, with three respondents having been born outside the UK, and one respondent being of Anglo-Asian ethnic origin. They represented a range of impairment groupings and self-identified as having differing sexual orientations.

THE NATURE OF RESEARCH AGREEMENTS

As part of inviting people into the project it was necessary to tackle difficult questions about why invitations were sent out and what people might be agreeing to. This was seen as the starting point for the relationship with participants; what might be called research agreements. There were two related sets of issues. First, why should disabled people be involved in a research project of this kind? Disabled people have been critical of research and what it has and has not done in relation to their lives. Some disabled people have seen research as part of the problem, not the solution. This takes us into underlying theoretical models and the messages conveyed through research about what disability means in people's lives. The possible risk-benefits here are collective. Could telling stories be part of disabled people's struggles against oppression, against abuse? Second, why be involved as an individual? This raises perhaps an even more complex set of issues concerning personal risk-benefits of involvement and takes us into the fraught realms of the ethical context. Ethical questions reverberate through all research. Research is a human enterprize encouched in interactions and communication between the researcher and the participants, the people telling their stories. In a project exploring the sexual abuse of disabled people issues such as respecting privacy become highlighted and accentuated.

Underpinning theoretical models: towards a research approach

Engaging in a research agreement raises a plethora of issues for researchers and participants, further highlighted by the subject of this research. From the standpoint of the researcher the agreements were based on practice that drew from both disability studies and feminism. The emancipatory research ideal, in particular, is recognized by many disability academics as being vital to any research relationship. It places emphasis on flexibility, power sharing and empowerment of the disabled person. The model arose from criticisms of traditional disability research methods, which sought to analyze the individual's personal difficulty created by their impairment, as opposed to understanding the social and cultural factors that work to marginalize and exclude us within society (Oliver 1992). Hunt (1981) argues that the early research process was largely non-reciprocal, self-servicing and exploitative. It failed to examine the power dynamics operating within the research relationship, and which then contributed to disabled people's classification as 'other'. Barnes (2003) elaborates further on the emergence of the emancipatory research principle:

> In contrast to traditional investigative approaches, the emancipatory disability research agenda warrants the generation and production of meaningful and accessible knowledge about the various structures – economic, political, cultural and environmental – that create and sustain the multiple deprivations encountered by the overwhelming majority of disabled people and their families. (p.6)

As a distinct theoretical research model, the emancipatory ideal emerged following a number of seminars funded by the Joseph Rowntree Foundation in 1991, which then provided a platform for the further development of this research model (Barnes 2001). Within the disabled people's movement, and within academic circles, the emancipatory research ideal has generated much debate. Oliver (1997) believes that emancipatory research can only be ever defined as such after the event. He suggests that a more pertinent issue to be considered is whether the researcher played a useful role in the participant's empowerment, or whether indeed they contributed to that individual's disempowerment. Barnes (2003) appears less cynical about the value of the emancipatory disability research. He argues that this research approach exposes inequalities and reinforces the need for change and, in that sense, has an important part to play in disabled people's emancipation at both an individual and collective level. When working to facilitate disabled survivor's sexual abuse narrative, a considered approach to the maintenance of the research relationship, and an engagement with its potential to disempower, served as major guiding principles throughout.

The emancipatory research ideal also owes much to other academic disciplines, particularly feminism. Of significance are the writings of Stanley and Wise (1983) who see mainstream (malestream) research in the social sciences as occluding the significance of women's contribution. Stanley (1990) and Stanley and Wise (1983) write about the typical 'maleness' of traditional research production, where women are over-represented as research subjects, yet male experience depicts the 'norm' in terms of research evaluation. Clear parallels can be drawn here for disabled people's involvement in research, where non-disabled people's experiences determine a standardized notion of normality. Similarly, the situation becomes more complicated for disabled people when race and sexuality are added to this equation. The process of 'repositioning' the subject is also common to both disciplines. The emergence of 'standpoint' theory within feminism brought women to centre stage and analyzed issues from a female perspective, including their marginalization (Stanley and Wise 1990). As Harding (1987, p.185) writes:

> To achieve a feminist standpoint one must engage in the intellectual and political struggle necessary to see natural and social life from the point of view of that distained activity which produces women's social experiences instead of from the partial and perverse perspective available from the 'ruling gender' experience of men.

A similar situation currently exists within Disability Studies, where issues are now being critiqued from disabled people's perspective. Within this process, there is a modification of language, and disability denotes the 'norm' from which non-disabled people are categorized as other (Swain and French 2000).

With reference to their earlier work, Stanley and Wise (1990) suggest that feminist ideals should be ingrained in both the specifics of the research encounter and the subsequent analysis of the research data. They write that feminism 'should be present in positive ways within the research process' (p.23) and demonstrated in a number of researcher practices, which determine a distinct feminist approach. For research involving disabled people, we argue that the emancipatory disability research ideal should inform both the research relationship and the later data analysis. Both of these aspects should serve to empower and ultimately validate participants' narratives. A children's rights perspective equally brings about a comparable research responsibility. In the research context, it determines a need to attribute responsibility for the abuse to the adult and make linkage, if required, between current difficulty and perpetrator behaviour. This perspective should also be visible in the analysis of data.

In this project the research was generated by a set of principles underlying emancipatory research. The challenge throughout was to realize the following key principles in actual practice and processes off the research:

- The adoption of the social model of disability as a basis for research production.

- The need to only undertake research which will be of some practical benefit to the self-empowerment of disabled people.

- Giving control of the research production to disabled people.

- The need to adopt a number of methods for data collection and analysis in response to the changing needs of disabled people.

- The ability to give voice to personal experience, whilst drawing out the political substance of disabled people's exclusion within society.

(Priestley 1997)

It is against these characteristics of an emancipatory research approach that this project can be judged.

The ethical context

The above principles reverberate through the ethical context of this project. Ethical issues were of paramount importance in stepping across the divide of such private, personal and deeply emotional concerns into a public arena, both in the direct relations between the researcher and the participants and, ultimately, the dissemination of participants' stories through publication. Swain, Heyman and Gillman (1998) believe that the question of ethics needs to be 'constructed and confronted' throughout the research process, from submission of the initial research proposal to publication. They argue that the actions of the researcher, and the development of the research relationship, impact on the lives of participants and confer particular researcher responsibilities. This might involve a responsibility to iron out any difficulties should they arise. The authors also propose that the more control the participant has in the research process, the less likely it is to infringe their rights. Implicit in their work is a commitment by the researcher to sustain an open and honest partnership. These general principles of openness, respect for the participant and respect for the participant's autonomy are consistent with what French (2004) describes as the deontological model of ethical decision-making.

Part of the process, which strives for openness and honesty, relates to how the research is explained to a participant in the first instance. The explaining process is important, as it will hopefully then facilitate the acquisition of informed consent. In addition to written information preceding an interview, verbal explanations require a number of important considerations. In particular, consideration should be given to how detailed the description of the research is, and how much information the researcher decides to give of themselves. Walmsley (1993) stresses the interactive nature of this part of the process. Explanations generate feedback, which often require further elaboration. This interactive process gives the researcher more information about the participant and their understanding of the research topic.

Lee (1993) cautions on the difficulties created by defining the research topic too tightly in these early stages, arguing that this may impact on the participant's ability to understand the research in their own way. From a researcher perspective, it may prevent them later from raising other seemingly unrelated issues. But when is the most appropriate time to seek informed consent? Is it realistic for participants to be asked to sign consent forms in the very early stages of the research process, or should informed consent be sought once a research relationship has been established? A number of writers believe the latter to be the case. Sin (2005) argues that, in reality, consent seeking is not a single event, and that different levels of consent are necessary at different points in the research procedure. This is particularly the case in relation to later publication.

Control should also extend to a choice about how a participant's story is told. This viewpoint is consistent with the work of Ochs and Capps (1996) who describe how narrative performance can take many forms. In this piece of research, participants chose to tell their stories using face-to-face interviews, poetry, a written story, photography, artwork and email, and frequently their story involved a combination of these methods. Electronic methods of participation are increasingly becoming a valuable method of data collection, particularly for hard to reach groups (Brownlow and O'Dell 2002). Mann and Stewart (2000) suggest that internet research can often provide anonymity for participants, where the visual cues that contribute to the development of power relations may be by-passed. For disabled people, it provides a level of accessibility, facilitating participation in an alternative and safe format. When commenting on a previous piece of his research, Mann describes email as being a 'flexible, sensitive, responsive and informative communication medium' (p.174). Despite the obvious benefits, email research in emotionally charged topics does remove the non-verbal dimension, which gives the researcher information about how the research process is being experienced.

Participant control was implicit in the ethical guidelines mailed to potential respondents before their participation commenced. The research agreements discussed issues such as confidentiality, anonymity, the storage and destruction of tapes, and exit strategies should the research process become too painful. Collaboration was encouraged when compiling both the transcript of the interview and the final narrative, with encouragement given to add or omit information as necessary. When constructing the final narrative account, a model was adopted that was used by Goodley (2000) when researching self-advocacy in the lives of people with learning difficulties. Issues relating to narrative (and the narratives produced in the research context) will be given further consideration in the next chapter. Needless to say, a partnership approach was adopted, with a free-flow of information between participant and researcher at different stages of the research process. This was intended to increase the sense of participant control and reduce the likelihood of a misrepresentation of data.

SEVEN DISABLED PEOPLE WITH STORIES TO TELL

Through the process of introducing the project, seven disabled people who wanted to tell their stories became involved. These stories are 'telling' both as a process of personal narrative and in terms of the broader understanding they provide of disability and child sexual abuse. The following are descriptive summaries gleaned from the interviews and agreed with the participants to introduce themselves. They provide background information to the narrative which appears in the forthcoming chapters. All the names referred to below are pseudonyms which were chosen by participants to protect their identity.

Lyn

At the time of interview, Lyn was in her early 40s, and living with her partner. Both her parents are no longer alive. Lyn was born in Singapore where her father was stationed with the RAF, returning to England at about the age of two years. On arriving back in the UK, she initially lived with her father's extended family in west London, who were of Anglo-Asian ethnic origin, and then later relocated to a new housing estate in a different part of London.

Lyn had a disabled mother, who had spent a significant period of her own childhood in children's homes. She still has her mother's old photographs, and her mother's letters which were written to her grandmother from the children's home. Lyn describes her father's family as having a huge hang-up about darkness and ascribing importance to having a pale complexion. Lyn described her father as an immigrant, and as somebody not fitting into the Indian world when he was in India, or the English world when in England. She believes this to be the reason for him being a bully in the home.

Lyn acquired a hearing impairment at eight years of age, as a result of meningitis; this is an illness episode that she still has vivid memories of because it was so traumatic. She remembers a lumbar puncture, being given the last rites and losing pretty much all of her hearing. Following her return home from hospital Lyn describes her mother as having an exacerbation of her mental health difficulties and her father's drink problem spiralling. As a child, Lyn felt responsible for her parents' difficulties, despite the prior presence of these illnesses.

Lyn believes that the abuse by her father had started before she had meningitis, but has a lack of clarity about that. What she does remember, however, and in some detail, is getting involved in sexual activities with strangers in the park, in return for rewards, and she describes this as not being particularly traumatizing. As she entered secondary school, Lyn describes the abuse by her father stopping or tapering off, and her father starting to have affairs with other women. Around that time, Lyn talks about getting involved in another abusive relationship, this time with a friend of her father's.

When Lyn was 14, she describes things as going wrong for her. Although managing to succeed at school, she talks about being incredibly unhappy and needing to self-harm. It seemed to Lyn that nobody managed to pick up on the signs of her distress. Later, she also describes getting obsessed with her weight, a preoccupation which continued up until her early years at university when she managed to get help with this. Lyn sought out therapeutic assistance in her mid-30s when her usual self-defence mechanisms began to falter.

Lyn talks about therapy in very positive terms, as a productive method of helping to make sense of the past. She describes therapy as having turned her life around, despite still being prone to getting quite shaky about the abuse experience. Her involvement in research she describes as being an experiment for her; a means of sharing her narrative outside the safety of her personal network of friends and her therapist.

Lyn shared her narrative during a face-to-face interview.

Josh

At the time of interview Josh was in his mid-40s and living with his wife and two teenage children. His mother, father, and his stepfather (who was also his abuser) are no longer alive. Josh comes from a large family and has five brothers and sisters, and three stepbrothers and stepsisters. His mother had a difficult labour and as a result Josh was later diagnosed with cerebral palsy, attributed to oxygen starvation during the birthing process. He maintains some contact with his siblings; one who has confirmed abuse, and others whom he suspects have also been abused.

Josh believes his abuse started when he was five or six when his mother was away convalescing, and continued for the next four or five years when the opportunity presented itself. It was often combined with physical abuse, or threats of physical violence for noncompliance with his stepfather's demands.

Josh attended a mainstream primary school and talks about his teachers having little understanding of how his impairment impacted upon his ability to participate in a number of school activities. During his school years Josh felt that he was less concerned with his impairment and the difficulties that it created, and more preoccupied with surviving abuse.

Josh felt that his mother began to get suspicious of his stepfather's activities when Josh was nine or ten and when his stepfather's behaviour became more reckless. At about the age of 11, when he was due to transfer to secondary school, his mother and a doctor decided that he should go to residential school and be taken out of the family, a move he describes as wrecking his education. The school was not geared up to dealing with bright children and he felt that it presented few educational challenges. Josh's abuse continued when he was home during the school holidays, and at age 13 he also talks about being sexually abused by an older child resident at the residential school he was attending. Josh talks about leaving residential school at 16 years of age totally ill-prepared for life. In adolescence he describes being confused about his sexuality, since his learning experiences, up until that point, had been homosexual learning experiences.

Josh's emotional difficulties came to a head in his mid-20s and when he was at polytechnic. He describes having a nervous breakdown, which led to a number of self-destructive behaviours. Despite the pressures of doing a three-year course in two years, being in a strange city without any support systems and being in an emotionally fragile state, Josh still managed to complete his course and get his degree.

Later, when Josh was ready to talk about his abuse, he was unable to find a counsellor, particularly a counsellor who worked with male victims of sexual abuse. Instead he shared his experience with several friends and his wife who validated what he had to say, and continues to provide support today.

Josh shared his narrative during a face-to-face interview and by sharing a childhood photograph.

Jean

At the time of interview, Jean was in her early 40s and in regular contact with her mother and stepfather. Jean's sexual abuse took place whilst she was in hospital for the investigation of unexplained symptoms occurring in her knee area, which later turned out to be rheumatoid arthritis. Jean's abuser was a nun who worked as a nurse on the children's ward, and subjected her to repeated physical and sexual assaults over a six-month period. During her stay at this hospital she also experienced other physical assaults by what she believes were male nurses and witnessed the murder of another disabled child resident on the same ward. In addition to these abuses, Jean describes having to contend with painful medical procedures and a total neglect of her physical and emotional needs. These abuse incidents came to an end when her mother removed her from the hospital, having become concerned about her daughter's behaviour, which demonstrated signs of autism with a complete loss of language. As a result of not having a diagnosis, Jean's GP felt that she should go to a different hospital, where she had exploratory surgery and the family finally got the diagnosis. She was at this second hospital for a further few months.

Jean describes being a very active child despite the limitations created by her impairment. She also describes her parents separating when she was 11 years old, because of her father's threatening behaviour, which was directed at Jean's mother. This split was experienced by Jean as a relief and her mother subsequently met another man and remarried.

Jean describes her early childhood as being characterized by problems associated with bedtime; reluctance to go to bed and terrifying nightmares when she did go to sleep. She also describes fear of hospitals and fear of bath time. Jean attended mainstream school and experienced this as an isolating experience, since there were very few other disabled children at the schools she attended. Additionally, the teachers did not challenge other children's name-calling and their disablist taunts.

Jean had coped with her abuse by burying the memories, which then emerged later in life. Some of the triggers, she believes, were her mother relaying details of Jean's first hospital stay and her own child reaching a similar age to when Jean was sexually abused. At this point Jean's relationship with her partner broke down, as did her own mental health. Jean continues to try and make sense of her emerging memories. She has used both counselling services and continues to use her own creative methods of self-empowerment.

Jean told her narrative via face-to-face interviews and by sharing her art work.

May

May sent her narrative via email following a chain of email exchanges leading up to that point. At that time of the research she was living with her partner and did not share information relating to her age or her impairment.

May's parents' relationship broke down when she was two years old and May describes this event as being linked to her being born with cerebral palsy (an impairment description that she later chose to share). May has clear memories of being told by her mother that the parental relationship did not survive because of her condition. Her father was described as believing that May had a disease, and that as a consequence he would have nothing to do with her. Her father was also described as having a number of affairs to prove that there was nothing wrong with him. May feels that her mother's stories made her believe that she had wrecked both her mother and her sibling's life.

May was sent away to school when she was four years old, an event that had a huge impact on her life, influencing both her ability to stand her ground and creating an unquestioned compliance. Although residential school was a largely negative experience, she describes feeling sad to leave because she had made so many friends and because her impairment was not seen as an issue there. May was taken out of residential school when she was seven or eight, which she relates to disability benefits coming into effect. She has since been told by other members of the family that people were arguing about who was going to look after her when she returned home, and she concludes that money must have been involved as nobody had been interested up until that point.

At about this time, May's mother remarried and she describes life as settling into a set routine. She looked after her mother's new baby, did the housework, supported the family financially and had very few friends. May believes her sexual abuse to have started when she was approximately 14 and that her impairment, and the need for physiotherapy, created the opportunity for it to occur without detection. Her abuser was her stepfather. Later May found out that her mother did know that she was being sexually abused but failed to do anything to stop it. May feels that her sense of powerlessness in her family expressed itself in the development of a number of psychological difficulties.

May's abuse continued into her 20s, despite making many attempts to move out the family home and live independently. Part of the problem related to a lack of adapted housing stock, and part of it related to her deteriorating health condition. She uses counselling services and continues to see her mother and younger sister, who she suspects has also been abused. Her stepfather/abuser is no longer alive.

Thomas

Thomas chose to tell his narrative by taking part in a face-to-face interview and sharing a written story about his early life, an impressive collection of poetry and a family photograph. At the time of interview Thomas was in his early 30s and living with his wife and five children. Thomas was sexually and physically abused by his stepfather, who came to live with his family following the collapse of a previous marriage. Thomas's abuse started when he was five years old and he holds vivid memories of abuse incidents that spanned many years.

At both primary and secondary school Thomas struggled for a number of reasons, partly to do with having undiagnosed Asperger's syndrome, and partly because of his abuse, which meant that he was often disruptive in class and unable to learn. Despite Thomas feeling that he was giving off clear distress signals at school, very few teachers attempted to broach the subject with him, apart from one teacher who had noticed bruising. The situation was made more complicated as Thomas's stepfather was also a school governor at his secondary school.

Thomas talks about not being fully aware that his abuse was wrong until he reached the age of 14. He also describes a confused early sexual identity, which was fed by his stepfather's homophobic taunts during abusive incidents. Thomas's story describes him as becoming involved in criminal activities as he was growing up, but the full consequences of his abuse did not begin to show itself until after his stepfather's death, when he describes a loss of a 'victim identity'. At this stage, he then started to use drugs and alcohol, to self-mutilate and get involved in violence at football matches and other criminal activities. This lasted until he met his current partner. Thomas explains that the well-kept family secret began to be exposed in the mid-1990s, and following a family argument, when his sister started to make indirect references to it. This led to discussions with his wife (who had no previous knowledge of it), his mother (who denied knowledge of it), and discussions with his other five siblings, some of whom had also been abused and others who had not. The uncovering of the abuse led to Thomas recovering other previously forgotten memories. It also resulted in a period of emotional instability and his involvement with counselling services.

Since his stepfather's death Thomas has built up a detailed picture of his stepfather. He now knows that his stepfather had abused children from his previous relationship, and he has put together information that offers some explanation for why his stepfather behaved as he did.

Chloe

Chloe told her narrative during a face-to-face interview and by sharing poetry. At the time of interview Chloe was in her mid-20s and living with her daughter. She had recently separated from her partner. Chloe has a brother and a sister and both her parents are still alive. In early childhood, Chloe describes living in a number of different European countries because her father was stationed there in the army. Chloe talks about the problems that an undiagnosed impairment created, both for her mother and for her teachers. She explains that her mother struggled to cope with Chloe's behaviour, and that her mother became depressed as a result of being isolated from her family and friends. At school, Chloe describes feeling different from the other children in her class, pretending to fit in and feeling more comfortable in adult company.

At the age of 13 Chloe was sexually abused by someone who she now suspects was also in the army, and operating as part of an organized network of paedophiles. The abuse took place whilst she was babysitting, and a friend, who she also believes to have been involved in this network, had set the arrangement up. She has memories of being plied with alcohol prior to the event and possibly been given drugs as well. Chloe believes that she had been specially selected for this abuse and that her difficult relationship with her parents had contributed to her vulnerability. At the time, she didn't realize that she had been abused, despite knowing that she didn't want to get involved in the sexual act. She felt that she had been at the babysitter's house through her own choice and partly expected something to happen that night.

Around this time, a teacher detected that Chloe was having difficulties at school. Chloe describes a meeting being called, which involved an educational psychologist and other teaching professionals, where the possibility of schizophrenia was raised, but then discounted. Chloe also describes having partial recollections of abuse occurring within her own family, but is unclear as to who the abuser was and where the abuse took place. These events she believes to have happened at a much earlier time, and that there are more abuse memories yet to be recovered.

Chloe talks about only realizing that she had been abused much later in life, and as her daughter was growing up. The trigger was her daughter reaching the same age and developmental stage that corresponded with Chloe's early sexual abuse memories. Chloe responded to this realization by having a psychotic episode, and a lengthy period of mental ill health.

Chloe talks about having a positive counselling experience which then determined a need to contact the police and launch a formal investigation into the abuse that she experienced as a teenager. She maintains a distanced relationship with her parents and siblings, believing that her sister may also have experienced abuse. She believes that her abuse narrative is incomplete.

Lizzie

At the time of interview Lizzie was in her mid-50s and living with her husband and two daughters. She has an older sister and her mother is no longer alive. Lizzie shared her narrative during a face-to-face interview. Lizzie describes being born abroad and then returning to the UK at a young age for surgery. A nurse who was working on her paediatric ward and covering a night shift sexually abused her. She also describes experiencing physical abuse and has memories of other children on that ward also being abused, some of whom did not have impairments. The abuse lasted for approximately four months and Lizzie describes dealing with her trauma by forgetting the abuse. Lizzie also describes having some other memory of something else happening with a neighbour when she was quite a lot older, but has less clear memories of that.

Lizzie describes attending mainstream school and being excluded by her peers. This was particularly noticeable in adolescence where she talks of being asexualized or desexualized and experiencing hostile comments from other girls when she did have a boyfriend. For her, this early relationship validated her emerging sexuality. Lizzie describes never having a need to rebel as a teenager, or do things to wind her parents up, as she got more support from her parents than anyone else.

When talking about the effects of sexual abuse on her life, Lizzie describes sexual abuse and disability as overlapping in a fairly confusing way, since issues of anxiety and depression could have equally been attributed to effects of disablism. She describes having sleep problems as a child and emotional difficulties as an adult, attempting suicide when she was working away from her support systems and in an unhealthy work environment, where there was a devaluation of children and a lack of regard for her impairment.

Lizzie recovered memories of her abuse when she was in her late 30s and involved in peer-counselling. Lizzie explains that the trigger for these memories was a physical assault that she had experienced. When working on the assault incident in counselling, the abuse memories began to emerge and since that time she describes being able to slowly piece together her abuse narrative, gradually making sense of past life experiences and her own personal characteristics. Amongst other things, Lizzie feels that her own abuse experience has made her far more aware of the potential dangers for her own children.

Martina

Martina was a doctorate student at Northumbria University when she undertook the research project. The project involved interviewing participants, transcribing the tapes and, in conjunction with the participants, producing a narrative account. This partnership approach extended to subsequent publications.

Martina is a disabled person herself and the parent of a disabled child. Consequently, she has first-hand experience of the prejudice that disabled people encounter, overtly and covertly. In her professional career she specialized in child protection; working as a practitioner and manager.

John

John was principle supervisor of Martina's doctorate at Northumbria University. This involved reading everything she produced, including interview transcripts and discussing together all the issues as they arose in the research.

CHAPTER 2

Narrative and Enabling Stories of Child Sexual Abuse

INTRODUCTION

This chapter addresses the idea of narrative and telling one's story. It starts from the premise that we are the narrative that we tell of ourselves and of our lives. Yet this is an inherently dynamic and continuing process of affirming and re-affirming, telling and re-telling, doubting and realizing, constructing and deconstructing, asserting and denying – a process of being and becoming. It is also a shared process. Narratives are recounted in particular contexts, as dialogues rather than monologues. The stories we tell of ourselves are shaped by who they are told to, why they are told, the circumstances in which they are told and the interpersonal dynamic of the telling. The complexities are highlighted and have a particular resonance when narratives disclose experiences of sexual abuse and problematized even further when they are disabled people's narrative. The particular context here was a research project and the factors that contributed to a person's ability to tell their abuse story in the research setting. We look at the question of what a narrative is, and what purpose a narrative serves for the individual in terms of their personal identity formation. We explore, to some degree, the stages of disclosure that generally precede, and build up to, a person's involvement in research. In the final section of this chapter, the research context, we further explore some thoughts on what might emotionally support the research partnership and the creation of the research narrative, and what other factors might determine what an individual might tell of themselves.

TELLING THE ABUSE STORY IN THE RESEARCH CONTEXT

We begin by turning to the participants. It was clear that volunteering to be involved in a research project was a significant event in each individual's own personal process. For these survivors, it marked the fact that they had reached a particular benchmark in their recovery process where they fell confident enough to allow their narrative into the public domain. Undoubtedly, the research narrative has a political function, with an intention to raise public awareness of disability and child sexual abuse. Participation, however, was a hugely personal matter, as can be observed in the following different viewpoints:

> Being involved in research is an experiment for me in that I haven't had this sort of conversation in a non-therapeutic context before except with my partner. Talking about it to an almost stranger is different, but I do feel that the reason that I have gone through all of this in the past couple of years has been to sort out my life and try to be happier. (Lyn)

> The final thing I wanted to say is that my process of recovery has been about looking at the story of my life, so it's something that I'm continually working with in a therapeutic way and in my visual arts work. It feels good to be reflective about my past, to be able to see it all in context. (Jean)

> Having it (the narrative) all in one place is useful because when you have counselling you deal with separate bits at a time. I know people say that (by breaking it down) you can see how that relates to that, but I don't think that it sinks in the same as having it in front of you. (May)

The importance of telling your story, producing a narrative, is clearly evident in these quotes. It can be a powerful, self-affirming process. We turn next, then, to the storytelling process – what is a narrative?

WHAT IS A NARRATIVE?

A narrative is more commonly referred to in literature as a story, with a story being given less credibility and being more directly associated with fiction. In everyday life a sizable chunk of our interaction with others is devoted to the process of storytelling, and storytelling can form the basis of our more intimate relationships by providing the means of gaining insight into one another. Oral traditions of storytelling appear to be more prevalent in particular cultures, where stories are passed down between generations, so creating distinguishable cultural identities. In academia, narrative is experiencing a renewed interest in particular disciplines, and as a research method it can have an interdisciplinary application (Maine 1993). It creates a means for collating rich research data, which provides a valuable insight into the complexities and contradictions of an individual's life.

When talking more generally about narrative, McAdams (1993) describes narrative grammar as usually having a number of distinguishing features. It begins with contextualization – a setting and characters. The middle section of the narrative involves an initiating event and an identifiable goal. The narrative ends with a climax and the eventual resolution of a problem. McAdams describes a story as having a typical 'narrative tone', which is either pessimistic or optimistic, and related to our early experiences of being parented. An optimistic tone stems from a secure attachment and a pessimistic tone is derived from an insecure attachment. A narrative tone, he argues, can be applied to both the quality of an explanation or the substance of an entire life history account. McAdams (1993) also believes that individuals utilize a range of 'mythical forms' in the creation of their narrative:

> The different forms our story may take are many. But they are not limitless. Despite the diversity, there are a finite number of basic story forms... Literary scholars have found useful the discrimination between four very general forms – comedy, romance, tragedy and irony. (p.50)

In psychological terms, storytelling and the construction of the personal narrative plays a very important role by providing a means of organizing different types of information in the mind (McAdams 1993). McLeod (1997) proposes that the production of the narrative enables individuals to reflect upon their experiences and give meaning to life events. Narrative construction, therefore, is characterized by its ongoing quality. Some would say that there is an inseparability of the narrative, the act of telling one's story and the self (McAdams 1993). In that respect, storytelling is seen by many to be fundamental to our identity formation (McAdams 1993; Swain and Gillman 2000). Polkinghorne (1988) elaborates further on this point:

> ...we achieve our personal identities and self-concept through the use of the narrative configuration, and make our existence into a whole by understanding it as an expression of a single unfolding and developing story. We are in the middle of our stories and cannot be sure how they will end; we are constantly having to revise the plot as new events are added to our lives. Self, then, is not a static thing nor a substance, but a configuring of personal events into a historical unity, which includes not only what one has been but also anticipations of what will be. (p.150)

With reference to the work of others, Jenkins (2004) suggests that between the ages of two and four years, a child develops an understanding of the self in relation to others in their life, which is reflected in the substance of their narrative. The child's narrative, at this stage, is essentially influenced by the style of the parent–child conversation (Eder 1994), where a narrative may be developed with a parent's encouragement and possibly a turn-taking structure (Fivush 1994). As a result of their developing social networks and educational opportunities, the young person gradually builds their identity (McAdams 1993). In doing so, they may acquire a more developed ability to reflect and construct meaning, which might then suggest a more adept ability to story the self.

Polkinghorne (1988) emphasizes the interactive nature of storytelling. He proposes that people produce their stories together and with reference to one another, and that this social dimension of storytelling allows the self-narrative to be adapted:

> The concept of self is not the discovery or release of some innate 'I'; it is a construction built on other people's responses and attitudes towards a person and is subject to change as these responses, inherently variable and inconsistent, change in their character. (p.150)

Linde (1993) stresses the importance of the individual being able to produce a coherent narrative, which helps affirm and validate the self. The importance of this process becomes most apparent when a new life event (such as trauma) interrupts the individual's ability to produce narrative. Initially this new event creates confusion and even anxiety until it can be successfully incorporated into the ongoing narrative, or until the narrative is adapted to include the new information. Child sexual abuse is an example of such an event. Undetected, it can significantly compromise a young person's ability to comfortably narrate the self for many years. In these instances, the child's narrative development is significantly impaired and cannot be easily developed (Neimeyer and Stewart 1996), as it falls outside both their knowledge base and their cognitive capacity. The consequence is that the majority of children are unable to make sense of the abuse event, and find the necessary language to describe it (Crowley 2000).

Approaches that see narrative as entirely a product of our social interactions with others (postmodernism) stress the temporary nature of a narrative and the fact that it is in a constant state of flux. Determining factors might include the context of the encounter, the predisposition of the narrator, and who the listener might be. Freedman and Combs (1998, p.22) highlight four factors related to this more fluid view of a narrative:

- Realities are social constructs.

- Realities are created via language.

- Realities are organized and maintained through storytelling.

- There are no essential truths.

When applying this more fluid approach to the study of child sexual abuse, some authors argue that the experience of child sexual abuse should not be seen as a 'fixed truth' but as a story which is subject to continual change, and one which is relevant to an individual's social and cultural climate (Reavey 2003). In contrast to this approach, others would argue that whilst narratives are not straightforward phenomena, which contain a definitive truth, they do have a strong connection with reality. A research narrative gives a snapshot of an individual's life, at a particular moment in time, and provides some insight into how an individual has gone about constructing their narrative truth (Spence 1982). Overly fluid perspectives, which focus on the cultural and linguistic construction of the narrative, according to Crossley (2000), detract from the need to understand the individual experience, which this book aims to do.

TELLING THE ABUSE STORY FOR THE FIRST TIME

As participants talked about the process of telling their abuse stories, it was clear that the outcome of sharing the narrative will determine whether the individual will then go on to make further disclosures:

> … but talking about it and having some friends to whom I could say, gradually over time, that this happened. Some of them, who have known me since university, have said that they knew something was wrong, but they were never going to push me to say anything before I was ready and that's nice. It's confirming because it means they sort of trusted my pace, and it also illustrates the fact that somebody outside noticed that there was something wrong. (Lyn)

> The first person that I disclosed to was a friend and he was okay about it. I disclosed quite early on to some members of my family, and my mother, but they didn't want to talk about it. They were quite happy to know about it, they just didn't want to damn well discuss it. (Josh)

As in Thomas's case, disclosure may not be planned or anticipated:

> In 1993 I met Sharon who unknown to me had only been living 300 yards from my front door, yet we'd never met, and in 1994 we wed. The well-kept family secret really started to become exposed in about '94, when my sister really brought everything to the fore. It was a big family argument and slowly but surely I could see where it was leading to and I said to her, 'Look, you know, put the brakes on, forget it, leave it', I didn't want it coming out. But she'd start making comments around my mother like, 'He wasn't everything he was cracked up to be, you go on about my dad as though he was somebody special, he wasn't everything that you're making him out to be.' And Sharon kept saying, 'Why does Carol keep going on about your dad?' By this stage we were married but we hadn't talked about

it at all and I thought, 'Christ everything's going to come out now.' I'd been leading this completely different life with Sharon, I mean I'd told her that I'd been at boarding school just to cover everything up and I thought, 'Oh Christ, now my sister's going to spill the beans,' and it really came to a head. (Thomas)

Also, I'd got into some trouble with the police through one thing and another and my sister knew about it. And I said to her, 'Look don't go telling my mother, keep it to yourself, it's only a minor thing, it's not major, just keep it to yourself.' But of course she went and told my mother and my mother came to the house this particular day and said, 'Our Carol's told me that you've been in trouble with the police and that is just disgusting, you're a thief, we've never had a thief in the family before.' And I just snapped; I lost it totally. And I just said, 'You have had a thief in the family before and he took far more than I've ever taken and it's called childhood,' and she said, 'I don't know what you mean.' And I said, 'You do know what I mean, you do, you know that my stepfather was abusing me, was abusing Carol, was abusing John and was abusing David too, you know it.' She tried to say that she knew nothing about it and we basically ended up having a real shouting match. I was swearing and cursing at her and eventually told her to get out of my house. (Thomas)

Disclosure to family members can sometimes be a positive experience but, conversely, it may also increase the likelihood of psychological isolation. Research indicates that disclosure may be a catalyst for another family member to share their own abuse experience, whilst others may find disclosure too painful to even contemplate (MacFarlane and Korbin 1983). This was probably the case for other members of Josh's family. For those whose disclosure is unplanned and met with hostility and denial, such as in Thomas's case, the impact can be potentially damaging.

The limitations presented by many family networks often result in survivors initially seeking support and validation of their abuse narrative through discussion with partners and friends (as was the case for Lyn and Josh), then involvement in counselling, and perhaps later through their participation in research. Chapter 9 will discuss the function of counselling/therapy in some detail, but the next section of this chapter considers issues that relate to facilitating a sexual abuse narrative in the research context.

Turning to the literature, although statistical information relating to the age at which an individual first feels able to talk about child sexual abuse varies slightly, it predominantly illustrates that disclosures taking place around the time of sexual abuse are limited. London *et al.* (2005) paint a consistent picture having reviewed 11 retrospective studies. An analysis of the reviewed data suggested that between 60 and 70 per cent of survivors have no memory of making a disclosure of sexual abuse in childhood, with a significant proportion of the respondents describe making their first disclosure during the research process. London *et al.* highlight a number of issues related to the accuracy of retrospective studies, and raise the possibility that some adults may have discussed their abuse in childhood and failed to remember this, or may have misdated their disclosure, placing it at a greater distance from the abuse experience. Despite these question marks, the findings of London *et al.* confirm a view that childhood disclosures are less common.

A child's tendency for non-disclosure adds weight to a previously expressed view that children are cognitively and developmentally unable to process and narrate the abuse experience particularly easily. It also validates the writings of Summit (1983) concerning the accommodation syndrome. The accommodation syndrome describes how a child psychologically manages the sexual abuse experience, illuminating why disclosure is not a realistic option for the child. The five phases of the accommodation syndrome are as follows:

- Secrecy.

- Helplessness.

- Entrapment and accommodation.

- Delayed, conflicted and unconvincing disclosure.

- Retraction.

Secrecy

Child sexual abuse usually happens when nobody else is present. Children are told by the perpetrator not to tell others about the sexual act and may even be threatened to remain quiet. The message is clear – this is a forbidden activity. Most children do not tell and may believe that somehow they are to blame.

Helplessness

Children will keep their silence, feeling that they have no choice but to comply with the perpetrators wishes. Self-hate grows for allowing the abuse to happen.

Entrapment and accommodation

Because of the compulsive/addictive nature of the perpetrator's behaviour, sexual abuse continues. The child feels they have no option but to live with the experience; however they will start to demonstrate self-punishing behaviour such as self-mutilation or anorexia. The perpetrator will continue to give the child strong messages about their responsibility to keep the family together by not disclosing.

Delayed, conflicted and unconvincing disclosure

Children may often stay quiet until they reach adolescence, when they attempt to become somewhat independent from their family. Family conflict and the perpetrator's jealousy may be responsible for disclosure. The requirement to accommodate the abuse is seen as less of an imperative, yet the risk of disclosure is the prospect of not being believed.

Retraction

Once having made a disclosure the young person is likely to retract it, as the family is launched into a state of chaos and disbelief, with potentially traumatic consequences. The young person sees no other option available to them other than withdrawing their allegation.

As can be seen, the factors which act as a deterrent to a child's disclosure, particularly in intra-familial abuse, are numerous and complex in their origin. For disabled children, these factors will be considered in more detail in Chapter 4. Undoubtedly, the child will carry an (unrealistic) burden of guilt related to their involvement in the experience, a fear of not being believed by adults (both parents and professionals) and, in cases of intra-familial abuse, a fear of the consequences of disclosure for other family members, which might involve such things as care proceedings and criminal prosecution.

As highlighted in Chapter 3, child protection systems present many obstacles to children being able to freely deliver their abuse narrative. Child protection teams undertaking investigative interviews grapple with the necessity of incorporating increasingly legalistic frameworks, such as the *Memorandum of Good Practice* (Home Office 1992) and the subsequent *Achieving Best Evidence in Criminal Proceedings* (Home Office 2002) into their work with children, needing to demonstrate, along the way, the child's capacity to distinguish between truth and lies (McCarron, Ridgway and Williams 2004). If the child's case proceeds to criminal proceedings, in addition to any corroborative evidence (which is generally absent), a range of developmental factors will dictate how the child delivers their narrative of abuse, which will then determine whether a juror will consider it a credible account of events. Problematic issues for interviewers and jurors can be ambiguity and gaps in the child's narrative. Spontaneous allegations and free narrative may prove helpful (Westcott and Kyman 2004). Frequently the legal system fails to meet the child's needs and sometimes it can be experienced as unhelpful by the young person, particularly when there is a significant delay in the case coming to court (Prior, Glaser and Lynch 1997).

Delayed or partial recall, in addition to the difficulty in disclosing when young, creates a situation whereby the majority of survivors of child sexual abuse only feel able to 'speak out' later in life, often in the context of a safe long-term relationship. Baker (2002) proposes that preceding therapy there is often no particular catalyst for disclosure. Disclosure can range from concern about other children's safety who may still be in contact with the perpetrator, to a more general build-up of psychological distress by the individual concerned.

Research indicates that the reaction of others to a disclosure, in a person's social support network, plays a critical part in the well-being of the survivor (McNulty and Wardle 1994), as was clear in the experiences of the participants (above). Additionally, 'disclosure of sexual abuse, especially to family members who are directly involved, may well represent a serious life stress in its own right, and would increase the incidence of illness' (p.551). In fact, Baker (2002) feels that validation and support by the mother, in particular, can be more significant than the abuse itself. By drawing on the work of others, McNulty and Wardle (1994) suggest that for those who experience positive responses to their disclosure, they are more likely to experience successful psychological adaption.

SUPPORTING AND FACILITATING IN THE RESEARCH CONTEXT

The development of the sexual abuse narrative in the research context is bound up with a number of ethical complexities. It involves consideration of three distinct areas of concern: the support mechanisms required by the participant whilst sharing their narrative, the support required by the researcher and, finally, a reflective evaluation of the research processes that facilitate the narrative. The ultimate goal is to produce a narrative that is acceptable to the narrator – a narrative which is self-affirming, self-absolving and which provides some degree of empowerment.

Supporting the research relationship

Castor-Lewis (1988) suggests that an important consideration when embarking upon research with survivors of child sexual abuse is the need for participants to have a counsellor/therapist in place before the work commences. Or, at the very least, the researcher might obtain a list of agencies who could offer counselling should this be required. A precondition of participation in this particular research project was the existence of an adequate and verifiable support system, namely, a support system that could provide some reassurance that the participant would not have to deal with any difficult emotions generated by the research process alone. This support would be beyond what could be offered by a researcher working at a distance. The presence of a support system also reduced the chances of receiving fresh disclosure material, which posed an immediate risk to the current safety of children (Swain, Heyman and Gillman 1998).

The research interview can be an anxiety-provoking event and participants dealt with this in their own particular way. Several participants had the support of their partners; either in the next room to where the interview was taking place or in the actual interview itself. Others relied on friends or chose to participate at a distance via email. Clearly, people had weighed up the personal cost/benefit of participation before responding to the research advertizement. This finding is consistent with the research of others where benefit is shown to outweigh cost (Newman, Walker and Gefland 1999).

Newman *et al.* (1997) consider a commonly cited ethical objection to participation in trauma-based research, i.e. the potential for re-traumatization as a result of involvement. They propose that a lack of distinction made between the effects of talking about trauma, and actually experiencing it hinders the risk-benefit research debate. Newman *et al.* evaluate this view in terms of others' research findings, and despite appreciation of the psychological difficulty created by trauma, believe these claims to be unsubstantiated. Bruzy, Ault and Segal (1997) found in their experience that whilst participants may describe negative effects relating to the interview process (such as anxiety when anticipating the interview, distress whilst discussing issues and nightmares after the interview) careful interview preparation and support from the researcher after the interview go some way towards countering any upset caused by their involvement.

In order to provide a more scientific method for weighing the risk-benefits for participation in trauma-based research, Newman, Walker and Gefland (1999) undertook intensive research with a large sample of participants. They found that the majority of participants reported benefit from involvement and for the minority who did report a degree of distress, this distress appeared tolerable and didn't prevent continuation. In interviews with abuse survivors in particular, the distress generally stemmed from evaluating past events from a current perspective. In research which looks specifically at the issue of sexual abuse by professionals, Disch (2001) found that when people participated through their own free will and were fully informed about the nature of the research, they were able to handle the feelings that the research generated. In fact, these survivors were able to use these feelings to further their own personal healing process.

Castor-Lewis (1988) advocates the need for the researcher to also have a support system in place. In particular, Castor-Lewis talks of having someone to share any feelings generated by the overwhelming nature of the material. Bruzy, Ault and Segal (1997) support this view and offer some other advice related to interviewer debriefing, including the usefulness of researchers recording their response to their involvement in the process. As well as providing a helpful medium of expression, they believe that this can often create emotional insights into the research encounter. The work of Thompson (1995) might indicate the need for note-taking immediately after the interview. With reference to others' research, she proposes that the same psychological dynamic of dealing with trauma (blocking, minimizing and forgetting) can also be mirrored in the researcher's own process.

Castor-Lewis (1988) draws researchers' attention to the need for reflection when examining their contribution to the research relationship. In particular, she highlights any perceived threat of boundary invasion, which might mirror the dynamics of the original abusive relationship. Castor-Lewis comments that 'researchers would do well to ask themselves how their particular approach, manner, or instructions will be experienced by someone whose boundaries were flagrantly, aggressively, often repeatedly, and sometimes violently violated in the context of early trauma' (p.74). The need to give a sense of control to the participant has been discussed already in Chapter 1, but the need for control also extends to a sensitivity to the pace set by the participant when telling their story (Thompson 1995). Thompson suggests that it is body language that provides the necessary information, which determines when it is appropriate to move on and whether it is acceptable to return to enquire further about certain events. She also maintains that good eye contact is important in the interview and can be compromised when researchers refer back to their notes.

Facilitating the narrative

I (Martina) encountered a number of issues in this whole process of facilitating narrative. One significant issue was whether to share information about myself. By drawing on the work of another, Cotterill and Letherby (1993) propose that the research narrative is, in fact, an amalgam of two narratives – that of the researched and that of the researcher. They suggest that the researcher needs first to give consideration to their own autobiography and then 'place herself in relation to the issues she is researching' (p.72). Although reciprocity is vital for relationship building, this approach is not without its own set of problems. The sharing of autobiographical detail considered to be largely unproblematic, for example, can sometimes subtly interfere with the research process. Identifying myself, as a parent of a disabled child, affected how freely one participant in this study was able to verbalize their opinions on how disabled children can be problematically perceived by their parents. This dynamic highlighted one particular source of contradiction for researchers working as 'insiders'. Whilst there was a shared identity of belonging to an oppressed section of society, at the same time I represented a potential oppressor. The reality of this situation reflects the fact that when researching the experiences of oppression, there is no neutral position for the researcher (Vernon 1997).

Examination of the role that reciprocity plays in facilitating a positive research relationship has been a concern of feminism some time. Oakley (1981), for example, challenges the traditional research model and questions the presumption that research could be a non-reciprocal process. In other words, she would question whether it is possible for the researcher to be a recipient of information, yet resist any wish to share their own views, feelings and experiences. Ribbens (1989) would perhaps be the first to question a researcher's reluctance to offer any personal involvement, or self-exposure, when engaging in research that expects participants to share intensely personal information.

Ribbens (1989) suggests there are several levels of reciprocity in an interview, the first being how a researcher might tackle direct questions from the participant. The second level concerns researcher risk taking – should the researcher play a more active role in volunteering information? Despite the obvious necessity for reciprocity in sensitive research, the risk incurred with this type of approach is when a researcher contribution might interrupt the narrative flow (Ribbens 1989). The most accurate predictor of how things should be in a research encounter is the participant; they invariably lead the way in terms of how the discourse will unfold. When interviewing survivors of sexual abuse, Castor-Lewis (1988) believes that several other aspects to researcher behaviour are important to the process. First, that the researcher is 'emotionally and cognitively present' (p.80) in the interview, with the researcher demonstrating an active engagement with the process. Additionally, Castor-Lewis suggests that it is important that the participant knows that there are two people involved in their journey.

The practicalities of facilitating a life story interview have been considered by a number of authors. It is probably fair to say that once volunteers have got to the point of agreeing to be involved in research they are generally keen to tell their story, but often need to prepare and get their thoughts together beforehand (Atkinson 1998). Other writers' work indicates that asking a 'generative narrative question' can be helpful in terms of preparation and stimulating narrative (Flick 1998). In this research, the question took the form of 'could you tell me the story of your life with reference to the experience of child sexual abuse, including more general happenings of relevance?' I supplied a list of additional questions, which could be used if these issues were not covered in their life story account. This list included questions such as:

- What factors do you believe put you at risk of child sexual abuse?

- What are your thoughts on why perpetrators commit such offences?

- How has sexual abuse affected your life and do you believe that non-disabled people would identify the same types of problems?

- What strategies have you used to survive the experience?

The use of a 'time line' or 'life map' (Walmsley 1998) was also introduced as an aid to narration. This involved the breaking down of their life story into more manageable chunks, so that the recounting of information might be made easier. This approach is consistent with the writings of Flick (1998) who suggests that our experiences are 'stored and remembered in forms of narrative-episodic and semantic knowledge' (p.106). Episodic knowledge is linked to concrete situations or events. Semantic knowledge relates to the meaning derived from those events. Rosenthal (1993) proposes that the process of choosing what to share in the interview is not a random choice for the participant, but the result of the ever-changing meaning attached to the narrative. It is a snapshot of a person's interpretation of events at a particular moment in time and further influenced, to a lesser degree, by the research dynamic.

CONCLUSION

The production of a research narrative is determined as much by the quality of the research relationship as the stage of recovery reached by the participant. As can be seen from this chapter, the production of a research narrative is a highly complex matter and in the investigation of sensitive subjects it usually involves a reciprocal approach. Factors related to the researcher's own experiences (personal and professional) are inevitably entwined with the participant's narrative to produce a jointly constructed written product. Cotterill and Letherby (1993) believe that, through the differing facets of the research process, researchers actually become the participant's biographer. Narratives are influenced by the research relationship, analyzed and interpreted using the researcher's own life experiences and, in that sense, they suggest that researchers become the filter through which a participant's life is understood.

CHAPTER 3

An Abusive Society?

INTRODUCTION

We turn next to the broad context in which disabled people have 'telling stories'. We shall begin this chapter by examining the social context of the sexual abuse of young people. The social context is one of devaluation to the point of dehumanization; the dominant view of disabled young people and their lives is inherently tragic, abnormal and ultimately, in eugenic terms, 'life unworthy of life'. We begin by exploring this dominant ideology as expressed in media representations, or misrepresentations, of disabled people, their lives and the lives of their families. We look at the ways in which cultural misrepresentations of disabled people have adversely influenced the attitudes of others, propagating numerous offensive stereotypes, which categorize and objectify.

The second section of the chapter considers how the disabled person's de-valued status is reflected in the lack of attention that 'child abuse and disability' receives in research. This factor becomes glaringly obvious in the field of sexual abuse where, for non-disabled children, the subject matter has been examined from every possible angle including its prevalence, its consequences for the child, the adult survivor, the non-abusive parent and the perpetrator. For disabled children, whilst incidence figures are slowly emerging, the crushing impact for the disabled child is hugely under-researched, to the point of being dismissed.

Section three explores the impact of dehumanization on service provision for disabled children living with their family of origin. It considers how a 'whole-system' approach can detract attention from the possibility of child sexual abuse occurring within and outside the immediate family. It further considers the issue of communication and the isolating consequences of failing to facilitate communication. Finally, it investigates the frustrations of those practitioners who want to communicate, but are held back by the financial constraints of their departments.

CULTURAL MISREPRESENTATIONS OF IMPAIRMENT

Disabled people are a de-valued section of society, a factor reflected in the cultural misrepresentations of impairment within society. These cultural depictions are layered with inaccuracies that often far exceed the reality of disabled people's impairment, commonly perpetuating a fear of difference (Grewal *et al.* 2002) and ultimately contributing to the creation of prejudice. The power to devalue certain sections of society, such as disabled people, lies in the status/power of the dominant group. The dominant group produces ideas of normality, and categorizes those who fall outside those norms as other/abnormal/tragic (Drake 1996). The requirement, set by society, relating to a need to attain bodily perfection creates one of the most significant sources of disabled people's oppression (Barnes 1996).

Thompson (2003) offers a useful categorization of mechanisms, which serve to maintain the power of the dominant group and maintain the oppression of others. These mechanisms include such processes as: stereotyping, marginalization, infantilization, medicalization, dehumanization and trivialization. Stereotypes, in particular, are argued by some to be one of the major embodiments of others' hostility, with Thompson (2003) contending that stereotypes are so ingrained in our society that it is easy to become oblivious to their existence and the ways in which they shape our perceptions of others. Stereotypes are also firmly embedded within our language, and for disabled people they can endorse and strengthen non-disabled people's negative attitudes (French 1996a). They can also work in an insidious fashion to erode the self-confidence of the disabled person (Reeve 2002). When describing disability hate crime in the UK, Quarmby (2008) writes, 'The motivating factor stares us in the face:

a hostility and contempt for disabled people based on the view that disabled people are inferior, and do not matter' (p.26).

Sutherland (1981) suggests that disabled people generally attract a range of offensive stereotypes. He asserts that we are frequently referred to as visually repulsive; helpless; dependent; too independent; brave and courageous; bitter, with chips on our shoulders; evil; mentally retarded, etc. The bravery stereotype, in particular, which highlights an individual's courage when 'fighting' or coping with their impairment appears on the surface to be innocuous. Sutherland proposes that this stereotype further adds to disabled people's oppression by constructing impairment as 'a purely individual responsibility' (p.68). He suggests that often a non-disabled person's dehumanizing behaviour can act as a catalyst for the disabled person's assumption of a particular (and subservient) role-type, which then reaffirms the non-disabled person's behaviour. One of the end products of this process can be a distortion of the disabled people's own sense of reality. Similarly, disabled children are described and perceived in negative and inaccurate terms. With reference to the work of others, Davis (2004) proposes that disabled young people are frequently defined in terms of 'deficit' and are seen to have an inability to express their views.

Contemporary cultural representations of impairment can often build on stereotypes, and generally centre on notions of tragedy and dependency. These portrayals have remained largely unchallenged until very recently. With reference to other writers, Priestley (1999) describes the etiquette of the tabloid press who tend to focus on particular impairment-related topics such as 'personal interest stories', which are generally accompanied by patronizing text. Here there may be a depiction of the disabled person as 'triumphing in the face of adversity' or surviving as a result of a non-disabled person's generous donations of cash/body parts. Barnes (1992) writes that the language used in this type of news media is often emotive, frequently linking impairment with illness and suffering. Barnes further makes the point that these types of news broadcast use depersonalized language, referring to, for example, 'the disabled' discourse which relegates disabled people to mere objects.

Shakespeare (1997) believes that charity advertizing operates along similar lines. Disabled people are represented in a demeaning and pitiable light with power differentials being widened by inflating non-disabled people's egos, often at the cost of disabled people's integrity. Also, a significant amount of inaccurate and irresponsible information can come from the advertizing campaigns of impairment-specific charities, which overwhelmingly depict impairment as deficit and dependency (Barnes 1992). Sheldon (2004) maintains that for disabled women, impairment adds another layer of complexity to the negative stereotype of femininity, which is also described in terms of passivity and dependency. For disabled women, the stereotype is further exaggerated by a perceived asexual identity.

Wilde (2004) considers the portrayal of disabled people within soap operas. In this type of medium, the range of impairment-related narratives are restricted, and examples are given of impairment being resolved by the 're-establishment of non-disabled identities' (p.360) or, in situations where impairment can't be resolved, it becomes associated with other forms of 'deviancy'. Barnes (1992) cites a number of invariably negative characterizations that commonly appear in media plot structures. These include depictions of the disabled person as sinister and evil; the disabled person as atmosphere or curio; the disabled person as a super cripple; the disabled person as their worst and only enemy; and the disabled person as an object of ridicule. In relation to this latter point, Clark (2003) examines the ways in which comedy has contributed to disabled people's disempowerment. Humour, he asserts, is commonly derived from an individual's impairment, and is often exploited to get laughs. The reality is that this type of media coverage can adversely affect public perception.

In their totality, cultural portrayals of impairment within the media serve to compound disabled people's de-valued status within society (Grewal 2002). We argue within the following sections of this chapter that some of these devaluing assumptions about disabled people have contributed to the abuse of disabled children taking a lower profile both within research and professional practice.

GAPS IN THE RESEARCH

Turning to research, the devaluation of disabled young people is expressed in a number of different ways when we examine the available literature, and is predominantly expressed in prevalence figures. Though there are complex issues involved in interpreting findings the evidence is clear: disabled young people are at a greater risk of sexual abuse. Yet the research is sparse. Why? Here we examine some of the research literature, comparing research involving non-disabled survivors (which is plentiful) to their disabled peers.

Itzin (2000a) makes the point that child sexual abuse is a significant area of academic and professional concern, drawing particular attention to the work of Bagley and Thurston (1996), for example, who have produced a two-volume synopsis detailing 500 studies on differing facets of the sexual abuse experience. A significant number of prevalence studies have originated from North America, and whilst there is recognition of the general under-reporting of child sexual abuse, there is also recognition that a relationship can exist between prevalence rates and research methodology, which can create variations in figures. Having considered a number of studies, Doyle Peters, Wyatt and Finkelhor (1986) cite prevalence rates, within North America, that vary enormously (6–62% for females, 3–31% for males). This is a factor they attribute to either the definition of sexual abuse used in a particular study, the possibility that findings may accurately reflect the prevalence rates in that particular section of society, or the fact that certain research practices distort the data. In particular these research practices might include how participants are recruited, the type of research method employed (questionnaires or face-to-face interviews), and the type of questions that are asked.

Cawson et al. (2000) give an example of the potential difficulties that definitions may present by referring to a study conducted by Kelly, Regan and Burton (1991) involving a sample of students aged 16–21. These authors discovered that one in two girls and one in five boys reported unwanted sexual experiences (flashing and sexual suggestions) before the age of 18, but when a more restrictive definition of sexual abuse was employed (penetration and coerced masturbation, and more than a five year age difference between parties) prevalence was significantly reduced. Cawson et al. also highlight a more general issue relating to definitions that pose problems for researchers. This includes the difficulty created by a need to establish where a cutoff point lies between 'normal sexual play and what has become known as "peer abuse"' (p.73). With reference to others' work, Cawson et al. describe how issues relating to child experimentation, fear of labelling, the minimization of the seriousness of peer abuse, and low reporting rates cloud the issue.

Bolen, Russell and Scannapieco (2000) refer to several of the more accurate reviews of this research literature in the US and Canada, which have been analyzed for methodological factors: Bolen and Scannapieco (1999) and Russell and Bolen (2000). From these two reviews, which considered 31 studies in total, using a mix of methodology, Bolen, Russell and Scannapieco conclude that both studies provide similar prevalence rates. These rates fall in a range of 30 per cent to 40 per cent for female child sexual abuse, with Bolen and Scannapieco finding 13 per cent or more for male child sexual abuse.

One of the most significant large-scale studies of child maltreatment conducted in the United Kingdom (2869 participants, aged 18–24 years, with a small percentage of disabled young people) cites prevalence rates for sexual abuse as 6 per cent of their total sample (Cawson et al. 2000). Of the self-assessed sexual abuse subgroup, 28 per cent considered themselves to have been sexually abused, reporting, amongst other things, sexual activity against their will, more than five years' age difference when under 16 even when consent was given, or sex in return for money/drugs/favours. The gendered division of sexual abuse proved to be 35 per cent for women and 15 per cent for men.

In marked contrast to this wealth of prevalence data investigating the sexual abuse of non-disabled children, studies specifically focusing on the prevalence rates amongst disabled children have been comparatively limited. Westcott and Jones (1999) imply this neglect of research, concerning child abuse and disability, may relate to societal indifference concerning the subject matter. We argue here that devaluing attitudes towards disabled children contribute to a situation whereby disabled children, for a whole number of reasons, are at an increased risk of child sexual abuse (as indicated in observations from professional practice), yet the slow growth in related academic research continues. In other words, in academia the abuse of disabled children matters less.

Much of the work that has investigated the prevalence of child sexual abuse among disabled children has also been conducted in North America, and predominantly taken from studies looking at the full range of child abuse experience. One of the most commonly cited large-scale study is that of Sullivan and Knutson (2000), which is a replication and extension of their previous work (Sullivan and Knutson 1998). Both of these studies involved control groups. Sullivan and Knutson (1998) examined the occurrence of child abuse using a hospital-based sample (cross-referenced for accuracy using a merger of other databases), finding that impairment was a significant risk factor in child abuse and, in addition, that impairment can be a consequence of some forms of maltreatment.

Sullivan and Knutson (2000), in an attempt to counter criticism that hospital data 'over-samples' children with impairments, combined their earlier findings with school databases taken from the same geographical region as the Sullivan and Knutson (1998) research. This more recent study found that there was 'major evidence' supporting the fact that disabled children were at greater risk of child abuse than their non-disabled peers, citing prevalence data of 31 per cent, by comparison to the 9 per cent rate for non-disabled children. Overall, they concluded that disabled children were 3.4 times more likely to experience some form of child abuse than their non-disabled counterparts. This study also concluded that disabled children are more likely to experience multiple forms of abuse, and they caution on the misleading consequences of treating types of abuse as distinct categories (so obscuring the overlap). They found no significant relationship between the type of impairment and the type of abuse. It was also noted that immediate family members were usually the perpetrators of physical abuse, emotional abuse and neglect and that extrafamilial perpetrators were more often responsible for sexual abuse.

Focusing specifically on the sexual abuse of disabled children, Sullivan and Knutson (2000) found that disabled children are 3.14 times more likely to be sexually abused than non-disabled children, a fact which is relevant to other, associated research (Crosse 1993; Jaudes and Diamond 1983; Knutson and Sullivan 1993; Kvam 2004; Sobsey and Mansell 1994; Sullivan, Vernon and Scanlan 1987). Sullivan and Knutson (2000) report that children with learning difficulties and children with speech and language impairments are at a slight, increased risk of sexual abuse compared with other disabled children. In terms of gender difference, Sobsey, Randall and Parrila (1997) found in their study that significantly more disabled girls (62%) than boys (38%) had experienced sexual abuse, but that disabled boys formed a much larger minority compared to non-disabled boys. Looking more closely at the group of sexually abused boys, Sobsey, Randall and Parrila found that more disabled boys were sexually abused in the 6–11 age range compared to girls within the same age banding.

In terms of European studies, Kvam (2004) investigated the prevalence of child sexual abuse in Norway, specifically amongst individuals with hearing impairments, using questionnaires and a comparison group. Kvam reported that females with hearing impairments experienced contact sexual abuse more than twice as often as hearing females (39.6% and 19.2%) and males with hearing impairments more than three times more often (32.8% and 9.6%). Approximately 50 per cent of the research participants described the fact that the perpetrator also had a hearing impairment and that half of the abusive incidents took place in schools for hearing impaired children. These individuals also spoke about having fewer friends at home, bullying experiences at school and poor parental relationships compared to the non-abused hearing-impaired group. Kvam found that the results of his study were consistent with North American research (Sullivan, Vernon and Scanlan 1987), with both studies indicating that the risk for hearing impaired children could be associated with residential education.

There is a paucity of prevalence and incidence data in Great Britain relating to the sexual abuse of disabled children. This situation has partly arisen because the Department of Health does not ask local authorities to indicate a child's impairment status once their name has been added to the child protection register (Morris 1999; Westcott and Cross 1996). Cooke and Standen (2002) investigated this issue further by sending a postal questionnaire to the chairs of 121 Area Child Protection Committees in England, Scotland, Wales and Northern Ireland. Whilst 51 per cent of respondents reported that they recorded a child's impairment, only 14 per cent of authorities could give an actual figure. Morris (1999) found, in her research, that disabled children are treated as 'largely invisible within the child protection systems' (p.92). The difficulty involved in recording information for one local authority stemmed from the following factors:

- Failure to establish a common definition of impairment.

- Failure to ensure that the information was consistently recorded.

- Failure to include children considered to have 'mild to moderate learning difficulties' within specialist disability services.

Two of the most commonly cited pieces of UK research that provide some incidence data relating to the sexual abuse of disabled children include that of Kennedy (1989) and Sinason (undated). Kennedy looked specifically at children with hearing impairments who were known to the teachers and social workers of children with hearing impairments. Sinason's cohort included children with learning difficulties and emotional problems who were in therapy (Westcott and Cross 1996). Bearing in mind the recruitment bias of the samples, both studies reported a significantly high incidence of child sexual abuse. Overall, it seems that research on child sexual abuse in Great Britain is limited with research being conducted through discussion with professionals known to the child, such as teachers (Stuart-Green and Stone 1996), or via retrospective case note review (Firth et al. 2001).

One of the most glaring differences that become apparent when comparing research looking at the experience of the disabled and non-disabled survivors is in the field of qualitative research. Whilst research examining differing facets of the abusive experience is plentiful for non-disabled survivors, the same cannot be said for research involving disabled people. Probably one of the most frequently cited pieces of research conducted in Great Britain, and addressing the issue of abuse and disability, is that of Westcott (1993). This study is a generalized piece of work using a sample of disabled and non-disabled adult survivors. It looks at the abuse of disabled adults and children using semi-structured interviews where, amongst other things, the disabled participants themselves highlight factors that contribute to the increased risk of abuse.

A similar situation exists in relation to narrative-based research. Increasingly, narrative methodology is used to investigate the sexual abuse experience and its far-reaching impact on the non-disabled individual's life (Crowley 2000; Durham 2003; Etherington 2000; Itzin 2000). For disabled people, who are at increased risk in childhood, there is a notable absence of this type of literature, with some limited examples of narrative-style research appearing outside the UK (Zavirsek 2002). This book aims to address this imbalance in our current knowledge base by illustrating the complexity of the disabled survivor's individual experience. In particular the book represents a need to consider, in some detail, the enmeshed and complex relationship between child sexual abuse, the impaired body and identity formation, with a consideration of the implications for this intricate relationship for practitioners working in the field.

CHILD PROTECTION: PAST AND PRESENT

It could be argued that little appears to have changed for disabled children living within their family of origin, as the possibility of child abuse is often eclipsed by a number of other matters that are seen to be perhaps more salient. In some local authorities child protection and disability are still viewed as two distinct specialisms, each with their own particular focus and value system, and a degree of neglect for the overlap continues to be the case. This means that indicators of child abuse can be overlooked or misinterpreted by practitioners. It also means that the lack of knowledge about impairment, in child protection teams (Morris 1999), has the potential to interfere with processes associated with facilitating disclosure and achieving a criminal prosecution.

In social work practice, a pattern of service delivery has evolved which recognizes the impact of a child's impairment on the day-to-day functioning of the family system, and appreciates the potential energy required by parents when dealing with a large assortment of professionals. This model of care, Statham and Read (1998) suggest, is characterized by a focus on particular methods of service delivery, which can include the necessity to work in partnership with parents, the use of a single key worker system and the provision of short-term breaks for the disabled child so that the family can have some respite. Whilst these three detailed components of service provision are recognized as providing many benefits for the disabled child, Middleton (1999) cautions on the potential dangers that respite care, in particular, can create for disabled children. Respite care can re-inforce the 'status of the disabled child as a "problem" for a family' (p.51). Respite care also carries the same risks of child abuse, with multiple carers increasing that risk of abuse. Separations can also potentially compromise parent–child attachments. Middleton suggests that the sympathy that social workers might feel for parents should not detract from a need to keep child protection issues on their agenda. The situation becomes more complex when the parent also has an impairment:

> She went to day centres, so we always had a social worker, and yet I don't think anybody ever asked me really. If somebody had asked me directly if there was anything I would like to stop, then I would have been able to say that, 'I wish he wouldn't drink so much, I wish he wouldn't grope me, I wish he'd listen to me', and that kind of thing. And that might have given them a clue. (Lyn)

> The relationship with social services was also very complex; my mother relied on their support, but there was also a resentment of the control that they had to provide support. Going to social services would have been a betrayal as well. Maybe one of the reasons that things didn't get noticed was that whenever I cropped up in the problem category it was always with the focus of hearing loss and the provision of hearing aids, and people maybe felt that once they'd done that bit, they'd done what was necessary. They were so concerned that I should hear enough at school and at university to succeed, and if that was achieved then the rest of it was almost too much to take on board. (Lyn)

In addition to the dangers of maintaining a fixed focus on the provision of hearing aids, Lyn's quotes also raise the issue of communication with disabled children. Middleton (1999) describes how the Social Services Inspectorate found (in their 1994 inspection) that the basic requirement of local authorities to consult with children, as detailed in the Children Act (1989), was not being achieved for disabled children. Furthermore, Middleton details how the inspectorate found that local authorities did not have the skills required to consult directly. Morris (1999) discovered, in her research, a contradictory state of affairs within disabled children's services. Whilst the local authority's client base was predominantly made up of children with significant communication requirements, there is an absence of specialist training to facilitate communication and support professional practice. In fact, Morris found that many disabled young people:

- did not have access to a communication system that suited their needs

- did not have routine access to people who understood the ways they communicated

- did not have access to independent facilitators.

(Morris 1999, p.101)

Rabiee, Sloper and Beresford (2005), when conducting more generally focused research with young people who have complex communication needs, found children keen to engage in a process of expressing their views. These authors, in addition to Marchant and Page (2003) and Kennedy (2002), highlight that, with the exception of speech, there are a significant number of other methods available to enable practitioners to gain access to disabled children's wishes and feelings. These methods can include augmentative communication systems involving communication boards, technology aided systems, signing, facial expressions and vocalization. There are also communication tools available that are designed to enable disabled children to express emotions related to their safety (Triangle/NSPCC 2001). Often communication involves a multi-agency approach and also may require creativity on the part of a practitioner. Morris (1999) found that despite the desire of some social workers to facilitate effective communication, the financial pressures faced by many local authorities may act as a deterrent to this process:

> There was someone, a psychologist I think it was, who was absolutely brilliant at telling you how you could interpret body language and the sounds that some children make. That's the kind of thing we need, and we need help with doing it... I paid to do a Makaton course myself. I wanted to do a more advanced course but the department wouldn't fund it. (p.100)

Both Morris (1999) and Marchant and Page (2003) conclude that lack of access to communication tools is a breach of a basic human right. It ultimately makes disabled children more vulnerable to abuse by compounding difficulties associated with disclosure. From a child's perspective, the inability to communicate intensifies their feelings of isolation:

> I think that there were reasons, not just to do with the family situation, that I was more isolated from other children. I did have difficulty communicating with people outside my family for

a long time; my lip reading wasn't very good and I wasn't offered any lip reading classes. I could usually understand my mother; I often had difficulty understanding my father, and people outside the family were often quite difficult. So I read a lot, I didn't really have many friends, and the habit of speaking to people about things stopped, I think. It's not the only reason, but it sort of compounded it and made the barriers harder. (Lyn)

Within this under-funded financial context, children's health and disability services have been classified as the 'Cinderella service' (Audit Commission 2003). Some writers make the link between resourcing issues for particular services, and the de-valued status of their client group (Wardhaugh and Wilding 1993). Resourcing issues are also reflected in the transitional services offered to young disabled people looking to live independently of their parents. In families where the parental perspective has been prioritized, and communication with the young person has become of secondary importance, the consequences for the young person can be incredibly problematic:

I also think that disabled people have to face issues with social services that others don't (although I hope that this has changed now). I tried to move out at an early age because I felt that this was the best way to change things. I approached my social worker, who then went to my parents to ask what they thought. Of course they said that I would never manage. I was told that I was better off at home. Other non-disabled people would have said, 'I'm having problems at home and want to move,' and been supported. I know this because friends that I have known have done this. (May)

For those young people, such as May, whose welfare benefits have been diverted into family funds, the usual difficulties associated with transition and independent living become exacerbated. The financial incentive for some parents to keep the abused disabled child at home for a longer period of time can slow down an already lengthy process created by the lack of adapted housing stock, in this instance. It also means that the duration of abuse is extended. In this situation, not only does the individual lose all control of their body because of the sexual abuse experience, but the matter also becomes more complicated since the prospect of escape to independent living seems more elusive. As indicated below, the diversion of funds can compound a child's sense of isolation, so reducing opportunities for disclosure:

My abuse lasted until I was into my twenties; this was a direct result of my disability. Like I said, I had been trying to move out from an early age but the lack of suitable properties meant I spent longer on the housing list than other people would. Anyone else in my position would have been able to move in anywhere, but I couldn't. My health was worse so I needed more help, and I think that this makes social services reluctant to re-house you because of the cost. My way of coping with things during this time was to stay away from home as much as possible. (May)

As indicated earlier, difficulties in facilitating communication can extend to formal investigation and court proceedings; an issue which will not be covered in any great detail here. Some difficulties relate to the lack of appropriate training given to police officers who undertake investigative interviews with disabled children (Aldridge and Wood 1999) and may determine a decision not to interview. Other problems relate to Crown Prosecution scrutiny which results in low numbers of disabled children's testimony reaching the courtroom setting. The decision not to pursue a case may be made because of inaccurate and ill-informed assumptions relating to the disabled child's ability to communicate (Kennedy 2002; Love, Cooke and Taylor 2003). Such factors, attitudinal and process-related, denies the right of the individual to even be heard in court. The disabled child witness, who actually manages to get into court, then faces many hurdles when trying to give their evidence, despite the existence of facilitative guidelines.

Overall, Middleton (1999) calls for a broadening of the social work knowledge base. For child disability practitioners, that should mean a requirement to undertake child protection training. Training that would enable them to keep issues of child protection continually in the mind's eye, investigating concerns as they arise, and according to child protection procedure. It would guard against the misinterpretation of indicators of sexual abuse, as behaviour stemming from a child's impairment (Middleton 1999; Kennedy 2002). As a preventative measure, Middleton (1999) suggests the need for practitioners to be alert to the significance of the disabled child's presence within the family system, in particular whether the child is seen in positive terms or construed as a burden (an issue which will be picked up and discussed further in later chapters).

On a finishing note, we need to stress that this section of the chapter has dealt ostensibly with practice issues relating to children living at home. In Chapter 6, child protection issues are raised once again, but this time in relation to disabled children living residentially, in both residential education or because of lengthy hospital admissions.

CONCLUSION

As a subject area, disability has lagged behind a general increase in public awareness of child abuse, despite this group of children's vulnerability. In part, the problem is linked to a societal belief that child abuse doesn't happen to disabled children (Kennedy 2002) and as disabled children are not considered in sexual terms, child sexual abuse is categorized as the 'unimaginable'. This chapter has looked at the ways in which the de-valued status of disabled people is reflected in the subject's downgrading as both a research priority and an area of professional practice. In comparison to non-disabled children's experiences, disability and child sexual abuse is an unforgivably neglected research topic. In professional practice, whilst there is some evidence of good work taking place in the field (Audit Commission 2003), services for disabled children and their families remain under-funded and take second place to services for non-disabled children. In reality, this means that communication between the disabled child and the practitioner can become less of a concern, the views of the parents remain more of a priority and issues of child protection are occluded.

CHAPTER 4

The Double Whammy Effect

INTRODUCTION

This short chapter lays the foundations for subsequent chapters where the implications of abuse are discussed in some detail and with reference to the child's developing sense of who they are. The double whammy effect, as it is referred to by Josh (see below), is the association between being disabled and being sexually abused, an issue which reverberates through all participants' experiences. Disability and abuse essentially reinforce each other.

The birth of a disabled child (or the subsequent diagnosis of impairment) marks a significant turning point for a family. Parents may have limited knowledge or experience of impairment, yet are required to make a rapid psychological adjustment to a diagnosis. Support/counselling at this stage may be seen as helpful, assisting parents to successfully make this major transition. Although most parents will form a close attachment to their disabled child, the development of difficult and undermining parent–child relationships do occur, and can have a destructive impact on a disabled child's sense of self.

This chapter explores the ways in which impairment interacts with sexual abuse; either by making disclosure of abuse a more difficult option for the child, or creating a view that they somehow deserved to be abused. A later section considers the implications of a compromised parent–child bond for the safety of the child outside the family environment. In particular, their vulnerability to further abuse by predatory paedophiles who they encounter in other parts of their life, and who are able to detect the child's emotional neediness and isolation. Let us begin first by considering what sexual abuse means for a child.

THE EXPERIENCE OF CHILD SEXUAL ABUSE

The experience of sexual abuse as a child, the experience of violence and violation, is an experience of powerlessness and worthlessness. It is the feeling that it was all you were good for and there was nothing you could do about it – the pressure to self-blame. The sense of powerlessness and worthlessness created by the experience of child sexual abuse is illustrated in the narratives of many non-disabled adult survivors (Durham 2003; Fraser 1987; Itzin 2000; Ward 1984). These quotes from Thomas and Lyn illustrate the wealth of emotion that is generated for the child and how these feelings are liable to carry over into adulthood:

> Later that evening, when I was in bed, he came into my bedroom and beat me up. He told me there was no point in telling my mother because she wouldn't believe me and that if I opened my mouth I would end up in the children's home that his mate ran, and that he would really make me scream. I heard him leave and go downstairs, laughing to himself. It was a laugh of arrogance, of one-up-manship. He had got away with it, convinced my mum so she believed him and lost me my milk (a drink I loved but cannot touch today without being physically sick). I remember lying in bed feeling useless, worthless, and knowing that he had all the power in the world to do what he wanted with me. I was totally beaten. (Thomas)

> A couple of years ago a film came out called 'Festen', which means the celebration or the party. It's a Danish film and it's about a father's 60th birthday party at which one of his children makes the revelation that he has abused them as children. It's almost comical in some places because it's so awful. It's deliberately, blackly comic, but it's also very painful. Anyway, I saw it with a group of people and one of the other people that I know had been abused – he is open about the fact that he's been abused by his father. There's this tiny bit of dialogue in the film where the son, who is actually by now very drunk, says in front of a lot of other people, 'I just want to know why it was. I never understood why you did it,' and the father was in a rage

and storms out of the room and almost in passing says, 'it was all you were good for'. When that happened, I remember that I looked across at this guy and he looked at me, and we both knew. (Lyn)

The emotional consequence of feeling powerless and worthless will be discussed in some detail in the next chapter, where the complexities of the process will be unravelled. When exploring the literature on child sexual abuse, differing facets of the experience are highlighted. By drawing on the work of others, Browne and Finkelhor (1986) refer to the significance of age, for example; illustrating that children in the 7–13 age range display more acute psychological distress than children in other age bandings. Others also comment on the subject matter from a gendered perspective, showing that girls have more of a tendency to turn painful emotions in on themselves, in comparison to boys (Feiring, Tasca and Lewis 1999). Some researchers emphasize the physiological implications of a trauma such as child sexual abuse on the memory (Sivers, Schooler and Freyd 2002). The emotional consequences of child sexual abuse are similar for disabled and non-disabled children. However, disabled children, as Josh describes below, have extra disability-related conflicts to deal with, which then become entangled with sexual abuse with potentially hazardous consequences and a double whammy effect:

> I think there are particular issues for disabled people who are sexually abused. Sexual abuse for any child is absolutely appalling, but it is worse in the respect that the disabled kid, whatever the disability is, whether it's learning disability or physical disability, it's worse in the respect that you're already at a disadvantage, you're already coping with lots of extras. Like I can't use my arm, I couldn't do up my buttons, I couldn't wipe my arse, I couldn't do this, I couldn't do that, and then somebody comes along and abuses you, sexually as well. So that's also taking something else away from you, so I think it's like having a double whammy; you know, you're hit once with your disability, you have to cope with non-disabled kids staring at the effects of your disability, then to get that on top, you're being hit twice. (Josh)

As can be seen in Chapter 7, perpetrators can also abuse disabled children who have a positive relationship with their primary carers, because they have managed to find employment within caring professions where they have regular access to children. This was the case for Lizzie who details a very loving relationship with her parents:

> When I was born, my mum just totally accepted me instantly and the nurses were really surprised. They said to her, 'Most women ask, has the baby got ten fingers and ten toes, and you didn't', and my mum was just a hundred per cent accepting of me, and my dad as well. So that was an enormous pillar of strength for me. And they did fight for me when fights were needed, as many of our parents do. (Lizzie)

A poor parent–child relationship, however, undoubtedly puts disabled children at further risk, as it has an additive implication for the child's sense of self-worth.

DISABLING PARENTING

A number of contributors to this book describe the difficulties that they encountered within the family home, where they were seen as a 'problem' or a 'burden'. This issue was reflected in the general quality of parenting that some children received, and invariably had an effect on their developing identity. It is important to stress at this point that these are the experiences of sexually abused disabled children, and are not representative of the experiences of disabled children per se, just as the experiences of sexually abused non-disabled children should not be taken as representative of the experiences of all non-disabled children.

In May's case, she describes a blatantly rejecting parenting experience. As can be seen, she felt that this influenced her ability to speak out about her sexual abuse later:

> My father felt that I had a disease and would have nothing to do with me. He also had a number of affairs just to prove that there was nothing wrong with him. So all this resulted in my mother leaving him, taking my younger sibling and me with her. From about the age of four, I can remember being told constantly, by my mother, that she could have stayed and had everything that she wanted, but instead left because of me. This made me feel like I had wrecked my mother and sibling's life. (May)

I don't think that there was ever a chance that I would have told, because of my feelings of having to make up for breaking up the family the first time round. For years I had been told I was an inconvenience, and that having someone with a disability in the house meant they couldn't do things. I was told that they couldn't have the holidays they wanted; they had to buy things they wouldn't buy normally, or replace things more often. These things just made me feel I was a nuisance, not good enough, and that I should support the family because I was costing them money. I came close to telling once or twice but just could not face the consequences of doing it. I thought my mother would hate me even more and I thought I would lose contact with my youngest sibling who I am very close to. (May)

Similarly, Lyn talks about her perception of herself, and her position both within her family and society at large. Her mother, who also had a physical impairment, had a significant impact on Lyn's viewpoint. Her feelings about herself also affected her ability to articulate sexual abuse:

You just feel apologetic the whole time within your family and in the rest of the world. You are a trouble and a problem and, however accommodating the environment, the accommodation has to be made, and you see it being made and you don't want to cause trouble. It becomes ingrained and, certainly, my mother's training had been, and what she handed on to me was, it must not show, you must not do anything which draws attention to yourself. (Lyn)

Social services were still coming to the house at that time but I couldn't tell because I still couldn't articulate what was wrong. All that I could have said was that there was something wrong and a large part of that was the feeling that it was me that was wrong. (Lyn)

In this next quote Lyn describes a complex set of emotions whereby being perceived as a problem or burden translated itself, in her mind, into feeling that she deserved to be sexually abused, or that being abused was one method of redeeming herself for being a problem:

The reverse of that is the feeling that you actually deserve it, really. If anybody deserves it in the family, you do. It's absorbing the problems. I used to have this fantasy that I was a sponge, and actually absorbing things like that (being sexually abused) becomes a good thing to do, it becomes your role. The many things that you can't do that other children can do in their families, e.g. being musical, or if you are in a wheelchair, being athletic, but you are able to do this! One thing that I did say to my therapist a while ago was that in all this time, between age eight and age 14, although there was a sense in which I didn't acknowledge that there was anything wrong, I also knew that there was a girl at my school called Jeanette, who everybody knew was being abused by her father. Everybody knew it. She was a wreck, and the awful thing is I can remember feeling contemptuous of her because she couldn't hack it, she couldn't handle it. There was pride there, there was the feeling of 'for Christ sake, I'm deaf and I can do it, and you're normal and you can't'. (Lyn)

It might be argued that the 'burden construct' marks the birth of a disabled child and symbolizes the first experience of social devaluation for that individual child. Again, we would emphasize that this is not the response of all parents of disabled children. Many parents welcome the birth of their child and engage in a struggle for the best possible quality of services for them (Murray and Penman 1996; Read 2000). Nevertheless, the event can be surrounded by a sense of misfortune and tragedy (Middleton 1992). Despite the very real emotional difficulties faced by some parents when trying to come to terms with their child's impairment, the medical profession can be accused of perpetuating this notion of 'tragedy'. Case (2000) found professional inadequacy when breaking the news of a child's impairment to the parents. The diagnosis was sometimes given abruptly and with little empathy, so increasing a parent's sense of alienation. Doctors should not underestimate the effect that they have on a parent's psychological adjustment, as their behaviour has the potential to influence how a parent might deal with their child's impairment (Case 2000; Cunningham, Morgan and McGucken 1984). By drawing on the work of other writers, Ablon (1990) suggests that for parents the birth of a disabled child can often mark the 'loss of the perfect child' (p.880), potentially influencing the parent's perception of themselves. Coming to terms and 'grieving' might involve a transition through a number of emotional states. It can also be understood in terms of the following set of behaviours:

- Awareness of the problem.

- Recognition of its nature.

- Search for a cause.

- Search for a cure.

- Acceptance of the problem.

Using such models, it must also be assumed that parents can get stuck at any particular stage, delaying their acceptance of their child. Some might question the usefulness of models of bereavement, seeing them as reinforcing negativity, rather than encouraging parents to embrace a child's individuality and difference (Middleton 1992). There is a necessity for parents not to define their child by their impairment, but to see past the label/diagnosis and see the child for the individual that they are (Middleton 1992), as many parents do.

Nevertheless, and in spite of parents' best efforts, the reality is that a sense of tragedy can often prevail in subsequent visits to health settings, where an early induction into the scientific language of abnormality takes place (Avery 1999). Tragedy discourse can then carry over into parents' encounters in the public arena. Here the reaction of strangers, which might create a sense of unease or even anger for the parent, can reinforce the tragedy message. As Avery (1999) writes:

> It does not help that perfect strangers ask us what is wrong with our child, or ask us about the nature of our child's problem. It does not help that the media inscribe our children as 'patients', 'victims' and 'sufferers'; or as being 'confined' to a wheelchair. (p.120)

Green (2003) undertook a survey of 81 mothers of physically impaired children, and then conducted in-depth interviews with seven from that group of 81. Green works with Goffman's concept of 'courtesy stigma' (1963), and examines the impact on the mother of others' reaction to their disabled child. Green's findings suggest that mothers, not surprisingly, may become parents yet still have some of the same prejudicial attitudes towards disabled people that are prevalent within society at large. She suggests that mothers who retain this sense of negativity, despite their parenting experience, may run the risk of becoming resentful.

The participants in Green's study reported many difficulties in their early experiences of managing others' reactions to their child. Family members and friends, who accepted their child, could still make negative comments about other disabled children. This could then trigger a mother's ambivalence. General coping strategies included re-interpreting others' behaviour as ignorance rather than malice, which then might necessitate a degree of re-education. These mothers reported exhaustion at having to tend to both others' and their own emotions. Green suggests that for some mothers, the anticipated response from others results in mothers limiting their child's interaction with peers, and their own choice of friends. Anticipated problems can also increase a mother's subjective sense of burden. Green suggests that assisting the development of maternal strategies for dealing with the public can potentially increase a disabled child's contact with their non-disabled peers.

Managing their own and others' reaction to their child is just one of the challenges facing the parents of disabled children. Other potential difficulties, highlighted by other research, include the impact on relationships within the family, particularly the parental relationship, which may come under a degree of pressure (Hornby 1992). This was a factor clearly evident in May's family where the parental relationship did not survive. Research indicates that there is, in fact, a polarization of parental responses to the appearance of impairment in the family, one of which is the strengthening of relationships, the other dissolution (Burke 2008). The work of Snell and Rosen (1997) identifies some of the important family strategies/attributes that enable parents to manage their child's presence. In this study, some of these attributes included family cohesion, which enabled family members to negotiate issues and include the disabled child as much as possible in family activities. In other families, cognitive strategies were adopted that enabled the family to see the child's presence in positive terms by identifying benefits, redefining events and normalizing issues. Both Snell and Rosen (1997) and Hornby (1992) comment on other positive consequences of being a parent of a disabled child. This involved a personal growth, or a shift in thinking relating to what they had perceived to be important in life.

Thomas's research (1998) approaches the issue of parenting from the perspective of the disabled young person, by gathering the views of 34 disabled women on their experiences of childhood.

This information was abstracted from a larger sample of 68 disabled women. Respondents told stories of parents, which ranged from supportive allies to obstacles to psychological well-being. Some of the undermining issues that Thomas's participants had to deal with are listed below; a number of these were also common to the experiences of participants in our study:

- Fathers blaming mothers for the child's impairment.

- Fathers resisting any physical contact with the disabled child.

- The disabled child emotionally supporting the mother.

- The mother's denial of her child's impairment.

- The child's fear of abandonment.

- The mother denying their child's emotional needs.

The picture that emerges from previous research and literature, then, is complex. Numerous factors impinge on the reactions of parents to their child and the development of the relationship between parents. These include: their existing relationship; their support network, including the extended family; the reactions of professionals; the information available; the reactions within the immediate community; and the broader social context reverberating through disabling attitudinal, environmental and structural barriers.

ATTACHMENT PROBLEMS

The above factors all have the capacity to impact on the parent–child bond, generating, in the experiences of the participants in this study, attachments that are less secure and less nurturing for the disabled child. In May's situation, the problematic attachment was added to by her placement at a residential school, which took her away from home for a number of years when she was still very young. May relates a difficult relationship with her parents to her vulnerability to sexual abuse later in life:

I know I do not have the same bond with my parents as my siblings. I think this is because boarding school is an environment where you are expected to be self-reliant as much as possible, both physically and emotionally. I think the lack of shared experiences also contributes, as you have your experiences from school, and your family have their experiences at home. I think the resulting lack of bond may make it easier to abuse a disabled child in the family setting. (May)

Chloe, who was sexually abused by an adult operating as part of a paedophile ring, talks about the difficulties her mother had in her parenting role. Chloe relates this to the stress created by an undiagnosed impairment, which meant that her mother was at a loss as to how to deal with her child's behaviour. The situation was compounded for Chloe's mother by her isolation and the lack of a support system:

My memories of when she talked about me as a baby were just of me being a problem. She was bringing me to the doctors because of my behaviour, because I was very demanding. It was because I had behavioural problems. I know now what it was. (Chloe)

I realize now that my mum probably did have depression, but was also having a hard time. She had a disabled child, actually, who wasn't understood by anybody else, or her, and no one to help her with it. And she was on her own in a foreign country, pregnant and then with a second baby, you know, she had a lot of stuff to deal with. (Chloe)

Additionally, Chloe talks about the continuing tension and conflict that marked her teenage years. What is significant for Chloe is that these patterns of parental behaviour contributed to her seeking adult attention outside the home:

She used to say 'you think you're very clever', and I didn't, you know what I mean. When you're a kid well you're just a kid, asking the questions that you ask and saying the things that you say. But I asked the wrong things and I said the wrong things. (Chloe)

One thing that came up in my counselling, when we actually talked it through, we actually worked out that at one point (and) half the time I was expected to be the parent with her and she still expects it now in a weird sort of way. My dad, my dad basically, once the problems got too bad with my mum, my dad did what he always does, which is not challenge my mum and just go quiet. But my dad probably goes blameless for a lot of stuff that he probably (should) share blame in, because again Mum's the easy target isn't she, if Mum's the one that's there, you know you expect Mum to sort it, when maybe your dad could have sorted it. (Chloe)

Turning to the literature, attachment theory has been a much studied area, which we do not claim to be able to do justice to here. Bowlby (1969; 1973; 1979; 1980; 1982) is perhaps the most well known writer on attachment theory. He stresses the importance of a warm, secure base for the healthy development of an infant. Bowlby highlights the centrality of the mother in the attachment process, with other authors such as Rutter (1972) questioning the necessity for the primary caregiver to be the mother. Pointing to the work of other writers, Marshall and Marshall (2000) refer to three types of attachment patterns that are commonly identified in clinical practice: the secure attachment, the anxious/ambivalent attachment and the avoidant attachment. Clearly, the secure attachment is considered to be the ideal where the child sees the caregiver as a consistent figure who can help them to deal with difficult emotions when such situations present themselves. The secure attachment allows the child to grow in self-confidence and later separate from the attachment figure, whilst concentrating their efforts on the wider environment.

Both May and Chloe detail how disability can interfere with the attachment process, for differing reasons. May makes a link between residential education and attachment. Chloe describes the difficulties involved in parenting a child with a hidden impairment. Muris and Maas (2004) look at the relationship between attachment, disability and institutionalization. They find that disabled children who are institutionalized, and who come from difficult family backgrounds, show an increased evidence of insecure attachments. This implies, therefore, that institutionalization does not necessarily create insecure attachments, but difficult attachments may be the reason for institutionalization. This piece of research may have some relevance for May, where family difficulties prevailed before she went to residential school. What May makes clear, however, is that institutionalization created a sense of distance, in her mind, between herself and the rest of her family.

Bacon and Richardson (2001) propose that research, which formulates a relationship between abuse and attachment, generally centres on neglect and physical abuse. The application of attachment theory to child sexual abuse has been a relatively recent development. Bolen (2002), in her extensive literature review, refers to the possible behavioural presentation of children who have problematic attachments. With reference to the work of others, compromised attachments, she proposes, can result in clingy and dependent behaviour, potentially creating a 'greater risk of sexual abuse by a trusted other' (p.104). Here, Lyn graphically describes what happened when her father stopped abusing her. Her sense of loss contributed to her seeking adult attention elsewhere, which also resulted in sexual abuse by a family friend:

> When he stopped I actually felt bereft, I felt lost. His attention was elsewhere. This was a reliable way of getting his attention and his attention was elsewhere. The end result of that, and the most dramatic thing in terms of actual abuse during my childhood, was that I ended up having an affair with a friend of his when I was 12. (Lyn)

> The affair could have been just a replacement of the attention, but it could also be to get back at my dad. It's a bit obvious that it was one of his best friends, a drinking partner. But that was also opportunistic in the sense that he was around most of the time, he was somebody that my parents trusted, and I would go to his house. (Lyn)

The re-traumatization of individuals following sexual abuse is discussed in Chapter 8, but with reference to adult survivors. The loss of a perceived identity in childhood, which then results in a re-traumatization elsewhere appears less frequently in the literature. Boney-McCoy and Finkelhor (1995) find a clear relationship between prior victimization and an increased likelihood of sexual abuse later in childhood. They cite a number of issues that are contributing factors, including prior sexual abuse and assault by a family member. With reference to the work of other writers, these authors suggest that traumatic sexualization may result in the child coming to perceive themselves as 'damaged goods', so increasing their vulnerability elsewhere. Others write about emotional closeness becoming associated with sexualized interactions for the child (Bacon 2003). This suggests that sexualized behaviour might then be re-enacted with others outside the family home. Such a dynamic could have been relevant for Lyn and may be accountable for her intense sense of loss when the abuse by her father stopped. Her father had, in effect, set her up for further abuse(s) by others.

CONCLUSION

Disability can impact upon the parent–child relationship in a number of ways. Mostly, parents find a way through the early years of a child's life by drawing upon their own strengths, the attachment they develop with their child, their support networks, the support services and, often not least of all, the support and experiences of other parents who have disabled children. Unfortunately, other parents cope less well and may slip into 'child blaming' patterns of relating, seeing the child as a significant problem or burden to the family. The communication does not have to be overt; children are experts at picking up on more subtle messages or interactions. A compromised sense of self may be the only signal that perpetrators require before targeting such children. Other children who are non-verbal are seen to be even more vulnerable. Sexual abuse creates further damage as it truly confirms a disabled child's bad body identity and produces what Josh refers to as the 'double whammy effect'. There are a number of possible implications for the child. The abuse combined with problematic attachments can influence children's ability to 'speak out' about their abuse (as in May's case) or it can impact on self-esteem with them coming to believe that they deserved to be abused (as in Lyn's situation); additionally it can influence a need to seek out adult attention outside the family home, which may result in involvement in other abusive relationships. Faced with a confusing assortment of emotions, the child's expression of pain usually follows a common self-destructive route. Chapter 5 will consider in detail the emotional consequences of sexual abuse for the disabled child.

Expressions and Survival of Pain

INTRODUCTION

As the title suggests this may be a difficult chapter to read. It documents the core of these narratives of violation and violated lives. It illustrates the complex processes of enduring and surviving sexual abuse. The consequences of sexual abuse are elaborately described by participants, including attacks on their physical being, the conversion of their trauma into bodily sensation and their criminal activities. A range of wholly predictable behaviours result from being silenced – being compromised to the extent that they were unable to vocalize their abuse experience. These behaviours can also be seen to fulfil a self-protective function, allowing a small part of the self to be free from contamination. The issue of impairment will be woven in and out of the chapter, highlighting points where difficulties become exaggerated for the disabled child – the double whammy. A later section of the chapter looks at the adult child's perception of the position of the non-abusing parent, in abuse taking place within the family.

COPING WITH THE EXPERIENCE OF SEXUAL ABUSE

Being able to deal with the physical and psychological intrusion of sexual abuse is a complicated matter for the disabled child. Some disabled children, as highlighted in Chapter 4, come to the experience with a compromised and shaky sense of who they are. They learn very early on in their life, that they are 'other' and that non-physical intrusion, in the form of staring, for example, may be a regular part of their experience – an experience that they also have no control over. Jean's quote illustrates the complexity of a situation whereby the disabled child has to try and grapple with two soul-destroying experiences:

> One of the things that I discovered during my recovery was this idea about our physical bodies being a piece of evidence of ourselves and that when you're young, and possibly this carries on to some extent, where is the line between my self and my body/mind? If this person is saying to me my body is bad and evil then that's saying I'm evil. The big message that disabled children get, regardless of abuse, is that you are a problem, your body, therefore you, are a problem, a disappointment, your impairment/difference or your 'self' has 'ruined' the idealized expectation of parenthood, and the perfect 'ten fingers and toes' baby. I felt that very much, I felt the pain that my mother had about what was going on with my body and me, I was causing that pain and there was nothing I could do to change that. I think that disabled children get that message very clearly, and then when you are abused as well, and when the abuse is happening with your physical body, they all just get muddled up into this big knot, which can become hugely self-hate focused on the body, mind and self. (Jean)

Coping with an experience such as sexual abuse creates a need for the disabled child to employ a number of behaviours that have a self-protective function. Whilst the child is unaware of the purpose of these behaviours at that time, these behaviours are used to deal with conflicting and negative emotions created by the abuse experience. These coping strategies commonly involve dissociation, a process which allows the removal of the 'self' from the body, so there is some psychological distance from the site of the trauma. As Jean describes, the relationship that the disabled child holds with their body may already be problematic, but sexual abuse can intensify the need to cut free from their physical being.

Turning to the literature, dissociation is something used by many of us, particularly when faced with repetitive activity, allowing the mind to slip into 'two or more streams of consciousness' (Putnam

1997, p.68). Dissociation can also occur in emotionally charged situations, which we might prefer to psychologically distance ourselves from. The risk of remaining fully connected, here, might be the creation of psychological conflict (Putnam 1997). The extremes of dissociation seen in children and young people who have been sexually abused, however, far exceed the 'normal' range. Mulder *et al.* (1998, p.806) refer to the DSM-IV definition of dissociation which is described as 'a disruption of the usually integrated functions of consciousness, memory, identity and perceptions of the environment'. In other words, the child is prevented from functioning as an integrated whole and fragmentation of the self occurs. Dissociation is a common and vital function for children who are faced with experiences that are overwhelming and who have little control with regard to what is happening to their physical being (MacFie, Ciccetti and Tooth 2001; Provus McElroy 1992).

A number of theories have evolved in an attempt to understand what processes are at play during trauma-related dissociation. These theories range from neurophysiological explanations, which explore such things as hippocampal damage (Bower and Sivers 1998), for instance, to more psychologically orientated theory. In terms of psychological theory, Young (1992) considers the problematic issue of embodiment and the difficulty that this might pose for the sexually abused child. She proposes that the child often responds to their spoiled/damaged/bad body by abandoning it, or turning on it in rage. The narratives of survivors of sexual abuse in the present study illustrate how impairment might provide yet another reason for the disabled child to step outside their body. As can be seen from a wealth of academic research, and contributors to this book, the process of disembodiment can take many guises, which will be discussed in some detail shortly. Consistent with the views of Young (1992) and the writings of Summit (1983), dissociation might be considered a logical expression of pain, hurt and confusion by a healthy child to a dangerous family environment. The child's pain can manifest itself in a disregard for their body; a view that is confirmed by the actions of their abusers (Young 1992). These psychological theories might assume that in early childhood the mind already has a capacity to keep separate traumatic experiences from a developing sense of self (Oppenheimer 2002).

Drawing on the work of Loewenstein (1991), Putnam (1997) has produced a classification of dissociative behaviours that develop following trauma. He describes amnesia and memory problems, and the commonly co-occurring post-traumatic symptoms (detachment, avoidance), as being primary dissociative problems. He sees alterations of bodily sensations and factors that destabilize the self (anxiety, depression and low self-esteem) as secondary responses, and self-destructive behaviours, such as anorexia and self-mutilation, as tertiary responses. Putman suggests that it is not possible to tackle self-destructive behaviour and secondary difficulties, until primary symptoms are resolved. This range of dissociative behaviour is illustrated in many differing ways throughout the narrative of the survivors in this book.

Forgetting

As described by Jean and Lizzie, one form of dissociation is amnesia or forgetting, only for the memory to be recovered later in life. Recovery of the memory of abuse usually follows periods of erratic behaviour in childhood and confusing life events in adulthood:

> I mean like a lot of abused kids I think I had that mixture, that range of reactions: some of the time I was displaying disturbed behaviour and acting out the abuse, other times I think I'd gone into a care-taking mode, being extremely responsible and displaying quite mature behaviour. (Jean)

> There were also things like the sleep stuff: I wasn't sleeping well and I was waking with nightmares a lot. A lot of the time I wasn't crying or crying out for help, I would just wake up completely and utterly terrified, sometimes covered in sweat and unable to speak, breathing rapidly, panic attack type stuff. I had the most bizarre nightmares. (Jean)

> I attempted suicide at a time when I was far away from my family. Things caught up with me then, but I didn't know what was catching up with me. I was 22 and I had no idea what was going on. I think now, I mean even now I'm not entirely sure to be honest, but I was surrounded by children... Do you know what's just dawned on me, goodness knows whether some deeply unconscious process was going on, years later it emerged that two of the staff who were there when I was

there, had been abusing children. Could I have had some kind of radar? I don't know. Or whether it was just being surrounded by children, or whether it was being so far from my support... it can't just be that, I don't know, I've not yet really worked it out. And again muddied by disability issues, because again the staff were abysmal in relation to my being disabled, and the kids were great but there was nobody, absolutely nobody amongst the staff who had an ounce of understanding. (Lizzie)

Recovered memory will be discussed in some detail in Chapter 9, but some writers suggest that amnesia is a relatively common occurrence if sexual abuse happens in the first few years of life when the child is unable to physiologically process the experience (Courtois 1999). Here, abuse might be re-enacted in play or it might appear symbolically in some other activity (Courtois 1999; Terr 1991). For older children too, partial or total forgetting may also be a feature of their experience. Some writers might argue that memory loss is linked to the severity and duration of the trauma, as the child needs to employ more powerful strategies including 'profound psychic numbing' (Terr 1991, p.16), although judgements relating to the severity of trauma can be difficult to make. Clark (1993) also maintains that forgetting is a form of self-protection. Forgetting might be later followed by disturbing behaviour in the child (as in Jean's case) or behaviours that are confusing for the adult and not clearly linked to one particular cause (as described by Lizzie). Undoubtedly, the repercussions of forgetting have a significant and profound impact on the developing sense of self.

Leaving the body behind at the time of abuse

Not surprisingly, some survivors of sexual abuse describe dissociation occurring during the abuse incident itself:

At the time, in order to survive the experience, I think I was probably doing a bit of dissociation, because I can remember something like that, though I always described it as 'holding my breath'. It was partly physical dissociation from the body, but also, in a sense, stopping time while it was happening, then you could experience the whole thing in a very different way, so it wasn't part of daily life. (Lyn)

Separating from the body in this way generally involves the induction of a self-hypnotic state, so that some psychological distance can be achieved from the event. It can involve becoming an outside observer to the abuse, or the child going on imaginary walks (Gelinas 1983). With reference to the work of others, Young (1992) suggests that this type of dissociation develops from a non-voluntary response to the abuse experience, to the later development of a self-hypnotic state as a voluntary response. As relevant to Lyn's experience, Herman (1992) describes these hypnotic states in the following way: 'Perceptions may be numbed or distorted, with partial anaesthesia or the loss of particular sensations. Time sense may be altered, often with a sense of slow motion, and the experience may lose its quality of ordinary reality' (p.43). Johnson, Pike and Chard (2001) found in their study that sexual abuse that involved penile penetration, or the creation of a belief that someone or something would be annihilated, increased the likelihood of dissociation at the time of the abuse.

Self-destruction

Eating disorders, self-mutilation, substance abuse and attempted suicide are also all classified as dissociative behaviours, where the body has been identified as something intrinsically 'bad' and then comes under attack, using a variety of methods. Herman (1992) suggests that most of these self-destructive behaviours go undetected by others, partly because they happen when the child is alone, but also because the child is usually able to present an exterior illusion of normality by employing the more socially acceptable 'false self'. This section of the text will consider these behaviours in separate groupings and explore what contributors to this book had to say on the subject.

EATING DISORDERS

May and Lyn talk about their experiences of anorexia:

> I cannot remember ever making a decision to stop eating, but I remember feeling very unhappy and not feeling like eating. I think one day just stretched into another and I only realized that I had a problem when I wanted to eat and couldn't. I found eating painful and chewing just made me feel sick. Looking back, I think I stopped eating because I was depressed, without

knowing it. I think I just got used to feeling unhappy, so didn't realize other people didn't feel the way I did. I can make this judgment now because I have learnt to recognize the signs of my depression, and one of the first things is that I stop feeling like eating. (May)

I got obsessed with my weight at around 15 and stopped eating and I think, from what I've read, that's also very characteristic of girls who've been abused. I can remember that part of the motivation for that was... It's very complicated, but one element of it was that I wanted to make people worried. I wanted them to pay attention and ask me questions, but I don't think anybody noticed that I'd lost weight. I never got catastrophically thin until I was at university and about 19 years of age. (Lyn)

Anorexia nervosa is a form of self-starvation, which is sometimes accompanied by bulimia nervosa, or binge eating followed by vomiting. On a political level, eating disorders have also been a concern of feminism, where women's relationship with food continues to be critically evaluated. Writers such as Orbach (1993) view anorexia as a destabilization of an individual's identity formation, where the female attempts to both conform to and reject the socially acceptable norm for body size and shape. Orbach proposes that the anorexic female behaviour represents an 'extreme, intense and rebellious relationship with the various struggles facing women' (p.10). Psychologically, there may be some inner conflict related to being denied expression of their emotional needs, and frequently having to defer to the needs of others (Orbach 1993). These issues can be combined with not having access to a legitimate route to protest.

When considering the relationship between child sexual abuse and eating disorders, there is a predominance of studies that make the association between the two issues. In terms of trying to unravel the dynamics at play for a disabled child who is sexually abused and who subsequently develops an eating disorder, little is known about the actual process which underpins this problem. Authors such as Orbach (1993) might view anorexia as the young person's attempt to become invisible; retaining some element of control whilst her psychological needs are being so outrageously flaunted. It can also be argued that the experience of 'othering' in a disabled child's life, together with being construed as a 'burden', might compound a desire to vanish from sight. As far as oral abuse is concerned, Nelson (2002) finds a relational link between this and facial/jaw/neck pain and difficulties involved in swallowing after the abuse event. She proposes that 'throat rape' might be a catalyst for subsequent development of anorexia and bulimia. May, who did not talk about oral abuse, made a connection between her problems with eating and chewing, but associated this instead with depression.

Other psychological perspectives vary in their emphasis. By drawing on clinical practice and the work of others, Young (1992), for example, theorizes the body as a foreign container of bad feelings. The child, by methods of abstinence, attempts to destroy this foreign container. The potential effect is liberation from unbearable memories and feelings. Miller, McCluskey-Fawcett and Irving (1993) suggest that eating disorders, such as bulimia, can symbolize an act of rebellion against a sexual experience that has been foisted upon them. With reference to the work of Heatherton and Baumeister (1991), Miller, McCluskey-Fawcett and Irving suggest that the binge–purge cycle in bulimia may produce an emotional numbness. This may help distract from the overwhelming feelings created by the abuse experience.

Hartt and Waller (2002) found in their small study of 23 women that whilst there was a strong association between the severity of sexual abuse and the severity of dissociation, there was no such link between the severity of sexual abuse and the severity of the eating disorders such as bulimia. In fact, these authors found that neglectful parenting is more predictive of dissociation for this group of women. Regardless of the exact relationship, the effect of an eating disorder is to unconsciously articulate that which defies verbalization:

> I think some of my behaviour then was expression of just pain and self-disgust. Some of it was about being lost and needing to feel in control of something. Some of it was almost a calculated attempt to get people to notice, and not simply for the sake of it, but to actually notice that there was something wrong. (Lyn)

Eating disorders, as can be seen from our and others' work, just happens to be one expression of emotional difficulty amongst many of a dissociative nature.

SELF-MUTILATION, EXCESSIVE DRUG USE
AND ATTEMPTED SUICIDE

Lyn talks about self-mutilation in terms of needing to attract the attention of others to her distress. She also makes the connection between self-mutilation and the discovery of her father's infidelity:

> When I was 14 things started going overtly wrong. Up until then I'd been doing very well at school. I think I was a success story really in everybody's eyes, and then suddenly when I hit 14 I started doing self-mutilation. Whether it was a long-term response to Phil and my dad, I don't know, but it was around that time that I found out, and my mother found out too, that my father had been having all these affairs. So it kind of went kaboom! at home, and I responded by starting to cut, for all the reasons that girls do. I think I felt very desperate that nobody noticed that I was very unhappy, and that it didn't seem to occur to anyone that I could be doing well at school yet still would be in trouble. (Lyn)

Thomas started to self-mutilate after his stepfather's death and was precipitated by a need to punish himself for grieving for his stepfather, as well as holding together two sets of conflicting emotion: love and hate:

> After his death I continued to live at home for a while but my relationship with my mother was not a good one, and months after he died, then it hit me, and then all of a sudden I started crying, getting weepy about him and missing him. And I thought, 'What the hell am I missing him for?', and then I'd get angry with myself for missing him and that's when I started self-injury, cutting and being a prat basically. I used to do my arms quite a lot, can't see the scars so much now, but I was carving swastikas into my arms. (Thomas)

Similarly, drug and alcohol abuse were prevalent in the narratives of several participants. Thomas relates this to his desire to self-destruct following his stepfather's death, and a personal realization that his identity had become totally consumed by the sexual abuse experience with no other perceived purpose to his life outside of this:

> I mean now I look back and think, 'Christ, how I didn't kill myself I'll never know.' I mean it was like heroin, I can remember the first time I did that, we were all sat round in a front room and

they were doing heroin and amphetamine mixed, which is what they called speed balls, and they were going, 'Is anybody here going to have a go?' And I was, 'Oh yeah, pass it here, I'll do it.' And everybody else was worried about what I was going to do and were asking whether I was sure, but I was straight up with the trouser leg, bumf, straight in. And now I can see why: he was dead, I'd got no reason to live anymore, I'd got no reason to hate anymore, so I might as well top myself, who else is going to want me. (Thomas)

A number of participants made suicide attempts, which had varying causality. Josh talks about how the pressure of starting polytechnic led to a nervous breakdown. Lyn describes how the help she received in her first year at university with her anorexia created a positivism, which contrasted with the demands that were still being placed upon her by her family. May relates her suicide attempt to depression and her sense of isolation:

I had to do the course in 18 months and it was a bad time. I actually missed one of those five terms because I spent most of that time in hospital because of not coping with what had happened in the past. I was in a strange city, I was having a nervous breakdown, I was trying to do a three-year course in less than two years, I mean you're talking about pressure, and I had it. I tried to kill myself a few times because I couldn't deal with it, I took pills and I cut my wrists. I almost succeeded once, I was on a ventilator, I didn't realize I'd been on a ventilator until later. (Josh)

The first year at university, the first part was very happy, then the eating got worse and worse and I started to see a specialist in eating disorders who was at the university that I was at, and that was very good. But ironically enough the therapy made me feel that there was a way out, but my mother was so much pulling back at that point. She was feeling ill; she wanted me to come home every weekend. It got worse and worse and worse and at one point, in the August of that year, I took an overdose. It was not that serious an overdose, but it could have been had I not thrown it up again almost immediately. However, I knew enough about drug dosages to know that it wasn't enough really. It wasn't so much a gesture to other people, I think, as a gesture to myself to say 'this is actually how bad it's got'. (Lyn)

I also stopped going out all together and at my lowest point took an overdose of my medication. I knew that ten was enough to kill someone, so I took 20 and went to bed thinking that that was the last time I would have to go through that. Obviously I did not succeed and this just made things even worse in my mind, I felt 'how useless are you, you can't even kill yourself'. (May)

Self-mutilation, drug use and suicide attempts are also frequently referred to in the literature on sexual abuse (Harrison, Fulkerson and Beebe 1997; Moran, Vuchinich and Hall 2004; Turrell and Armstrong 2000; Young 1992; Ystgaard *et al.* 2004). They are also considered to be dissociative behaviours, which involve a different type of attack on the body with the same effect of numbing the emotional pain. During attacks such as self-mutilation, survivors often report intense feelings of agitation preceding the attack, little physical pain during the act (at least initially), but the creation of a sense of calm afterwards (Herman 1992). Research tends to indicate that the occurrence of these self-destructive behaviours increases if child sexual abuse has been accompanied by another form of child abuse, as is frequently the case.

As already indicated, physical assaults on the body commonly occur in young people who are attempting to deal with the sexual abuse experience. Turrell and Armsworth (2000) found that, when comparing a sexually abused student group of self-mutilators and non-mutilators, a number of factors were significant for mutilators including such things as ethnicity, multiple perpetrators, abuse duration and frequency, age of onset and the co-occurrence of other types of abuse. Particularly relevant to our research was if sexual abuse was accompanied by frequent incidents of physical abuse, as this increased the severity of self-mutilation. As can be seen from narrative in previous chapters, both Thomas and Josh reported experiences of physical abuse. In Thomas's graphic description of self-harm he raises an issue which appears less frequently in the literature, and which relates to the young person also having to cope with a range of other feelings for their perpetrator, some of which may be positive. In MacFarlane and Korbin's study (1983) survivors spoke of perpetrators providing the only source of affection for the child, or the perpetrator showing an interest in their early academic success. This issue is also alluded to in Lyn's narrative, but for Thomas he describes these positive feelings as being unbearable and punishable by directing his rage at his own body in the form of self-mutilation. Also significant in Turrell and Armsworth's study was the impact of emotional abuse, with some self-mutilators reporting that they felt a 'burden' to their family. This issue is detailed by several participants in Chapter 4, potentially adding an extra dimension to the problem of self-harm for disabled children.

Similarly, Harrison, Fulkerson and Beebe (1997) found that there was a strong link between physical and sexual abuse, and multiple substance abuse in adolescents. They found that survivors tended to use a greater variety of substances, had an earlier introduction to the substance, and reported 'more frequent attempts to self-medicate painful emotions' (p.536). Moran, Vuchinich and Hall (2004), using a similar research methodology, also found this strong relationship. They discovered that male survivors of physical and sexual abuse were prone to using illicit drugs. With reference to the work of other writers, these authors propose that if the abuse was forceful, and perpetrated by a male, illicit substance use may be the result of a confused sexual identity stemming from a same-sex encounter. This was a concern raised by Thomas, but was not linked directly to substance abuse. Thomas's words highlight the problem of identity formation for a sexually abused child, whose purpose is seen to have become totally consumed with meeting the sexual needs of adults, and whose experiences influence their view of themselves and their sense of self-worth.

With regard to suicidal behaviour, Ystgaard *et al.* (2004) found that suicide attempters who had a background of both physical and sexual abuse demonstrated more self-destructive tendencies than others. Barker-Callo (2001) analyzed suicide in relation to the blame that a survivor was seen to have attached to their sexual abuse in childhood. She found that children who were abused by a family member, or a stranger when under the age of ten, tended to report blaming themselves as a child, and demonstrated signs of psychological difficulty and suicide attempts later in life. For both Lyn and Josh, their suicidal behaviour occurred at university/polytechnic where they also had to cope with pressures in the academic environment. Lyn, who was receiving counselling at that time, which allowed her to acknowledge her emotional need within the context of a safe adult relationship, describes how the neediness of her family countered the positive effect of therapy. As indicated, for Josh, the pressures of higher education and a growing awareness of the significance of his abuse led to a nervous meltdown, a number of suicide attempts and periods of hospitalization.

We propose, here, that all these self-inflicted attacks on the body carry added significance for the survivors of sexual abuse in the present study, as they symbolize double jeopardy. The process of 'othering', experienced by the participants as disabled young people, transmits a 'bad body' communication; sexual intrusion truly cements the message.

Distortion of bodily sensation

Some sexually abused individuals carry their emotional distress as alterations in bodily sensations. Josh elaborates further on the issue of contracture, feeling strongly that his emotional turmoil was also reflected in his physical being:

> I mean it was like I had these tight bands wrapped around me and they were holding me in, and I needed somebody to come along with the wire cutters and just cut me free. And then, when that happens you're okay and that happened to me gradually. I mean up to being 30 years old, before I began to feel better, I used to wear a size 9 shoe, now I wear a size 11; that's how powerful the feeling of being constrained was. (Josh)

A change in bodily sensation occurred whilst Lyn was resident at university. It followed a rape incident, which compounded the emotional pain created by child sexual abuse. Here, Lyn describes the sensation in more detail:

> Physically, I remember I had a sense of my body being an odd patchwork of bits that weren't quite connected with each other and that lasted until about November. It happened in June. Until about November there was the thing that any bit that they did touch didn't feel quite right, and the only bit that they hadn't was my left hand and that felt normal, it was very strange. (Lyn)

The literature suggests that the emotional reaction to child sexual abuse, in the form of sleep disturbance, phobic behaviour and anxiety, are common phenomenon for individuals who have experienced trauma. Psychosomatic complaints may also be prevalent, including unexplained aches and pains, gastrointestinal disturbance and conversion symptoms. Conversion disorders refer to when intense emotional pain is housed in body parts. Conversion symptoms are eloquently described by both Josh and Lyn, and are defined in the literature as 'deficits affecting the voluntary motor or sensory functions' (Roelofs *et al.* 2002, p.1908) with no apparent physical cause.

The diagnosis of conversion symptoms is not a simple and straightforward matter, since symptoms can mimic neurological conditions. Examples of conversion disorders date back many centuries and can be seen in the early writings of Sigmund Freud, who referred to these symptoms as 'conversion hysteria'. Conversion symptoms commonly follow a trauma such as child sexual abuse, with research indicating that these symptoms are present when survivors report varying types of physical abuse and longer lasting periods of sexual abuse and incest (Roelofs *et al.* 2002).

Conversion symptoms may present themselves in a number of different forms including:

- Weakness/paralysis of a limb or the entire body.

- Contracture.

- Impaired hearing or vision.

- Impairment or loss of speech.

- Tremor.

- Non-organic seizures.

Outwardly directed behaviour

Additionally, expressions of pain can be outwardly directed and targeted at others in society. Thomas's anger could sometimes be observed in his involvement in criminal activities, such as burglary or arson, or his violence at football matches. In Thomas's first narrative episode, he believes his behaviour was aimed at a need to make others aware of his situation. In the second, he describes his behaviour as bringing about some kind of cathartic release:

I would get up in the morning and think to myself, 'I'm going to be a bad boy today and I hope that I do get caught, and I hope that the coppers do bring me home, and I hope that you're shamed and I hope that all the neighbours do see the police car, and see me not giving a toss basically that I have been caught. Make them realize that this local trade union official and Labour Party chairman has still got this terrible awful son that won't behave. I'll bring some shame on you; I can't stand up in the middle of the street and say, "This guy is abusing me," but what I can do is make your life a living hell through living with me, through you being in my space.' (Thomas)

I mean I often hear it said, especially by that generation above us, 'Oh they make me sick these young criminals, they go into court and say that they come from a broken home or they've been abused and what's that got to do with nicking a car?' Well it's got a bloody lot. It had a bloody lot to do with me wanting to go to Man United matches and kick the complete crap out of a perfect stranger simply because he swore at another team. I used to walk away from that and think I've inflicted on some-body what I had inflicted on me and that's good. (Thomas)

Turning once again to research, and with comparison to other forms of child abuse, some research refutes the fact that a signifi-cant relationship exists between an increased involvement in criminal activity and a history of child sexual abuse (Spatz Widom and Ashley Ames 1994). Other research, by comparison, finds a strong relational link (Swanston et al. 2003). By looking at groups of both abused and non-abused young people, Swanston and her colleagues found that criminal, delinquent and aggressive behaviour was equally re-ported for both male and female participants. This was dissimilar to other research which shows a clear gender differential – girls show-ing more of an inwardly focused pattern of destructive behaviour, whilst boys had a propensity for delinquency. When using a number of measurements, including self-reporting by the young person, and adjusting for a number of factors (age, sex, socio-economic grouping and residency) the authors noted the prevalence of crimes such as assault, intentional damage to property, break and entry, and theft, all of which Thomas describes in his grand narrative account.

MISSING ALLIES?

Here, we consider the child's perception of the safety of their immediate environment in cases of sexual abuse occurring within the family, which is where most child abuse occurs. Central to the operation of perpetrators within the family context is their capacity to isolate the child from possible avenues of support, including other siblings who may also be experiencing abuse, and more crucially the child's mother. Such strategies facilitate an individualizing process whereby the child feels somehow responsible for the abuse, and perceives the non-abusing parent as complicit by failing to see the child's predicament. All the participants in this study who had siblings were unaware in childhood that some of these siblings were also being abused. Additionally, perceptions of their mother's position varied from suspecting that they must have known about the abuse yet failed to act, to being absolutely certain that this was the fact. For some, as detailed in Chapter 4, the disabling attitudes of parents were already part of the equation and may have influenced the child's sense of safety. The following narratives vividly illustrate the child's perception of the non-abusing parent, from their adult perspective. Thomas, Lyn and Josh's detailed information suggests that their mothers could have been aware:

> It was one Tuesday night that, in my mind, confronted my Mum with the truth. It was just before my seventh birthday: September 1974. We had started back at school that day after the long summer holidays and as always she had gone to bingo. Dave, who was 12, was out with his mates and not due in until later. He raped me and beat me, but before I had the chance to wash and dress, in walked Mum, she had forgotten something. So there I am in the living room, naked and bleeding from my anus; how would he get out of this, I thought. He told her I was constipated from drinking too much milk. He told me to bend over and said that I came down from the loo like this and that he was going to clean me up. I just stood there, and out of fear of not being believed I said nothing, even when he left me and Mum alone and went to the bathroom to fetch the Germalene, I said nothing. To this day I wish I had, but fear prevented me. She applied the cream, said that I wasn't allowed any more milk and went back to bingo. She must have known that there was more to my injuries than constipation, she had to, what kind

of mother can apply Germalene to a boy's backside believing those injuries were caused by constipation! (Thomas)

I know that my mother must have seen a considerable amount of what was going on, and apart from a couple of sentences like, 'Leave her alone,' I don't remember her intervening in any way. I have been very resentful of that. I wonder now whether she actually went through something whilst she was in the children's home, because you read so much now, you hear so much about abuse within children's homes. She had very difficult relationships with men when she was an adult and I suspect that something may have happened to her that made her totally unable to deal with it. Or perhaps she just simply took it for granted: that it might have seemed more normal to her than other people. (Lyn)

When I got to the age of 19 my mother suspected something because one day she came upstairs… I mean this is how crazy it was getting, she was actually in the house and came upstairs, and I think I'd been ill, and it was the afternoon and I was ill in bed, and so she came upstairs. So he leapt off the bed, but of course he had left his belt on the bed, I remember that belt, I had been hit with it. And so she started to get a bit suspicious and then when I was 11, and this is where they ruined my education really, I was about to go to secondary school, I was going in the middle stream, the B stream, which was fine, but they decided to send me away to a special school for people with disabilities. (Josh)

May's situation differed in the respect that her mother did know about the abuse, and even acknowledged it with May. This increased May's sense of culpability and worthlessness:

Things had been happening to me for some time when one day my mother told me, 'Your father is your special friend.' At the time I thought she meant I was being treated differently to my siblings, but a few months went by and then out of the blue, my mother told me she could hear everything. I then thought back to what had been said earlier and realized she had known all along. This made me feel, 'What is the point in saying anything; she doesn't care what happens to me.' I am sure my mother felt that it was my fault and that it was better than my father having an affair outside. It also meant that she didn't have to do things that she didn't want to, like having sex, which she told me she was not interested in, but kept the financial security. I started to think about the things that had happened and realized not only did my mother know, she also created opportunities for it to happen by going out all day, making my youngest sibling go as well even when she didn't want to. (May)

There needs to be acknowledgment here of the difficulties faced by individuals (researcher in this instance) when trying to truly understand the internal dynamic of an individual's family situation. However, we believe that some of the major research findings, relating to the position of the mother, may have some relevance to the experiences of Thomas, Josh, Lyn and May. The motivation to explore this subject area further rests in the necessity to illustrate the importance of the child's perception of their immediate environment, since, as can be seen in Chapter 4, it determines a child's ability to 'speak out' about the abuse and affects their future healing. The four participants' quotes illustrate a range of perceptions, ranging from a degree of suspicion about their mother's awareness of their abuse, to absolute knowledge of the fact, demonstrated by the mother's admission.

When trying to understand the role of the mother in cases of intra-familial abuse, conflicting ideologies and differing theoretical stances become apparent. Some of these theoretical approaches are considered too individualizing (and hence pathologizing) as far as mothers are concerned, and others' broad-based sociological perspectives are seen to eclipse clinical practice (Baker 2002). Hooper and Humphreys (1998) outline a debate which sets family systems approaches against feminism. With reference to the work of other writers, the authors see family systems theory as proposing a circular causality which analyses the positioning of, and interaction between, key family members (the incestuous triad). Feminism, on the other hand, depersonalizes the issue, to an extent, and cites the problem of child sexual abuse as stemming essentially from power inequalities within society, which are reflected in relationships within the nuclear family. Feminist readings highlight the issue of male dominance and the process of maternal disempowerment. Attributions of blame and responsibility lie squarely with the perpetrator. Hooper and Humphreys (1998) respond to a need to understand this complex interaction by pointing to an integrated model, based on Finkelhor's four preconditions (1984), and referred to in Chapter 7. They write:

It is only after the abuser has become motivated to abuse (the first stage), and overcome his internal inhibitions (the second stage), that the mother–child relationship may become significant, either via the child's supervision, which may affect the abuser's ability to overcome external impediments (the third stage), and/or the child's vulnerability, which may affect the abuser's ability to undermine or overcome the child's possible resistance (the fourth stage). At all stages, explanation requires attention to the interaction between individual, familial and social factors. (p.568)

The research of Hooper (1992) and Bell (2003) has confirmed that it is possible for a mother not to be aware of the abuse of their children by perpetrators living in the home. This fact is supported by the reality that abuse is invariably a secretive matter, kept hidden from the mother by the perpetrator's psychological tactics, or overtly aggressive threats to the child. Additionally, Hooper also demonstrates that some mothers may also know about their children's abuse, as was the case for May, and fail to act for a number of different reasons.

In Hooper's study (1992), which involved interviews with 15 mothers, the issue of mothers' knowledge relating to their child's abuse was explored in some detail, where 'children had both thought their mothers knew when they did not and thought they did not know when they did' (p.55). For the mothers who did not know, many felt that something was amiss for their child, but had explained this to themselves in a variety of ways, with sexual abuse not being part of the equation. This could, in fact, have been the situation for Josh's mother in the early stages of his sexual abuse, since Josh describes her, in other parts of his narrative, as being, essentially, a naïve person. A number of mothers were concerned with surviving domestic violence, which impacted on their emotional availability for their children. One mother was desensitized by her own childhood experience of sexual abuse, which could have possibly been the case for Lyn's mother. From the group of women who experienced domestic violence, one lacked confidence in her own parenting abilities, and another demonstrated a degree of detachment and a non-confrontational approach, which could have been the case for Thomas's mother, who was mothering within an overtly violent familial context.

Women who suspected sexual abuse in Hooper's study had to grapple with a number of issues including the problem of having to differentiate between abusive and non-abusive interactions between the child and their partner. This created uncertainty and impacted upon their ability to make interpretations. This too could have been the experience of Lyn's mother, whose husband abused within a context of the confusion he created in the minds of others, including Lyn. Additionally, women faced situations which made it difficult to confront the issue with both the child and the perpetrator. A minority of children told their mothers about the abuse, but only when the abuser had left the family home. Confrontation of abusers had variable results. The process of reconstructing a reality for some mothers often took a significant period of time, where information needed to be re-evaluated in line with acknowledgement of abuse.

For a number of women, confusion operated on many levels after they learnt of the abuse. Although there was recognition of its wrongness, some women showed ignorance relating to the psychological implication of abuse for their child. In several cases, Hooper related this to the women's subjective sense of powerlessness in their own lives. Lack of clarity skewed one mother's ability to see through the justifications of the abuser, who interpreted his behaviour as non-harmful sex education. The mother who knew about her children's sexual abuse at the time of its occurrence, expressed confusion about what her partner's behaviour meant. For three women, although responding angrily to the disclosure, they showed little awareness of power differentials, referring to their children as having equal capability. One of these mothers saw the child as the seducer, and the other two showed little understanding for their children. Clearly, some of these themes are relevant to May's experience, particularly her mother's ignorance to the fact that her husband's behaviour constituted child abuse, and also her disregard for the devastating consequences of his behaviour.

Bell's research (2003) was based on interviews with 11 women. Of the 34 children born to the interviewees, 17 disclosed abuse. Five had disclosed to their mothers when they were under five years old, four as teenagers and two as adult children. Five participants also talked about unconfirmed suspicions in relation to their other children. All the mothers in this study described the child's disclosure as a shock, which brought into question their maternal identity.

They described their relationship with their children in positive terms, with some referring to their partners' attempts to sabotage this relationship. Similar to the writings of Hooper (1992), Bell also problematizes the concept of maternal knowledge, suggesting 'the reasons why they don't "see" may be related to the fact that what there is to "see" varies greatly' (p.131) and generally not apparent to the outside world. In her analysis, which is embedded within feminist discourse, Bell raises various aspects of the 'ideal of motherhood' that had been adversely affected by their child's disclosure. In particular, she cites: motherhood as protection; motherhood as selflessness; and motherhood as a source of power, all of which place mothers and children in an untenable position given their social and economic positioning. Motherhood as selflessness, in particular, presents a contradictory source of information for abused children, since their mother's tolerance of domestic violence is, understandably, replicated in the abuser–child dynamic.

The findings of other researchers, who have considered the implications for mothers on discovering child sex abuse, may also have some relevance to participant's experiences in this study. In particular, we note the research of Bernard (2001) who investigated the experiences of 30 black mothers whose children had experienced sexual abuse either within the family, or by someone known to them. In particular, Bernard raises the issue of 'stigmatizing deficit models of motherhood' where racist stereotypes of neglectful and promiscuous identities, in this instance, influenced how mothers felt other people might see them. Bernard suggests that such societal prescriptions can compound feelings of inferiority once disclosure is made. Similar issues must impact upon a disabled mother's ability to 'see' and 'act' where there are suspicions of child sexual abuse. These factors could have possibly been relevant for Lyn's mother. Several mothers in Bernard's study had children with learning difficulties, one of whom had difficulty reporting her concerns to agencies involved because of their reluctance to take her concerns seriously. This mother's experience clearly illustrates how the combined effect of race and disability further marginalized her child. Frequently, the mothers in this research relied on informal networks of support, rather than formal support.

In concluding, we return to the work of Baker (2002) who contends that, in reality, a mother's validation of a survivor's discourse is one of the most fundamental elements to their future healing process. Only after emotional disconnection from the maternal narrative, are survivors able to stand back from their personal experience and consider other interpretations of their mother's behaviour. Others, by contrast, might refute the importance of maternal validation for future healing.

CONCLUSION

Surviving sexual abuse is a complex issue for the disabled child. The impaired identities of some children are fragmented further by abuse, so disrupting the usual developmental sequences of childhood. In order to deal with incomprehensible intrusions of both disabilism and sexual abuse, disabled participants employed a range of dissociative strategies to protect their inner integrity or sense of self, as they understood it. This was by refusing to incorporate the sexual abuse experience into their developing self-concept. The consequence, however, was the dissociative spectrum of symptoms described, which were accommodated to the best of their ability. Some would suggest that these outwardly worrying behaviours, designed to protect the self, have little to do with the 'real self' who strives to find some element of control. Blumstein (2001), defines the real self or true self as 'a personal intrapsychic structure and is only knowable by the person to whom it belongs' (p.183). Throughout adolescence and adulthood, and through a process of healing, participants have acquired a number of collective identities, which will be considered in Chapter 8.

CHAPTER 6

Organizational Abuse

INTRODUCTION

This chapter considers disabled children's experiences of large organizations, most notably the medical profession and educational systems. Organizations can often reflect the same prejudice that is present within society at large (Salaman 1979) and detailed in Chapter 3. Notions of validity and worth can permeate organizational cultures, influencing, to varying degrees, professional attitudes and practice. The abuse of disabled children happens to be one of the potential outcomes of a dysfunctional organizational system, where organizational mores determine that some individuals feel they are just in misusing their professional power to gain some level of personal self-satisfaction. In previous chapters it has been clear that sexual abuse is closely associated with physical abuse. Indeed, it can be argued that sexual abuse is a pernicious form of physical abuse. It is a physical violence, a violation of body and being. We have seen, too, the double whammy and the association between sexual abuse and disablism. This chapter further expands our understanding of abuse. We look at abuse in its widest sense, from activities that can be clearly labelled child abuse to others that are also seen to be a breach of a child's human rights. We discussed the meaning of the term sexual abuse within the introduction. Brown's analysis of a broader view of abuse is relevant at this point. She states:

> 'Abuse' is a rather loose term that has been critized from opposing points of view. Williams (1993) has argued that it minimizes the impact of incidents that are often serious criminal

offences, such as theft, assault or rape. Others have argued that it is too heavy-handed. Often the word is only applied to harm caused or sustained within an ongoing relationship marked by dependency and other inequalities. This focus on family, or other 'carer' relationships, draws the attention away from the abuse and exploitation which vulnerable adults experience in day or residential services or their neighbours and communities (Flynn 1987), including assaults from other service users or mistreatment by staff. (1999, p.292)

We will begin by considering disabled children's experiences of the medical profession and the ways in which participants felt they were objectified and marginalized within this system. Their experiences relate to their general treatment by medical staff, their experiences of child abuse whilst resident on hospital wards and their observations of how other disabled children were treated.

We will then explore their experience of mainstream and 'special' school. For those children who attended special schools, they talked about the school's failure to provide a level of education that was consistent with their academic ability, their socialization by the institution into compliant and unchallenging behaviour and their experience of sexual abuse. In mainstream, and for children with visible impairments, they spoke of teachers failing to intervene in incidents of bullying and a lack of awareness of the implications of impairment for the child's ability to participate in certain curricular activities. For children with hidden impairments, they felt that their educational struggles, and the consequential frustration that this created, meant that their behaviour was misread as naughtiness and disruptiveness, with their educational requirements not being adequately addressed. Both educational systems were considered problematic with neither fully addressing the disabled child's educational and social needs.

As in previous chapters, it is essential to recognize that the picture painted here is generated by the experiences of survivors of sexual abuse. This is not a denial that there is good professional practice and, indeed, several participants spoke of the occasional professional who recognized the child's distress and, despite being unsure about child protection procedure, did their best to help them out in whichever way they could. Nevertheless, the participants' narratives make bleak reading with the challenge that abuse is not simply a private affair but reverberates throughout society to touch all citizens.

THE MEDICAL PROFESSION

Medicine in western society operates within a hierarchical power structure, where doctors sit at the top of the pecking order, differentiated according to consultant status, and an acknowledged expertize (Hughes and Furgusson 2000). MacKay (2003, p.820) asserts that 'the power of medicine lies in its intellectual knowledge of the body' which grants its legitimacy and permits a set of objectifying practices that a large section of society feels are justified. Leder (1990) proposes that the patient's body is seen by medics to be a physiological machine. An object which, when invaded by illness and disease, requires the medical profession's assistance in 'fixing the machine' (p.148) and restoring it to an acceptable standard. Lupton (1994) suggests that the division of the mind and body is the philosophical ideology underpinning contemporary western medicine. Disease is essentially confined to the body and the mind is of secondary importance. The division of mind and body is responsible for many of the professions' practices that result in the patient feeling depersonalized and alienated from their body (Wendell 1996). When searching for cure and the resumption of normal functioning, the expectation of patients' behaviour is clear. They are required to be suitably attentive and compliant with the doctor's assessment and proposed treatment regime (Oliver 1998). As indicated, doctors' behaviour is not deemed by society to be oppressive; it is just what is required of them (Lupton 1994).

Disabled children's general experiences of health care

Medical practice adopts a functionalist stance to illness, which often equates impairment with deviancy (Oliver 1998). As a consequence, this influences the language used by the medical profession, where the term 'abnormal' is common currency, and interpretations of disabled people's ability are commonly described as deficit (MacKay 2003). Within medicine, quality of life arguments dominate decision-making and resource allocation, and become more salient when medical conditions are seen to deviate from what is considered to be the societal norm (Koch 2000). For disabled people with severe impairments, many are considered to have a poor/no quality of life (Marks 1999a).

This can culminate in a variety of medical practices, some question-able, which are sanctioned by medicine's scientific knowledge base. These practices can include such things as withholding treatment (e.g. do not resuscitate), aggressively applying treatment to those felt suitable (Koch 2000) and the utilization of measures designed to eliminate impairment. This latter category can include the following medical procedure: advice about the benefit of undertaking pre-natal screening, advice about aborting an unborn disabled baby approach-ing full gestation, withholding nutrition or treatment and infanticide (Crow 1996; Marks 1999a; Wolfensberger 1994).

Within this oppressive medical framework, it can be argued that disabled children's tendency to be objectified and dehumanized be-comes heightened, potentially impacting upon the way that their medical treatment is delivered:

> They tied me into a cot, they put on my right leg what's known as a 'Jonathon splint', which stretches and keeps your leg straight. They were also testing me for different things. I was allergic to the plaster they used to attach the splint to my leg, so that when they took that off, it just took off the top layer of my skin, so I had raw wounds from that. I wasn't getting the pain relief that I should have been getting and I wasn't being fed properly. I was hungry and thirsty a lot of the time. I don't know why they tied me into the cot; I think it was to stop me moving about. (Jean)

> A couple of times I was given too much medication and I ended up in a children's hospital because I was a bit dopey. My mum only just told me this. She said that I was half awake, half asleep, 'You weren't asleep but you weren't awake.' She called it co-matose, but it wasn't a coma, obviously. They took me in and changed the pain medication that they had me on. That hap-pened again when I was about eight, over Christmas time, where, again, I was given too much medication. (Jean)

Some disabled people report feeling dissatisfied in the relationship they have with the medical profession (Begum 1996; Crisp 2000). This can be an even more significant problem for disabled children. Although research indicates that disabled children have a desire to be informed about medical procedure and included in medical con-sultations (Garth and Aroni 2003), other writers propose that dis-abled children's perspectives continue to be overlooked because of misguided assumptions relating to competency and agency (Davis 2004). Similar to Jean's narrative, hospitalizations can still be experienced by disabled children as traumatic, despite medical progress. There needs to be recognition of children's need for honest, age-appropriate and sensitively delivered information (Closs 1998). The process of objectification and the imbalance in power can also be seen in some of the other more routine medical procedures that disabled children are regularly subjected to:

> In one hospital I was photographed because I'm quite unusual, because I have such extreme symptoms in one joint, and also because after my surgery one of my toes stopped growing, so one of my toes is the same size as it was when I was nine. And they said, 'Oh, that's interesting. How did that happen?' Nobody would actually acknowledge any possible connection to the surgery. Many other disabled people talk of similar experiences of being examined and photographed in an abusive way. (Jean)

> I also think that, like other disabled people, I lacked a sense of my own body belonging to me, and being private, of not having to be touched if I didn't want to be. This came from having to have many visits to the doctors and physiotherapists, and needing help to do things. I remember being paraded in front of doctors with very little on and feeling I was a thing for discussion rather than a person in my own right. This feeling got stronger as I got older. I was 13 before I was given a choice about whether I kept appointments. When I exercised my choice by not going, then I was made to feel guilty by other professionals, which reinforced my feelings of 'what is the point?' This lack of a sense that your body belongs to you is an issue that non-disabled children do not have to face. And, again, I can't say that this makes us more of a target, but it does make us better victims as we are less likely to object or tell. (May)

Begum (1996) found that within a primary care settings, disabled women report experiencing medical practices that were considered to be both offensive and intrusive. Begum highlights a tendency for some doctors to show great curiosity towards a woman's impairment. This could happen even when the individual was visiting the health locality for some other unrelated medical complaint. This medical curiosity, which in Begum's research was felt to be inappropriate, has the potential to become more blatantly abusive, particularly in the case of disabled children who have less power to protest. As can be seen, May's quote draws some parallels between a continued process of medical objectification and the potential for later sexual victimization.

On a separate but related matter, some writers draw attention to the fact that the medical profession's power also extends to them holding a disproportionate amount of influence over other aspects of a disabled person's existence by acting as gatekeepers to many other resources (Bricher 2000; French 1994). Josh's case is one example of where the unquestioned and inappropriate use of medical power provided access to a non-medical facility as a means of dealing with suspicions of sexual abuse occurring within the family home. One would hope that Josh's view that procedure is different 30 years down the line actually holds true.

> It was a decision made by my mother and the doctor, and the reason why it happened, I found out subsequently when I spoke to my mother, was that she was concerned that I was being abused and special school would take me out of the situation. The doctor was the one that dealt with my particular disability. I think his name might have been Clarke; he's been dead a long time now. And she'd obviously gone and said, 'Well look, something's not quite right.' And, of course, these days they'd send the child protection team in, and goodness knows what else, and they'd remove the child and they'd have banged him up in the nick, but in those days they didn't, did they? And so I was taken out of the situation, but they still allowed me home at holiday time to be abused. (Josh)

More blatant experiences of abuse

When writing about professional perpetrators Sullivan and Beech (2002) state that 'any organization or institution, whether statutory or voluntary, where children are cared for, is vulnerable to infiltration by professionals who wish to abuse' (p.159). This can be both a male or female perpetrator. High profile child abuse cases, which have attracted a significant amount media attention, have demonstrated that the police check system is fallible. One example is the murder of the two Soham schoolgirls in 2002, where the perpetrator, Ian

Huntley, had previously sexually assaulted children, yet no data relating to allegations was kept by Humberside police force, and nothing remained on police records indicating the risk he posed to children. He was later able to gain employment as a school caretaker, and as a consequence he came into contact with the two children he subsequently murdered. Similarly, and more recently, allegations of sexual abuse have been made by over 150 adults who were cared for as children at Haut de la Garenne children's home on the Isle of Jersey. Both cases clearly illustrate the inadequacy of the child protection system, past and present. Perpetrators, such as Huntley, possess the necessary skills and ability to slip through the child protection safety net, by using other identities and moving around the country (BBC News 2004). Undoubtedly, such abusers will demonstrate some of the same perpetrator characteristics, which are detailed later in Chapter 7.

Hospital day care admission has reduced the number of children experiencing lengthy periods of hospitalization, so creating fewer opportunities for abusers to offend. However, not much more than 30 years ago disabled children were routinely hospitalized for months at a time, sometimes even years. Often these children had no medical need, only a requirement for physiotherapy, education, or even a home. Inevitably, these children ended up demonstrating clear signs of emotional and social deprivation (Oswin 1971). These types of placement took place with little awareness of issues to do with attachment (Robertson 1952) and child protection. As can be seen in the experiences of some participants in this study, who had lengthy periods of hospitalization, sometimes parental contact was compromised by the hospital being some distance from the family home. The inflexibility of the hospital-visiting regime meant that parents had limited contact with their child. Consequently, the signs of a child's distress remained undetectable or, in cases of more frequent contact, a parent's wish to discharge their child from hospital was met with medical opposition:

> I was brought back at the age of about 14 months and fairly promptly put into hospital for an exploratory operation and also for a frog plaster. And what I have uncovered, starting when I was something like in my late 30s, yeah, in my late 30s, I uncovered the abuse and that it was a night nurse. I was in hospital for four months and it was in the days of parents visiting for an hour a week, and it was god knows where, but a long

way from where they lived, and there was no awareness of the issue then, issues to do with abuse. So I don't think my parents could have known or guessed or worried. (Lizzie)

Anyway, my mum was coming everyday to the hospital. She was young, in her early 20s, and was in some ways quite a trusting kind of person. She was brought up to believe that the doctor was a man to be trusted so she had a very strong belief and trust in medical people. Although they still hadn't given her a diagnosis they were talking about serious medical conditions so she was very frightened. She obviously didn't want to take me out of there because she thought that they were going to find out what was going on with my leg. On the other hand, she also had just qualified as a teacher and so she knew something about child development and she realized that I was becoming disturbed. She says that the reason that she took me out of hospital was because I started displaying the early signs of autism. I'd stop speaking; before I went into the hospital I was speaking, and I stopped completely, and I could not even hold her eye contact, and that was the point when she said to herself, 'She's disturbed, there's something not right about this, I've got to get her out of here.' She took me out against their advice, and still with no diagnosis, which took a lot of guts. (Jean)

In the following narrative episodes, Jean talks about her experiences of sexual and physical abuse, which preceded the behaviour observed by her mother. Jean's perpetrator was a nun who was working as part of the nursing team. Abuse by members of the clergy, particularly nuns, appears in the work of other writers (French 2006), and here Jean elaborates further on her experience:

They had a variety of nursing staff there and they had quite a few nuns who were medically qualified, who were part of the nursing staff, I think. There was one nun there who abused me, repeatedly over that time, in a variety of ways. One of them was enemas, and I now think that they were giving me enemas because I was constipated due to lack of movement. But the way she was doing them was sexually abusive: she did it in a very rough way, so that I was injured by her roughness... and one of the things that she would do would be to put her rosary beads inside my rectum and then pull them out very fast, and that was all a part of this ritual that she created around the enema, and it was about getting me clean and getting the 'devil' out of me. It was very painful; physically painful, and very frightening because she went from, at times, being, kind of, very strapped down emotionally, talking in a quiet voice and mumbling prayer, then it would become quite frenzied. So she seemed out of control and all over the place. It was very frightening, obviously, and physically very painful. (Jean)

I would be sitting in this wide tub and she would be pouring water all over me, and also pushing me down. She would grab the back of my head and my chest and push me down into the water. So I would be spluttering and trying to breathe, and not being able to breathe. And, again, all the sort of frenzied religious stuff was happening in what she was saying to me; full of hate. Hatefulness was the thing that came across so clearly to me. Of course, I got better at being able to time my breathing and predict what she was going to do, but it's very hard to do that because there was not a fixed pattern to it, and part of what she was trying to do was to push it, you know, to shock the 'devil' out of me. I realize now, looking back on it, how lucky I was because, accidentally, she could have killed me and she could have killed me on purpose too. The injuries to my anus would sting in the water. She also would pour extremes of hot and cold water over my head, and sometimes salt-water, it was very confusing and very frightening. So, that also happened on a regular basis; I think probably daily, or every couple of days that would happen. That would usually happen after the anal abuse, which would make sense that she would do an enema and then give me a bath. (Jean)

Both Lizzie and Jean also describe seeing other children being assaulted by members of hospital staff. In the second quote Jean refers to witnessing an incident of infanticide:

And I must say that I have memories of other children on the ward being abused. I know it wasn't just me, and most likely a significant proportion of them were not disabled, and that's what I mean. We were a pool of available children and I was one of them and none of us could get away. How old the others were, I really don't know, but we were a pool of available children in an era when it wasn't even expected, or on the agenda, so I'm sure that he was very typical and that I was abused, not so much because I was disabled, but because I was available alongside other children. But that's very individual, that's very particular to me in a sense, it's a particular circumstance and I'm sure other children, well, I know that other disabled children are targeted in situations in which they're the only disabled children around. (Lizzie)

But the worst thing that happened was that I saw two male medics take the life of a child in the cot next to me. It's still a really difficult one for me. I saw, in the dark, two white coats come in and they were mumbling, speaking in low voices, and they came to the cot next to me. I saw one of them put his hand over the child's mouth, covering the mouth and nose, and I saw the alarm in the eyes of the child and some 'convulsion' type movements, and then the child went still. They picked him up by holding his clothes at his chest, so his limbs were dangling, and then they took him away. I think he was probably about three or four, and I think, probably, had cerebral palsy. He was very thin, and kind of lanky with dark, short hair. I always call him a 'he' – I'm not sure, of course. He had beautiful, dark brown eyes. That was terrifying. It was actually, at the time, terrifying, and I know it's very shocking, and I know it's very difficult for a lot of people to believe, but it was absolutely horrendous. I mean, I know that that was happening and still does; that severely disabled infants often are left and given no water and food, but this was actually taking a child's life, this was suffocation. I've since read of a woman who witnessed a child killed by drowning. That woman was also talking about the 60s. I'm not saying that that kind of eugenic murder is happening now, in that way. It may not be, there's other ways that they do it; I mean there is pre-natal scanning and abortion isn't there; they are quite effective ones. There is also lack of resuscitation. The TLC one, tender loving care and no food and water, is still commonly used. (Jean)

Wardhaugh and Wilding (1993) build on the work of Goffman (1961) and Martin (1984), who had broadened their analysis of institutional abuse from the exclusive focus on the psychopathology of the offender to the consideration of organizational structures and processes that harbour such things as abuse. Such an analysis is applicable to practices such as sexual abuse and infanticide. They describe this phenomenon as 'the corruption of care' and cite eight dynamic features that can operate in large organizations, playing a role in the creation of abusive environments. Below we present a number of these features, several of which we apply to the disabled child resident in hospital:

- Children, particularly disabled children resident on a hospital ward, can come to be considered 'less than fully human' (Wardhaugh and Wilding 1993, p.6). Cultural stereotypes of impairment and a perceived poor/no quality of life, may aid this process of dehumanization. A person's normal feelings of compassion and sensitivity to others' pain can lead to depersonalization and moral distancing.

- Children resident in institutions such as hospitals, particularly disabled children, often have a minimum amount of power or influence over their situation, since they are oblivious to how the organization functions and how they might obtain what they need. This is in contrast to staff who appear to have total power, but who, at the same time, may feel that they are rendered powerless by their organization. Expressions of power by staff in these situations may be inappropriate and ultimately dangerous.

- There are groups, such as disabled children, who are devalued by society. The low value placed upon such groups of individuals is reflected in the limited resources that are ascribed to their services, demonstrating to staff the lack of importance given to their work. Shortages of resources can create situations of risk. Emphasis is placed on containment, and past enquiry evidence indicates that service users can be harmed. Management can demonstrate little interest in such situations so long as control is being maintained.

- The corruption of care can often result from a failure of management systems, as demonstrated by a number of enquiries. Clear organizational aims and objectives (set by management) direct the workforce and instil a level of professionalism necessary when working with de-valued groups. Policy and procedure declare 'the basic humanity and rights of service users and reinforce ideas of good practice' (Wardhaugh and Wilding 1993, p.18).

- Tightly knit structures can work to prevent criticism from within and as a consequence nurture dysfunction. Research indicates that this can develop from a misguided sense of staff solidarity. In inward-looking organizations expectations of staff and clients are low.

- Certain ways of working and organizational structures can contribute to the corruption of care. Hierarchical structures can put a sizable gap between management and where the service is ultimately delivered. This can work to undermine legitimacy of a management perspective, as other more pressing practice-based agendas can be given more credibility. This distance also creates difficulty for allegations of ill-treatment to be voiced.

The act of taking a child's life (as referred to in Jean's narrative) is the subject of conflicting opinion, which sits within a broader and more complex societal debate. Within contemporary society, two polarized positions seem to exist in relation to the question of whether or not children with severe impairment should be given life-promoting treatment or, instead, be subjected to medical practices designed to take lives. Pro-life advocates believe in every individual's right to life, with some arguing that this begins at conception (Lee 2002). Any attempt to take life (in whatever form) is seen as being intrinsically wrong. Perspectives that advocate the termination of a disabled child's life are based on argument that not only question the quality of life of the disabled child, but also question the quality of life of their parents and other family members (Kuhse and Singer 1985). This is in addition to the economic cost of providing long-term care for disabled children. Singer (1993) suggests that because newborns do not possess rationality, autonomy and self-consciousness the taking of their lives 'cannot be equated with killing normal human beings or any other self-conscious beings' (p.182). Later, when talking about disabled infants he proposes that 'killing a disabled infant is not morally equivalent to killing a person. Very often it is not wrong at all' (p.191). Here, the author does not even credit the disabled child with person status. With reference to the views of other doctors, Kuhse and Singer (1985) raise the question whether it is better to keep a severely disabled child alive, or let them die in the interests of replacing them later with a 'normal' child; many doctors believing this latter option to be more preferable. Whatever the leanings of doctors, however, these complex decisions rest with the individual parent.

The acceptability of infanticide promoted in the earlier writings of authors such as Kuhse and Singer (1985) has promoted some controversy in recent years, where the views of seemingly explicit disablist writers have come under attack. In addition to the human rights discourse, the disabled people's movement has begun to offer other forms of challenge to euthanistic practices. Authors such as Shakespeare (1998) present a political and rights-based perspective on pre-natal screening, and Macfarlane (1994) raises awareness of infanticide using a narrative format. Shakespeare (1998) suggests that as impairment is part of life, it is time for society to promote more positive measures to include and value disabled people. This might include new parents being given the appropriate level of welfare and social provision to support their parenting and disability equality training for geneticists and obstetricians; the people who have a major influence on prospective parents' decisions in the early stages of pregnancy.

EDUCATION SYSTEMS

All of the seven contributors to this book attended mainstream schools at some point in their educational careers, with two of these seven also having spent some time at residential school. We begin this section by first looking at May and Josh's experience of segregated education, and then move on to consider the range of difficulties encountered by disabled children attending mainstream.

Special school

Segregated education was considered to be the most appropriate way of educating disabled children until relatively recent times. Kliewer and Drake (1998) theorize its evolution as part of a larger process of institutionalization, which attempted to manage individuals whose differing needs fell outside society's mainstream. As can be seen from the following narrative, the institutional regime was described by participants in this study as failing to see the child as an individual (with a particular range of educational competencies), neglecting to prepare the young person for independent living, or being preoccupied with control and order, which detracted from the child's ability to build self-confidence and see their opinion as valid and worthwhile:

> ...no educational challenges, no exam system in place for bright disabled people; because if they've got a disability they're probably thick anyway. I mean there were teachers and professionals with that attitude, which was, and is, an absolute disgrace. (Josh)

> Because of my abuse, I didn't get an education because I was easy to slot into a school for disabled people. The abuse made it worse for me, in that respect. The fact that I didn't have any qualifications, that I left totally confused at 16, totally confused about everything. (Josh)

> My experience of boarding school also made it less likely I would tell anyone about everything that was happening to me at home. Boarding school conditions mean you to fit into a system. I remember being told 'you are doing it because we say so'. If I complained there was always a consequence, the same was true if you had a disagreement with a member of staff, or said you didn't like something someone was doing. So you learned to put up and shut up. I felt very much that there was no point in saying anything because it would only make things worse. (May)

Josh also describes being sexually abused at residential school, this time by a much older child resident:

> ...but when I was about 13, I was abused by one of the older boys as well. He was probably 16; perhaps he was staying on longer so he could have been 17 actually, and that was a bit scary. That wasn't anal, that was just masturbation. At these times I was the submissive one, only interested in mutual masturbation because then it would be over quickly. No anal or oral sex because I had to ensure that it was over as fast as possible. Although I used strategies to protect myself so that I didn't have to endure the pain of penetrative sex, I did feel I was being done to yet again. (Josh)

Research indicates that justification for the development of the residential education systems appeared to have its scientific base in instruments such as psychometric testing (Kliewer and Drake 1998). It could be seen that such educational tools validated moving disabled children from a segregated classroom situation to an educational institution with the same low educational expectations described by Josh. Similarly, support for controlling and dominating behaviour were sanctioned through the application of crude and objectifying psychological theory, which approved Pavlovian-type behavioural methods to obtain acquiescence from the child (Kliewer and Drake 1998). French (1996b) describes how sometimes the determination of staff to maintain control of their charges could result in situations deemed physically and psychologically abusive. Wardhaugh and Wilding's (1993) analysis of the 'corruption of care' can equally be applied to residential educational settings. Within such regimes, pecking orders can also be established amongst the children themselves, and inadequately supervized situations have the potential to develop into sexual abuse amongst peers.

Descriptions of physical, sexual and emotional abuse, occurring within residential educational establishments, can be seen in the work of a number of writers (Durham 2003; French 1996b; French and Swain 2000; French 2006). Roets and van Hove (2003) comment on the impact on an individual's self-esteem and personal identity when encountering oppressive institutional practices. They write that 'if people are frequently in situations in which they have no control, their expectation and belief that they can do anything to effect or change events wears off' (p.609). This view is endorsed by May, when she cites this type of oppression as one of the reasons why she was later unable to disclose sexual abuse. French and Swain (2000) make reference to the consequences of a controlling regime on all aspects of a child's development, the implications of which carry over into adulthood. Some of these controlling staff behaviours, that are designed to limit the non-harmful bodily actions of the disabled child (physical restraint) can still be observed today in schools (Davis and Watson 2001).

Children end up in residential education for a variety of reasons, including a lack of suitable local provision or the impact of impairment on the functioning of the family unit (Morris, Abbott and Ward 2002). These authors might suggest, however, that residential placements can be unsafe environments for disabled children. They found much inconsistency in the local authorities' interpretations of their statutory responsibility once a child had been placed in special school.

Children funded solely by education departments received minimal, if any, input. In jointly funded placements, assumptions were made about social services taking the lead role. This study showed that rarely were 'looked after' procedures for disabled children fully complied with, despite one in ten children being of primary school age. The reviewing regulations (advocated by the Children Act (1989)) and 'looked after' policy and procedure go some way in providing a structural mechanism for ensuring a child's safety when placed away from home. If neglected they create situations of risk. For children such as Josh and May, who were educated residentially before the introduction of such guidelines, there were no protective measures in existence to monitor their well-being.

Mainstream education

The Warnock Report (1978) signified the beginnings of a change in ideology relating to educational provision for disabled children, with parts of it encouraging the inclusion of disabled children in the mainstream system (Davis and Watson 2001). However, in spite of this, the medical model of disability and its accompanying attitudes prevail in legislation. This has created a situation whereby 'special needs' discourse predominates, operating on the same objectifying continuum of normality–abnormality (Shaw 1998), with an emphasis on what the child lacks. This is at the same time as peddling educational policies that promote inclusion. The indifference located in the current educational philosophy becomes apparent when analyzing the problematic structures that fail to sustain it (Davis and Watson 2001). The difficulties include, amongst other things, the devolution of a child's support budget to individual schools and the appearance of school league tables that have the potential to create resentment amongst parents and children. More importantly, there is a lack of funding to enable the necessary training that might facilitate a shift in staff and pupils' attitudes. The difficulties encountered by the research participants in this study are still very relevant today:

> I got very little help from members of staff, no help at all with it. And again that's one of the things that I would say about integration for disabled kids. Yeah, I'm totally in favour of it, absolutely one hundred per cent, but we need to be paying attention to those issues. I know that there is more awareness

of that now, but for me it was very hard. For a while, at my primary school, there were two other disabled girls, and that was good, that made things a bit easier, it wasn't just me. We were all bullied and it was mostly a kind of low level bullying that teachers did nothing about. They heard it all, I mean, I was called 'spaz' all the time and 'hop along' and nothing was done about that, no comment was made. (Jean)

Josh describes the general lack of understanding of his impairment and the inappropriate expectation that he participated in physical education with no extra support or supervision. This lack of understanding also contributed, on occasions, to the misinterpretation of impairment effects as naughtiness or cheekiness:

Sports I used to find really, really difficult because they were expecting you to climb up these damn ropes, and they expected you to climb up these wooden things on the walls. They didn't make any special dispensation for me, and they should have done. The fact that I couldn't run as fast as somebody else, it was insensitivity, and so I suppose sports was the worst. (Josh)

And because of my disability, I sometimes ended up with a smirk on my face, which was no good in school because they'd chuck the board rubber down the back of the classroom, and I had the slipper a few times purely for me just being me. (Josh)

Despite the trend towards inclusive education, the system remains largely problematic for disabled children. Dorries and Haller (2001) detail a polarized debate, which surfaced in the US following a disabled child's exclusion from mainstream education. The debate represents an assortment of societal perspectives that surround the inclusion agenda. These attitudes range from positive arguments, such as promoting increased tolerance of diversity amongst non-disabled children, to more negative viewpoints. The negatives focus on a number of themes including the potentially disruptive influence of disabled children in the classroom and the lowering of educational standards. The debate also highlights a resource issue, with some parties contending, rightly, that poorly implemented educational policy is destined to disadvantage disabled children by placing them in unsupported situations. The authors suggest that this polarized debate neglects the complexity embedded in the reality of an inclusive system. It does, however, reflect much of the current debate within the British education system.

In terms of the British education system, a number of paradoxes currently exist in mainstream education. In spite of an acknowledgement of difference, disabled children's behaviour and performance is still measured against the standardized non-disabled norm (Davis and Watson 2001). Davis and Watson found that the process of inclusion was further complicated by the creation of segregated special units within an inclusive educational setting. They also found that bullying behaviour, such as that experienced by Jean, was interpreted in terms of the disabled child's shortcomings. This justified the continuation of the bullying behaviour. Little consideration was paid to the negative subcultures that developed and were nurtured by the organization, as a result of a non-interventionist approach. The 'difference' discourse led to an objectification of the disabled child in practice.

Thomas and Chloe's difficulties related to their hidden impairments were unrecognized by teaching staff. This meant that they didn't receive the help they required. It also meant that the teachers formulated an inaccurate assessment of these two children's ability. Thomas's behaviour was seen as difficult and disruptive, and Chloe's attempt to get help was eventually construed as attention-seeking behaviour:

> I would often run riot with teachers and could even be violent. This made life very difficult for me since I was always being put in isolation, preventing me from disrupting lessons. Looking back, my Asperger's made schooling an awful experience. (Thomas)

> The teacher talked to me, I told her what it was, they tried to get me help and they brought an educational psychologist in who talked to some of my teachers, not the one I'd talked to, and not me. And they said, 'Oh, we think she might have schizophrenia,' which my mum told me a couple of years ago. And another teacher said, 'Oh no, she's just getting carried away with a drama project.' (Chloe)

> When I told her (the teacher) I thought, 'what a relief someone's going to help me' and then all these people came along that didn't help me, and I had to sit in the sick bay, in the corridor. Our school was in an old hospital and I had to sit in the

corridor on a hard chair for about an hour while they were all in this room, a bunch of people who mostly didn't know me, talking about me, but not once involving me. Then they came out and I got took back to the head of year's office and told off for wasting everybody's time. So, yeah, I told her that my head was different... (Chloe)

In Thomas's situation, he felt that his sexual abuse exacerbated his learning difficulties, and even created a resistance to learning:

I was at secondary school and was trying to settle down and behave myself. I was trying hard in as many lessons as possible and started to get decent grades. I was still in the lowest group, but I was now among the top six in most of my subjects, apart from maths. My reading continued to be a bit of problem and my English teacher mentioned this to my stepfather at a school governors' meeting and, god, did he go on about it. He started making me sit with a book for one hour each night at home. I would have to read a chapter to myself and then tell him what it was about. He would come to my room to hear what I had to say and once I'd finished he would bugger me or do some other perverted act. I wouldn't read a word of any book he gave me; I'd lie on my bed and listen to the radio. He'd go crazy at me; shouting, punching and slapping me at my failure to answer his questions. (Thomas)

Despite the difficulties that are created by a labelling culture, both Chloe and Thomas illustrate the fact that diagnosis of impairment can be a useful, particularly for parents who will then know where to go to access information and support (Burke 2008). For teachers, the identification of learning difficulties can often provide an increased understanding of the prevailing issues for the child. In a school setting it may also facilitate access to the necessary resources to support learning (Malloy and Vasil 2002), promoting an inclusive ideology within the classroom setting and preventing other labels such as disruptive, naughty and attention-seeking. Assessment and the acquirement of a 'label' would have proved beneficial to Chloe and Thomas's education. The lack of recognition of learning needs may also have been symptomatic of a failure to recognize and understand impairments located on the autistic spectrum.

Lyn and Thomas raise other issues, not directly related to their education, but nevertheless significant. At both of these individuals' schools, teachers were able to see the child's distress, but dealt with it in their own particular and well-intentioned way. The response was probably typical for the 1970s and relevant to a desire not to compromise their professional role, or the child's safety. It resulted, for Lyn, in a need to 'up the stakes' in order for the situation to be recognized. In Thomas's case, a teacher's expression of concern was seen as supportive:

> She went to meetings (Lyn's mother), and one time she went away for a week's course on meditation, and when that happened I went to this teacher and said, 'Could I come and babysit for a week?' I remember, she said, 'Why?' I said, 'My mum's going away and I don't want to be home with my dad.' And there was this little beat of a pause and she said, 'That's fine, you come,' and I did. And after that, in my sixth-form time, there were periods when I would go and stay over-night there, and the excuse was always that I was babysitting. Years and years later, I said to her, 'Why didn't you pick it up?' and she said that she didn't know what to do; it wasn't something that people were given guidelines about. She said that I was a topic of conversation in the staff room; people knew that there was something seriously wrong and they just didn't know how to handle it, and they just didn't want to ask a direct question because they were frightened of getting it wrong. I can understand the not knowing what to do, being afraid that they would actually make things much worse. Perhaps there was a sense of, 'Well, if it's something at home, then she's nearly at university, and if we do something now then it could screw up "A" levels and stuff, so if we can sort of just keep going like this, it will be okay in the end.' I don't know. She said it wasn't that people didn't notice, they did. At the time, I felt nobody was noticing anything at all, and that made me feel very lost, and it made me feel that I had to escalate stuff. But I think it would have been helpful if somebody had said there's obviously something going on. (Lyn)

> He (the teacher) knew I hated my stepfather, he knew that something was wrong in my home life, and asked me what the problem was many times, or asked me how I'd got the cuts and bruises. He told my stepfather of his concerns, making out that he thought I was being bullied, in his own way warning him that he knew something was very wrong. It didn't stop the abuse

but at least he tried, he was on my side, he cared about me. (Thomas)

The appearance of the occasional professional who played a supportive role in the disabled child's life can be seen in the narrative of individuals participating in a study conducted by French (2006). Additionally, Zimrin (1986) found that abused children, who had access to adults who helped instil confidence and encouraged them, fared better. The complications faced by the teachers in Lyn and Thomas's situation still have some relevance today, as there continues to be a significant number of obstacles to reporting child protection concerns (Kenny 2001; O'Toole *et al.* 1999). Kenny found in her questionnaire-based research with 197 teachers, that many teachers were not aware of child abuse procedure and felt that they were ill-equipped to make reports. In fact the majority had never made a report, despite having on average ten years' teaching experience. Kenny believes that the deterrent to lodging reports relate to concerns about whether they will be adequately supported by senior staff members, concerns about making inaccurate reports and questions relating to the child protection service's ability to support the child.

Both O'Toole *et al.* (1999) and Kenny (2001) indicate the importance of staff training in the recognition of child abuse and the correct reporting procedures. This training should facilitate an increased awareness of what will happen once their concerns have been reported to social services. Most importantly, awareness needs to be raised about their professional responsibility to the child. This training should not only take place whilst students are undertaking teacher training, but should also be a feature of their ongoing professional development (Baginsky 2003; Kenny 2001). Such training has the capacity to increase teachers' confidence and help them to appreciate the importance of their contribution as effective partners the child protection process.

CONCLUSION

This chapter demonstrates how disabled children are compromised in many aspects of their daily lives. Disabling attitudes are seen to infiltrate the cultures of some of the key organizations that they encounter on a regular basis. Sometimes dysfunctional organizational cultures can evolve into abusive environments, which manage to escape detection. Some aspects of medical practice, identified by contributors to this book, are commonplace medical procedures that are often taken for granted and rarely challenged. Others can be classified as clearly abusive, yet infanticide still continues to be the subject of a polarized debate. Equally as potentially destructive, as demonstrated by these sexually abused survivors' narratives, can be the experiences of disabled children attending both residential and mainstream educational provision. Both systems are shown, in these accounts, to create a range of emotional difficulties for the child, with mainstream education seen to be struggling to promote a truly inclusive ideology. Neither of these educational systems appears to be ideally suited to the child's needs. Organizational abuse can infiltrate disabled children's daily lives, with experiences demonstrating that systems neither recognize nor meet their needs and rights as citizens.

CHAPTER 7

Who Abuses and Why?

INTRODUCTION

As is already evident, this research did not involve talking with perpetrators, or engaging with their narratives. There is much, nevertheless, in the stories of survivors; where they describe how they
have had to grapple to understand why and how they were subjected
to violence. Reverberating through the narratives is the search for
self-affirmation; that they are the victims and not the instigators of
sexual abuse. This chapter considers the issue of who abuses and
why. It begins with some factual data illustrating the extent of the
problem within the UK and Wales, and then goes on to examine the
perpetrator profile. The following section provides an overview of
the literature, addressing the question of why men (and occasionally
women) sexually abuse children. It looks at the issue of how perpetrators operate; more specifically the tactics that they use to ensure a
child's compliance, and whether a relationship exists between these
modes of operation and the emotional outcome for the victim. Within
that analysis, consideration is also given to paedophiles working as
part of an organized network, as opposed to men abusing within the
family context.

Finally, the chapter discusses issues more relevant to the disabled
child, and how factors associated with communication and dependency can significantly increase a disabled child's vulnerability. It
examines the distorted belief systems held by perpetrators, and how
society's devaluation of disabled children can adversely influence a
perpetrator's perspective and ultimately create justification for their

behaviour. In its totality, the chapter aims to broaden our understanding of the abuse experience and the emotional implications for the disabled child who strives to make sense of their experiences. It illustrates how, from the combined experience of a group of individuals, strategies for prevention can be formulated.

THE EXTENT OF THE PROBLEM

The NSPCC (2006) provide the following statistical information, which gives some sense of the extent of sex offender activity:

- There are 28,994 people registered as sex offenders in England and Wales. This figure does not, however, give a breakdown of how many offenders have abused children and how many have abused adults (Home Office 2005).

- A UK study discovered that 70 per cent of abusers had between one and nine child victims. This figure is supported by Home Office data which estimates that each sexual offender will have abused three children (Beech, Fisher and Beckett 1998). There have also been reports of perpetrators abusing up to 450 children (Elliott, Browne and Kilcoyne 1995).

- In 1993 it was estimated that 110,000 people had been convicted of sexual offences against children in England and Wales (Marshall 1997).

As indicated in Chapter 2, the figures relating to registration and conviction represent the 'tip of the iceberg' since many survivors do not disclose abuse until adulthood (London *et al.* 2005) and conviction remains fraught with difficulty.

WHO ABUSES

Who were the perpetrators in this study? Participants' narrative illustrates that five of the participants had been sexually abused by parents or stepparents living within the family home. Furthermore, two had been abused by professionals (nurses) working in the health care profession. Three participants had experienced both abuse within the home and abuse outside. One person described being abused by a perpetrator working as part of an organized network of paedophiles. Here, Thomas explains how his mother's financial and emotional vulnerability opened the door for his stepfather:

> She meets her first husband, he goes off to war and he's captured by the Germans, he gets severe frostbite, escapes, comes home and he's a hero. He gets sent to India, gets shot in the leg which has a huge detrimental affect on his health and dies not many years later, after the war, leaving her on her own with five children, back to where she was in the 1930s. She was dependent on welfare, nothing coming in, five kids to bring up and she hates everyone for it, because she's been dealt a dirty card. So all of a sudden Jack walks in, he's been living over the road with his wife and two children, David and Ann, from this first marriage, both of whom he's been sexually abusing. (Thomas)

One of Lyn's abusers was a friend of her father's — an ordinary family man whose pets provided the necessary hook for Lyn:

> But that was also opportunistic in the sense that he was around most of the time, he was somebody that my parents trusted, and I would go to his house. He was married and he had two daughters and three dogs, and the dogs were a big attraction for me; he had three Labradors, and I would go around to his house. (Lyn)

The word paedophile means 'child love' and according to Wyre (2000) it describes individuals who 'exhibit sexual arousal and attraction towards pre-pubertal children' (p.49). Research illustrates that paedophiles are generally men, who vary in age (13–76 years), marital status (50% married or co-habiting), levels of education, employment status and ethnicity (Fisher 1994). Typically, they can be manipulative, skilled liars and prone to denial, minimization and distorted thinking (Wyre 2000). Erooga (2002) refers to the work of Beckett *et al.* who describe the personal characteristics of 59 convicted male perpetrators, participating in seven treatment programmes. In evaluating the research data these authors write that the men involved were:

> ...typically emotionally isolated individuals, lacking in self-confidence, underassertive, poor at appreciating the perspectives of

others, and ill-equipped to deal with emotional distress. They characteristically denied or minimized the full extent of their sexual offending and problems. A significant proportion were found to have: little empathy for their victims; strong emotional attachments to children; a range of distorted attitudes and beliefs... (Beckett et al. 1994, p.5)

Craig, Browne and Beech (2008) build a profile of a sex offender based on a review of other writers' research findings. They propose that whilst for a number of years the average age of a convicted perpetrator was 40 (Elliott, Browne and Kilcoyne 1995), individuals age 17 and under now make up one third of sexual abuse allegations (Glasgow et al. 1994), with many receiving a community sentences for their offence (Masson and Erooga 1999). Retrospective studies also illustrate that 60–80 per cent of perpetrators started abusing young children as teenagers (Groth, Hobson and Garry 1982). In terms of the relationship between offender and child, and intra-familial abuse, family members such as father, stepfather, grandfather and uncle feature frequently, whilst acquaintances such as friend of the family or professionals comprise members of the extra-familial group. A third and smaller group of offenders are total strangers to the child (Faller 1990).

Having once been considered an insignificant subgroup of the sexual offender population, Jennings (1993) points to the work of Finkelhor and Russell (1984) who challenge the notion that women rarely sexually abuse children. Using data provided by the American Humane Association study, Finkelhor and Russell conclude that women are the perpetrators in 14 per cent of cases against boys, and in 6 per cent of cases perpetrated against girls. The research literature on women perpetrators, however, shows many differences of opinion, with incidence figures taken from other studies indicating much lower figures. With reference to the work of Fergusson and Mullen (1999), Craig, Browne and Beech (2008) highlight that more recent research indicates that 2.5 per cent of female survivors and 21.3 per cent of male survivors report abuse by female perpetrators, making this issue a significant societal problem. Elliot (1993) questions the notion that female abusers are coerced into sexually abusing a child by men, which is a common assumption. She discovered in her small-scale sample that invariably women acted alone, or in a man's absence. Elliot suggests that society's resistance to accepting that women commit sexual offences against children is rooted in a number of factors, including the fact that:

- 'Female sexual abuse is more threatening – it undermines feelings about how women should relate to children.' (p.8)

- 'It has taken years for people to accept that children are sexually abused, and such sexual abuse has been placed in the context of male power and aggression. Women are not supposed to be sexually aggressive, and the male power theory eliminates them as possible abusers unless they are coerced by males.' (p.8)

Similar to the victims of male offenders, abuse perpetrated by a female may bring about similar patterns of psychological distress.

WHY PERPETRATORS ABUSE

As a perpetrator's predisposition to abuse a child is independent of the child's impairment status, we feel it necessary to begin here with a brief overview of some of the existing theoretical literature addressing the issue of why perpetrators sexually abuse children. These theoretical models vary in their emphasis, but generally speaking they can be divided into models that see causality linked to dysfunction within the family system, models that consider differing aspects of the offender psychology, feminist theory that links causality to the ways in which men are socialized within our society and lastly multifactoral models of abuse. Within this section of the text, research participants' viewpoints are once again used to illuminate theoretical models, and it is clear that these theories of abuse reverberate through the narratives of these survivors.

Family systems theory

Models emphasizing family pathology dominated the early literature on sexual abuse. Some of these earlier writings on intra-familial child sexual abuse use a family systems analysis that highlight the development of dysfunctional family relationships as one aspect of the problem. As is illustrated by some of the experiences of Lyn and Chloe, these theories contend that it is the family's social isolation, chaotic modes of functioning and distorted patterns of relating that break down family boundaries:

> It was just getting out of control in a very weird way, in the sense that it was very structured. The boundaries of it were very firm, the external boundaries, I mean; my mother literally never went out, my father barely had a social life, and my going in and out was pretty controlled. No children came to our house; I never invited anyone home partly because of my dad's drinking. By this point it was heavy enough for his behaviour to be erratic, and my mum's behaviour could be a bit erratic as well. It was just not something I did. Also, the boundaries within the family were not quite as in other people's houses. (Lyn)

> And my family have actually been living with him (Chloe's grandfather) and tolerating this sort of behaviour and they think it's okay. Why, because my dad's behaviour is not quite right either. I remember my dad getting my mum wearing short skirts and talking about her knickers and talking about her being sexy. I didn't know that everybody's parents didn't do that. (Chloe)

Mayer (1983) refers to the mother–child–perpetrator relationship as the 'incestuous triad'. By drawing on the work of Gottlieb (1980), she suggests that often such families are characterized by their interdependency and impaired communication. The sexual abuse is seen as one method of allowing the family to function (Tomison 1995). The child, for example, might see the abuse as one form of adult attention in an otherwise emotionally depleted household. The need for control is seen to become a more poignant issue once the child reaches their teens and the risk of disclosure is greater (Mayer 1983; Summit 1983). Such models see marital difficulty and/or the sexual incompatibility of the parents as being responsible for the child fulfilling the role of the mother, both emotionally and sexually. Mayer (1983) believes that this pattern of relating has a number of possible causes including the mother's own sexual abuse. She contends that the mother can consciously or unconsciously reverse the mother–daughter role, as evidenced here in May's experience:

> I am sure my mother felt that it was my fault and that it was better than my father having an affair outside. It also meant that she didn't have to do things that she didn't want to, like

having sex, which she told me she was not interested in, but kept the financial security. I started to think about the things that had happened and realized not only did my mother know, she also created opportunities for it to happen by going out all day, making my youngest sibling go as well even when they didn't want to. (May)

Despite the reality of these observations in clinical practice (Baker 2002), feminist critique has drawn attention to the inherent patholo-gization of other family members present in these theories. This is particularly the case for the mother, who is seen to be partly re-sponsible for the abuse, with the culpability of the perpetrator being somewhat diminished (Westcott and Cross 1996). Family systems theory shows little regard for the male-dominated power structure of the family system, which results in the woman potentially becoming complicit in their partner's abusive behaviour.

Psychopathology of the offender

Both the earlier writings of Miller (1984) and the more recent work of Marshall and Marshall (2000) propose models of perpetrator pa-thology, which make the link between being sexually abused as a child and later becoming a perpetrator of child sexual abuse. Miller's theory (1984) is rooted in her own psychoanalytic practice and evolves around the notion of repression and repetition. In accordance with this model, a child's own abuse is seen to be repressed to ensure their survival, but at the same time it works to the detriment of the child's emotional well-being. Far from the repression process acting to keep a lid on the situation, the trauma becomes heightened, creat-ing a need to express the experience by repetition compulsion, which becomes more 'urgent and uncontrollable the more deeply repressed the original trauma' (p.163). Elements of this dynamic are clearly vis-ible in Thomas's narrative, where he struggles to find explanations for his stepfather's violent behaviour:

> I do believe my stepfather was abused as a child himself; ap-parently he had an awful time with his stepmother. His mother died when he was seven, and he left home when he was 11 be-cause his stepmother beat him, as he put it. He left home and went to live with his grandmother when he was 11. And I can remember him talking one day when all the family were around

and saying that he'd turned around and hit her back. He said, 'I hit the cow back, for the first time in my life, I stood up and hit her one back; she'd spent bloody years belting the hell out of me.' And I thought, that's where it comes from, the physical abuse side, that's where it comes from. The sexual abuse, I couldn't say. (Thomas)

Although repetition compulsion can be observed in some individuals' behaviour, the shortcomings of Miller's work relate to the implied inevitability of this process (if therapeutic assistance is not sought) and the fact that the majority of victims do not go on to become abusers. The theory assumes a lack of agency for the individual concerned and has an absence of any gender analysis.

Marshall and Marshall's work (2000) is, perhaps, more applicable to extra-familial child sexual abuse and also offers a fairly detailed and complex analysis of the process whereby a victim becomes an abuser. Drawing on both their own work (Dhawan and Marshall 1996; Marshall and Mazzucco 1995; Marshall, Serran and Cortoni 2000) and the work of Smallbone and McCabe (2003), they make the link between the poor quality of early attachment experienced by the abuser and the propensity to abuse later in life. They suggest that an insecure attachment creates a child with low self-esteem, poor interpersonal skills and the need to seek out attention/affection from adults. This, in turn, manufactures a vulnerability that increases the risk of being sexually abused. The possibility that some sexual pleasure is derived from the sexual abuse experience (or that masturbatory habits are established as a consequence) may result in the child perceiving the experience in positive, non-harmful terms, so removing one barrier to sexually offending later, when an opportunity to offend presents itself. Marshall and Marshall's theory is possibly limited in the same way that Miller's theory is, because poor attachment in early childhood does not necessarily increase a tendency for sexual victimization, followed by the perpetration of sexual offences against children.

The work of Glaser et al. (2001) counters Marshall and Marshall's perspective. They undertook a large-scale study investigating the proposed 'cycle of child sexual abuse' using a method of clinical case note review of individuals attending a forensic psychotherapy centre. They conclude that their findings do not give strong support to a cycle of abuse, and that a history of abuse is relevant in a minority of cases and is just one factor contributing to an individual becoming a perpetrator. The authors also caution on the distinct nature of their sample, and that being a forensic psychotherapy patient was 'not representative of the wider population of victims and perpetrators' (p.492). The large size of the sample may, however, offer reassurances to survivors of abuse. The authors found no significant relationship between problematic attachments and later becoming an abuser.

Feminist theories and patriarchy

In contrast to approaches that solely focus on individual psychopathology, radical feminists offer another valuable and very relevant social analysis of child sexual abuse. They theorize it as being just one form of violence perpetrated by men within a family unit (McLeod and Saraga 1988).

With reference to the work of others, Solomon (1992) proposes that within the family, men are socialized to be a dominant force and women are socialized to be passive, with the system perpetuating itself by the production of children with the same attitudes and values. Family dynamics reflect the power differentials of wider society. Walby (1990) describes a patriarchal system where male identity is conferred by the enactment of extreme masculine type behaviour and violence is sanctioned as a legitimate means of men getting what they want. She suggests that support for the use of violence can be most clearly seen in the armed forces. Not surprisingly, a significant number of perpetrators in this study had spent some time in the military. In addition to believing that it is a man's entitlement to sexually violate, the following narratives from Lyn and Thomas illustrate the various ways in which a belief in male privilege can manifest itself in some families. This can be seen in both the man's general behaviour (complicated in this first instance by factors related to ethnicity) and then in their frequent use of physical violence:

> My father's family had this huge hang-up about darkness, and it always used to enrage my mother that the first question anyone asked when she had me was not what sex I was, or even if I was all right, but how dark I was. So the one member of the family in that generation who went to university was actually a girl, and she wasn't the oldest but she was the lightest and they put the money into her. So, my father was an immigrant

and, as somebody not fitting into the Indian world when he'd been in India, or the English world, he had almost no status anywhere. And he did tend to dominate my mother and me, and was the classic bully, I suppose, in that it was the only place that he could, so tended to do it quite a lot. Understanding it doesn't necessarily mean condoning it, or feeling any better about it, but I can see where it might have come from. And he was the darkest in his family so he was very much the underdog amongst his brother and sisters, so he took it out where he could. (Lyn)

Stupid things like I sharpened a pencil when I was about seven and it had a rubber on the other end so I put the rubber in the sharpener as well, and he came in and saw what I was doing. It was one of these wind up pencil sharpener things, which he brought home from the office that he worked in. He came in and threw the pencil sharpener at me. It had got like a plastic draw in it and the sharpener went above my head but the draw came down and caught me on the head. So I went down and he came in and kicked me right under the chin, could have broke my neck quite easily, sent me flying, you know, into an armchair and said, 'You never ever sharpen fucking rubbers.' What was that about? And I sit here sometimes and I think to myself what was that about, what was so bad about sharpening a bloody rubber? (Thomas)

Solomon (1992) illustrates the relevance of a radical feminist analysis of child sexual abuse, which remains silent on other issues (why most men don't sexually abuse children). Her research clearly demonstrates that perpetrators are male and that girls are usually (but not always) the victims. If women do abuse, they generally have male accomplices, a factor detailed in the clinical research of Sgroi and Sargent (1993), but refuted by the work of Elliott (1993). With reference to the work of Finkelhor (1984), Glaser and Frosh (1988) write there are 'normative factors in the socialization of men that help explain why such abuse is widespread' (p.22). The social acceptability of sexual abuse can also be observed in the sexualized depiction of children in some advertizing and the relatively free availability of child pornography, both of which provide affirmation of the appropriateness of conceptualizing children in sexual terms.

Mulifactoral theory

Several authors have proposed a combined theory of sexual offending, which brings together a range of factors when trying to account for perpetrator behaviour (Finkelhor 1984; Wolf 1985). Oates and Cohn Donnelly (2000) write that Finkelhor's four preconditions was the 'first comprehensive, multidisciplinary paradigm for thinking about, understanding, studying, assessing and eventually treating and preventing sexual abuse' (p.173). The model was formed by using a mix of theory and knowledge acquired in clinical practice. It is an amalgam of psychological and sociological perspectives and offers an invaluable approach when trying to understand perpetrator behaviour. Put succinctly, the model includes first, that a potential offender would need to have a motivation to sexual abuse. This might be related to a person's re-enactment of their own childhood trauma, or it may relate to the individual finding children sexually arousing. Second, the person would need to overcome any internal inhibitors, by believing in male privilege, for example, or by becoming disinhibited by alcohol. Third, the individual would have to overcome external inhibitors, which would be aided by a socially isolated family unit, or an absent or ill mother. Last, the individual would need to deal with any resistance that the child might present, or equally the abuse could be understood in terms of the child's social powerlessness. Lancaster and Lumb (1999) describe Finkelhor's model as proposing that a 'range of social, cultural, developmental and psychological features interconnect within each individual and aid the creation of a paedophilic personality' (p.122) and no factor by itself would generally suffice.

UNDERSTANDING HOW PERPETRATORS OPERATE

When trying to gain some understanding of what factors are considered important to the perpetrator when targeting a child, Craig, Browne and Beech (2008) draw attention to the work of Elliott, Browne and Kilcoyne (1995). By interviewing a large number of convicted child abusers, these authors established that children are selected for abuse by paedophiles for a range of reasons. The following factors give some idea of what is considered important to the offender. Prettiness was seen to be significant for 42 per cent of perpetrators, how the child dressed (27%), being young or small (18%), innocent or trusting children (13%) and children who lacked confidence or had low self-worth (49%). It is notable, then, that perpetrators hone in on the most emotionally vulnerable children. What is also evident is there is no direct reference to disability or impairment here. In literature about the sexual abuse of children, disability and impairment tend not to be specifically addressed from the viewpoint of perpetrators. The line of 'prettiness', it would seem, presents a more acceptable and understandable picture, and disabled children remain invisible, despite their increased vulnerability.

Elliot, Browne and Kilcoyne (1995) also found that perpetrators who abused children outside the family unit hung around places such as schools, shopping precincts, parks and swimming pools. A percentage aimed to become a visitor to the child's home. In the majority of cases abuse took place at either the offender or child's home. A significant percentage said they abused in public places such as toilets, and parks. Again the implications in relation to disabled children are not addressed.

Of course, perpetrators also have their own modus operandi once with a child. Following interviews with 23 perpetrators (20 male and 3 female), ages ranging from 21–56, Gilgun (1994) constructs a continuum of sex offender behaviour. The categories are based on offender descriptions and evaluated in terms of closeness to the child. The behaviours are marked by their fluidity across categories and include the following classification: avengers, takers, controllers, conquerors, playmates, lovers and soul mates.

From the viewpoint of survivors in this study, the classification of perpetrator behaviour has some relevance in understanding how their abuser operated. 'Taker' type behaviour is illustrated by the words of Thomas and Josh and is marked by its aggression and brutality. As Gilgun describes, the abuser sees the child as an object and there is little concern for the consequences of their actions. As can be seen from the narrative, these perpetrators use violence and force, and the abuse can result in rape, which was the case for these two children:

Sexual abuse is evil, full stop; you can't say, well, some sexual abuse is mild and some very unpleasant. It is awful, and when it's forced upon you, that's what makes it worse, and his was a complete brutality. There was no, 'Okay, you've begged me enough, I'll stop.' It was, 'I will physically kick you to death to get what I want, I will batter you to a pulp to get what I want. You will be compliant. You will do as I say.' (Thomas)

And I got told, 'Well look, you've got two choices. You can either go straight to bed now (for sex),' and this was sometimes at five o'clock in the afternoon, 'or you can have the belt.' So, I mean, what sort of choice is that for somebody when there is a body function and you're not always in control of it? And I'd say, 'Okay then, beat me because I'm not giving in.' He'd beat me and then, quite often, I'd get abused as well. So apart from the physical abuse, I'd get sexually abused as well. (Josh)

Lyn's description of abuse by a family friend is illustrative of a per-petrator who assumes the 'playmate' or 'lover' role. This individual had a distorted belief system and an illusion that there is a degree of equity in the abusive relationship. The early stages of the seduction mimic a courtship ritual and sex was just one activity that the abuser involved Lyn in:

But at the time, he, Phil, was saying things like I was much older for my age than other girls. I was flattered by the maturity he was implying and I was flattered by his attention, and I was get-ting attention from him that I wasn't getting from my dad. It started with those jokes that are slightly edgy and then discus-sions about boyfriends, and then touching and stroking, and then step-by-step, over a period of probably weeks or maybe it was days, but I think weeks... (Lyn)

I don't remember, at the time, feeling that I was being exploited. I thought I was an equal partner, or even in control. I think from things that I remember him saying, that I have discussed now with my therapist, he either instinctively or consciously manipulated that to happen. On a few occasions, I remember when he got excited, when he got an erection, he said to me, 'Now look what you have done.' And it was half joking. And with equal partners it would have been a joke, you know, play, but because we weren't equal partners, it wasn't. And there was a part of me that felt, 'yes, that's something that I've done'. (Lyn)

One finding highlighted in a study conducted by Russell (1986) was that the severity of sexual abuse (i.e. intercourse) was generally related to an increased reporting of trauma by her research participants. Also significant in this study was the degree of physical force and violence used by the perpetrator and the consequence for the survivor. Niederberger's (2002) work balances this argument, finding that other aspects of the abusive relationship contribute to the severity of effect. He found a definite correlation between the use of force and the creation of anxiety and guilt feelings in the survivor. But he challenges the belief that the use of force worsens the outcome for that person (although acknowledging that the force used in his sample was not extreme). Similar to the experience of Lyn, he found that strategies involving affection can have a stronger implication. He found a greater depressive effect and a reduction in psychological well-being for the adult survivor. Also significant for the survivor was if self-blaming took place at the time of the abuse:

> For me, the kind of thing that happened to me is damaging in a corrupting kind of way. You feel so implicit in it; you feel that your edges aren't straight any more. I really don't want to say that there are some children who are assaulted who get off easier, that's not what I am trying to say. Their moral boundaries may remain the same because they know that what happened was very wrong and that maybe they had nothing to do with it. Where you have been put in a position, perhaps deliberately, by somebody else in which it feels like you are the one who is making all the moves, and you're the one who is in control, and you're the one who is making it happen, it's just corrosive in terms of redoing it afterwards. I'm only just beginning to see how hard that is to undo. (Lyn)

Any typology of perpetrator behaviour can equally apply to perpetrators acting alone, or to perpetrators acting as part of an organized network. However, it is worth highlighting factors which typify organized abuse. Wyre (2000), who has worked extensively with perpetrators, differentiates between predatory paedophiles, who can abduct to sexually abuse or abuse as an expression of anger, and non-predatory paedophiles, who demonstrate distorted thinking patterns relating to a child's ability to enjoy, and give consent to sex. Wyre proposes that the behaviour of this latter group of individuals, in effect, is also predatory. Wyre (2000) gives an example of more organized abuse by citing an example of a man who kept a large number of amusement machines in his garage, attracting children from the local area. When talking about the children involved in this network, Wyre writes 'they needed money to play on the machines. This created dependency on the offender, which led eventually to gifts being given for favours' (p.61). As described by Lyn in her last quote, Wyre refers to the corrupting nature of some perpetrators' behaviour. Wyre describes the typical characteristics of a fixated paedophile, which can include factors such as:

- They may belong to children's organizations.

- They may be in contact with other paedophiles.

- They show distortions in their thinking.

- They may create or participate in paedophile networks.

- They may work at gaining the trust of parents.

(Wyre 2000, p66)

Organized child sexual abuse is notable by the difficulty created in its detection. It often involves large numbers of children who may be drawn from specific neighbourhoods or communities. Gallagher (1998) proposes that, frequently, these children demonstrate resistance to authority. As described by Chloe, children may be recruited by their peers for the abuser and may be 'tied in' by the inducements, offered by the paedophile, including things like sweets, toys, money, alcohol and drugs. They may also include attention and affection that the child lacks in other parts of their life:

> A friend of mine did some 'grooming' for some people. I knew she was friendly with these people that lived near her and that she babysat, and I vaguely remember that there was something dodgy going on but I can't remember what. I think it was all a bit, not really being said. I got asked to go and babysit for these people and I went round on my own to these people's house. They gave me a few drinks and off they went out, and I don't remember any kids being there. It's a funny thing, I just don't know if the kids were there or not, I really can't remember. Anyway, because what I do remember is so significant, little facts like that are just... Anyway, later, somebody came round and it's so...even at the time it was obvious to me that it was

> organized, I think I knew he might come. What I didn't realize
> at the time was that it was abuse; I didn't realize that it was
> wrong and, also, I wasn't capable of saying no. (Chloe)

Often, these paedophiles employ strategies to throw officials off the
scent, including the intimidation of witnesses, or the removal and
destruction of evidence (Gallagher 1998). Their activities throw up
complex issues for those professionals who are involved in criminal
investigation and a child's protection.

CHILD SEXUAL ABUSE AND DISABILITY

In contrast to the neglect in the literature of disability and impairment as significant factors from the viewpoint of perpetrators, this
research unveils a different picture. From the perspectives of survivors, disability and impairment are deeply pertinent to understanding
why and how perpetrators act as they do. A range of complex factors
emerge in the individual narratives, but the starting point for many
are the barriers to communication faced by disabled children.

A disabled child's communication can create a number of potential difficulties for others. The non-disabled parent or carer might not
share the same communication system as the child, or the child may
not have the necessary vocabulary to describe their abuse experience.
For verbal children whose impairment presents itself as behavioural
difficulties, the nature of the child's impairment may mean that they
are less likely to be believed by adults. For some disabled children,
such as Lyn and Chloe, a poor parental relationship can limit the
child's communication possibilities, resulting in a need to seek out
adult attention elsewhere. All these factors have a part to play in a
perpetrator choosing such a child to abuse, as well as limiting the
child's subsequent disclosure opportunities:

> Phil, I think, could see that I was isolated and desperate for male
> attention. He may have been able to see the difficulties with
> communication that I had and been more sure that I wouldn't
> even think about talking about it. I still can't quite grasp this: he
> took a huge risk, I know that, in what he was doing, and some-
> how he felt safe enough to do it with me, and I'm not sure why
> that was and how much was what he observed and how much
> was the disability. (Lyn)

In childhood I was vulnerable because they would have known
that I was bad at remembering things; that I quickly moved on
from things and got on with it. They would have realized…be-
cause I spent a lot of time round at my friend's house, going on
about my terrible relationship with my mother. So, again, it's
the indirect stuff, it's not directly necessarily because I was disabled, but the consequences of being a young disabled person
without the support that I needed for a variety of things that
put me in a position of vulnerability, because I was needy, because I needed somewhere to get respect and support. I was
really there for the taking for anybody that would give me the
attention, you know. And a lot of it was to do with my impairment, and it's to do with not having the support at home. My
mother's relationship with my brother was fine so I have to see
it as being about my impairment. (Chloe)

For those disabled children who live at home, and require personal
care, their situation becomes complicated by a dependence on informal carers, some of whom may turn out to be perpetrators, and who
are then provided with the necessary opportunity to sexually abuse.
In this type of 'caring' relationship, where the disabled individual
is physically very reliant on the abusive caregiver for such things as
help with intimate care tasks or physiotherapy, for example, there
may be no other option for the child but to accommodate the sexual
abuse (Kennedy 1996; Shakespeare 1996a; Sobsey 1994). Josh and
May elaborate further on this point:

Also, I remember after that when we were still in the same
house where the toilet and bathroom were downstairs, that
occasionally I would mess myself and he would use the opportunity of me having to have a bath, or having to clean me up, to
abuse me. I was easily accessible; I was an easy target because
of my disability. Because I had a disability, there was more opportunity to access me, and because I needed cleaning up in
the bathroom, I was more available in the right places as well.
(Josh)

I think once a disabled person is being abused it is easier for the
abuser to find opportunities to be in close contact because of
the need for support and things like physiotherapy, which then
become used as excuses. (May)

Child sexual abuse literature clearly illustrates that perpetrators demonstrate a distorted belief system, which is seen to act as a justification for their behaviour (Araji and Finkelhor 1986; Marshall and Marshall 2000; Wyre 2000). As May describes, an example is a belief that the sexual abuse of a stepdaughter is permissible as the child is not a blood relative:

> I was first raped just after my 16th birthday, and I think he thought that this was not abuse because he was not a blood relative and also I was at the age of consent. I think he thought he was doing nothing wrong. I think that that was also why only touching happened up until that point. (May)

For disabled children, Shakespeare (1996a) and Westcott and Cross (1996) argue that perpetrators can use an additional range of distorted assumptions and justifications for their behaviour. This might include a belief that disabled children are destined not to have sexual relations, so any sexual encounter would be beneficial. These justifications may also include a belief that the damage created by sexual abuse is negligible, since the person is significantly damaged already. Lyn elaborates further on this point:

> One of my ideas is that people are repelled by disabled children, and they are also slightly attracted by them because they are odd. It works both ways, that there's a sort of feeling of 'you can't damage them any more than they already are. You can't break them any more because there's already something profoundly wrong with them', so, somehow, it's morally less bad to do it. I'm sure that people would never say that aloud, or very rarely say that aloud, but I think there may be something of that in it. He was punishing me for being defective, you know, I don't know. If I'd had siblings and I had been the only one, then that would have been clear. (Lyn)

Shakespeare (1997) identifies a wider social issue, which may contribute to the question of why perpetrators choose disabled children to abuse. Disabled people can symbolize a passivity and weakness for non-disabled people, which in turn creates fear. Unable to contend with their feelings relating to their own vulnerability, non-disabled people may project this fear and hostility onto those who represent weakness and who generate this insecurity in the first place. Thomas understands his abuse in terms of the contempt that his stepfather held for his learning difficulties. Jean describes how impairment can become a symbolic representation of something else; in this case evil.

> I do feel that my stepfather saw me as stupid and easy to target. He was always bragging about his intelligence and comparing my lack of intelligence to it. I definitely do feel this is why he targeted me and why I found it so difficult to stand up to him, unlike some of my older brothers. (Thomas)

> The impaired body becomes a target, largely because it's a symbol of something else. For the nun who was abusing me, my impairment was a symbol of something else for her (probably Satan or evil). Because of our powerless position, and because such little value is given to our lives, abusers can get away with it, conceal it and justify it by dehumanizing us – using terms like vegetable, for example. So I think there's a whole load of issues there about the body (including the mind) and about the body being the focus: being objectified and targeted because of the impairment or difference, and about others projecting symbolic ideas onto the impaired body – things like evil, ugliness, other, primitive, dirtiness, vulnerability, loss and death. (Jean)

Jean's quote problematizes the issue of impairment, and what that might represent or signify for members of the clergy, an issue debated by Barnes (1996), when analyzing the historical origins of disabled people's oppression. Barnes plots the process where a relationship has been established within Christianity between the devil and everything associated with this construct (including impairment, impurity and sin). He writes: 'People with impairments provided living proof of Satan's existence and of his power over humans. Thus, visibly impaired human children were seen as "'changelings"' – the devil's substitutes for human children' (Barnes 1996, p.55). In a similar vein, Douglas (1966) refers to the book of Leviticus, where holiness is equated with 'physical perfection', and emphasis is placed on the need for purification and ritual cleansing of those considered to be less than perfect before they worship (lepers are cited as an example). Clear parallels can be seen here between the writings of Barnes (1996) and Douglas (1966) and the ritual cleansing abuses experienced by Jean, and described in detail in Chapter 6.

CONCLUSION

This chapter provides an understanding of perpetrator behaviour from a number of differing perspectives. Included within this is an appraisal of family systems theory, a consideration of the psychological profile of the offender, a radical feminist viewpoint and a multi-factorial explanation. These theories can be applied to both the sexual abuse of disabled and non-disabled children, but for the disabled child factors related to their impairment, or their personal care arrangements, can increase their vulnerability by creating additional avenues for exploitation. Equally, a child's de-valued impairment status can add to the perpetrator's already distorted belief system, so providing another dubious justification for their behaviour. A true understanding of what motivates an individual to sexually abuse a child may never be truly achievable, but an analysis of the ways in which a disabled child's vulnerability can be significantly increased, by difficult early attachment experiences and differing care arrangements, is valuable knowledge for both professionals and parents alike.

CHAPTER 8

Collective Identities

INTRODUCTION

Within this chapter we shall be exploring the combined impact of disability and child sexual abuse on participant's identity formation and identity enactment. As can be seen in Chapter 5, the participants' narratives suggest that a variable and sometimes fragile sense of self, created by negative attitudes towards impairment in early childhood, is fragmented by the experience of child sexual abuse, so creating a series of dissociative behaviours and, for some, confused sexual identities, which persist into adulthood effecting both an individual's relationship with the self and with others. It is also evident in their stories that the reintegration of mind and body in adulthood, a process which may be influenced by impairment, is influential in terms of the ability to form a positive sense of self, rewarding relationships with others and sometimes empowering collective identities in a wider society.

Our focus, then, is the participants' thoughts on their collective identity, which they may share with others who have had similar experiences and/or share similar beliefs. Arriving at a personal ownership of these collective identities, which mostly exercise their power through providing affirmation of the self, signifies, for many participants, a point at which they have been able to become re-united with their sense of self and reclaim some of what had been stolen from them in childhood.

Participants spoke of a number of collective identities that they now own, partially or more comprehensively, and that have provided a degree of self-validation and empowerment. Of particular significance was their identity as a survivor of childhood sexual abuse raising, for some, the complexities involved in occupying this identity. Other social identities that were felt important included their identity as a disabled person and their sexual identity, with these latter two issues being intrinsically linked by society's denial of disabled people's sexuality. We shall now endeavour to consider each of these collective identities in turn.

SURVIVOR IDENTITY: 'COMING THROUGH YOUR OWN HOLOCAUST'

The road to arriving at a place where survivor identity could be assumed, partially or more fully, was a difficult process for all participants and was complicated further, for some, by disability. Numerous factors have been influential in helping them to reach a position where they have been able to 'speak out' about their experience, move forward in their lives and resist the ongoing destructive potential of sexual abuse. These factors have included, for instance, the input of family, the relevance of personal qualities and the contribution of allied professionals. We begin, however, by looking at the concept of 'survivor status' and explore several participants' views about the acquirement of this personal and social identity. Below Thomas talks about his survivor identity in positive terms and his realization that he had, in fact, come through a process of survival, a perspective that was probably implicit in all participant's narratives, yet rarely voiced. He had come through his own holocaust.

> I'm the survivor. And that word...when my probation officer first used it, I laughed. I said, 'What do you mean I'm a survivor, I thought you only became a survivor if you went through Dachau, Belsen or Auschwitz, what's this survivor thing?' But she said, 'You are, you have come through your own holocaust, you've made it, you're a living witness to that and you've done that.' And I thought, 'Christ yeah.' (Thomas)

In these next quotes, Lyn describes her ambivalence about the survivor identity, since it signifies, for her, the acquisition of yet another stigmatized identity and creates unease about the fact that, in reality, there is a relationship between the two issues of sexual abuse and disability:

> You struggle so hard to be seen as a person and not just as a disability that you don't then want to add something that you also can be labelled with and no longer be seen as being you. You know, an abuse case. It's quite subtle, that, and I can feel that sort of drive in me. I just don't want to have another handy label stuck on, because that particular handy label, disability, has been there all the time and it takes such an effort to get people to see past the label. (Lyn)

> That all feeds into not being able to talk about this kind of stuff (sexual abuse) because you are there as a victim again, as damaged goods again, just when you've done all that work to say, well, there may be a disability there, may be an impairment, but it doesn't get in the way of me being productive and happy and all the rest of it. And to talk about sexual abuse and to suggest in any way that the two of them might in some way be connected, it feels like cutting the ground away from under your feet, even though I know that it's true, even if I know that there is stuff to be explored there. (Lyn)

Below Jean relays her concerns about a survivor identity, feeling that it precludes and potentially overrides other important aspects of the individual's self:

> Having said that, I also feel very much that I don't want this identity that is about being a survivor, I am much more than that, a lot of other things have happened in my life. (Jean)

The actual healing process, which has enabled individuals to attain varying degrees of distance from the original experience, still presents an ongoing challenge for all participants who, inevitably, have to deal with the residual emotion generated within the context of their daily lives. Below participants elaborate further on this point and, by using an analogy, Josh describes his attempts to manage his distress:

> Now I see abuse like a piece of luggage really, so what I do as much as possible is leave it at the station. Occasionally I'm back round on the train and I pick it up for a short while, but I make sure I drop it off again pretty quickly because I'm not having that bastard still ruin my life. (Josh)

May's method of managing involves the creation of a degree of detachment from the experience. May also illustrates the point that, despite any amount of therapy, sexual abuse can continue to be an emotionally isolating experience:

> People may feel I must have it together to write this; don't be fooled. I can write this because I've had all kinds of therapy and I've gone over and over it, had the whys and wherefores explained. And I can detach myself, so it is like writing about someone else, even though I know it is me. The bottom line is, you can have all the support in the world, but you are the only one in your head, so no one can cope for you, and that is the problem. (May)

Lizzie describes the emotional consequences of her abuse experience, which can sometimes express itself in the form of self-harm:

> I guess the most persistent impact, I think, has been that I am hideously self-critical, and there are two key things that trigger it the worst. They are getting lost and losing things and it doesn't take a rocket scientist to work it out, does it? Depending on how tired I am, or how much pain I'm in, I'll either abuse myself verbally, or at worst slap my own face or pull my hair really hard. This is something I haven't yet been able to overcome, and it bothers me. (Lizzie)

When investigating the participants' actual recovery process and the means of identifying as a survivor, there have been things that have been clearly assistive in the process, and others that have impeded recovery. Here we offer a selection of quotes illustrating these important contributions. In Thomas's case, he credits the influence of a supportive partner who provided a safe base from which disclosure could be achieved. In Lyn's case, she talks about the security provided by a supportive network of friends:

> I know now, thanks to the support I've had, that it's not my fault and that there was nothing I could do. Today I am not a victim of abuse; today I am a survivor. Since my breakdown in 1995 when I told Sharon my story she has done nothing but support me, she understood and above all showed me something I had been missing all my life: love. Slowly I have come to terms with my past. (Thomas)

It sounds so banal but talking about it and having some friends to whom I could say, gradually over time, that this happened. Some of them, who have known me since university, have said that they knew something was wrong, but they were never going to push me to say anything before I was ready and that's nice. It's confirming because it means they sort of trusted my pace. (Lyn)

Jean refers to her resilient nature, which was demonstrated in her ability to survive the experience of sexual abuse. Additionally, she makes the link between resilience and her supportive parents, an issue which we will come back to later on in this section:

My general resilience I attribute to my experiences, but I also have a bit of a resilient nature, I know I am a very strong person and I think that's probably a mixture of my natural inclination and my hard life. In addition I had good loving relationships with my mum, stepdad and other adults, and I know this also helps children deal with abuse. (Jean)

Lyn and Jean talk about the influence of therapy. This included therapy occurring in a formalized therapeutic setting, as in Lyn's case, and the personal therapeutic process happening outside formal therapy, as in Jean's situation:

I'm a huge fan of therapy now, I'm probably too much, and I know that it doesn't work for everybody but it did seem to help. I could not imagine feeling like this three years ago. I couldn't imagine living another year, but certainly not feeling as positive as I do about things, and being able to talk about it like this. It doesn't mean that I don't still get very shaky about it. (Lyn)

That is where I've been able to make progress: really working on my relationship with myself and really building on self-love as the key thing and a way of fighting back. The very fact that I do have successful intimate relationships is a huge victory be-cause that's what they were stealing – the capacity for joy and self-love, to have an authentic emotional connection to myself and others, and being able to live my life and achieve my goals, this is the sweetest revenge! (Jean)

Josh and Chloe refer to the positive consequences of being able to channel their negative experience in a productive manner, in the outside world:

So that's why I got involved with the charity because I want to help other people. And I particularly want to help blokes, because there's plenty of help for women, there's Rape Crisis and all the others to help them work through it. But for the rest of us that find it more difficult to talk about those bloke things, you need somewhere safe to be able to talk about it. (Josh)

The (disability) movement has given me the chance to take out the energy that before was just internalized, or put out into the world to attract abuse. I have found ways that I can use it as positive energy. So I can take anger and make that into something positive. It has helped me deal with the abuse and I'm not going to let them fuckers beat me because I know what's right and wrong now, and I will fucking fight back. (Chloe)

Lastly, Chloe speaks about the influence of education. Her education, she believes, has enabled her to obtain a wider, less personal, perspective on the sexual abuse experience:

And it's a terrible thing to say that if you are not as educated or free thinking as the next person then you might have worse consequences and less opportunity to deal with it. Well that just makes me sad. I don't know if it's true or not. I mean, the thing is every person will just find whatever they have got, so you just draw on whatever you have and it is always one of the things that I have had. It's not always been a good thing but it's been a useful thing at times. (Chloe)

In terms of prohibitive factors, and following on from Jean's earlier quote, the support of parents, particularly the primary caregiver, plays a significant part in the healing process. Here Thomas talks about his disclosure to his mother, which occurred in the context of an argument, and was met with disbelief and a general attitude of denial, blocking the healing process:

There are times when she'll come over and she will say...let's give you an example, I've bought a greenhouse recently and she said, 'Oh that greenhouse is far too big, what the hell are you doing with a big greenhouse like that?' And I just feel like turning round and saying, 'So I can go in it and escape from shit like you.' But Sharon will say, 'Well, he wants to grow lots of different things, don't you Thomas?' And when she goes, Sharon will tell you, I just go in the study and I sit there and I'll roll fag after fag after fag. As far as what happened to us kids, see that rug

there, she sweeps it right underneath. Good, great and brilliant: Jack Brown, good, great and brilliant. She always talks
of his positives: 'It would have been our wedding anniversary
today; he always bought me roses on my wedding anniversary.'
(Thomas)

Denial is the theme that dominates this next quote from May. May's
mother's concern for children sexually abused within the context of
the extended family is not connected in any way to May's sexual
abuse, which her mother was aware of at the time. Her mother's
attitude compounds and heightens May's sense of worthlessness:

> I am not sure what I find most difficult; the fact that my mother
> knew and did nothing or that she has somehow managed to
> blank out what happened. I say this because she is very critical
> of the person that knew in the case of abuse in the extended
> family, saying they should have done something to protect the
> children. She also talks about it at every opportunity, saying
> how upset and devastated my stepfather would be if he knew,
> which just reinforces my feeling that she does blame me, and
> feels it was my fault. All of this makes me feel that she was quite
> happy to let anything happen to me because of what happened
> before she met my stepfather, as long as she kept the money
> she had and didn't end up on her own again. Counsellors, and
> other support I have, suggested to me that perhaps she raises
> the issue all the time because she feels guilty and wants to bring
> it out into the open, so she can apologize. I do not agree, I think
> she is scared that I might say something to someone and she
> will be in trouble, as this is what happened with my extended
> family. I think my mother thought that nothing would happen to
> her because she didn't take part, and also my stepfather is no
> longer around so in a sense it is over and done with. (May)

Lyn's inability to confront and disclose her abuse is hampered by the
deaths of both of her parents, leaving, for her, a degree of unfinished
business:

> I wish they were alive. They are both dead now and that makes
> it difficult because now I would like to talk to them about it. I
> would like to be able to say to my dad, 'Just what the hell do
> you think you were doing? What was it? What was going on?'
> I feel a mixture of things towards him, it's not just anger. With
> my mother I'd like to say, 'How much did you know?' To be

> able to say, 'Look I can understand if it was a big problem for
> you, I just want to know if you noticed at all?' (Lyn)

Turning to the literature, feminist author Naples (2003, p.1151) defines a survivor as a person who has 'self-consciously redefined their relationship to the experience from one of victim'. From the viewpoint of the participants in this study, this commonly cited and definitive duality of victim–survivor needs to be deconstructed. These concepts need to be given a further degree of consideration since they have the potential to become oppressive and limiting categorizations, with the full survivor status never truly being achievable. In actuality, as can be seen from participants' quotes, although essentially survivors of this experience, the status of victim and survivor are not, in reality, static concepts. Participants in this study have tended to oscillate between these two restrictive categories, influenced by factors associated with their environment. Naples's definition of the term survivor appears, to us, to rest in a subjective measure of the degree of emotional distance, which has been achieved from the experience, and how much sexual abuse is perceived to adversely affect the individual's life at that particular moment in time. This finding reflects, we believe, the limited and limiting number of identities currently prevalent in the child abuse literature.

Reavey and Gough (2000) propose that the act of 'speaking out' and 'breaking the silence' is seen to lie at the very heart of the therapeutic alliance. It has also been instrumental in the wider consciousness-raising process, founded in the activities of the Women's Liberation Movement, which broadened its concerns from domestic violence to child sexual abuse (Naples 2003). Naples suggests that the emergence of a depersonalizing discourse within contemporary society politicized the problem by moving it, more squarely, into the public domain. Undoubtedly, 'speaking out' creates a sense of personal empowerment for the individuals concerned. Some of these political factors have been influential in motivating participants in this study to become involved in the research process. Naples contends that the politicization of the issue, and the questioning of the sanctity of the family, also generated a societal 'backlash' with the formation of such groups as the False Memory Syndrome Foundation. The emergence of false memory discourse was also accompanied by a distrust of therapists and child protection social workers (Scott 2001).

Additionally, it undermined much of the political work that had gone before.

Naples (2003) acknowledges the variety of ways that individuals use to 'speak out' and then reinterpret their childhood experience. With reference to the work of other writers, she also raises the issue that the articulation of abuse can be complicated or compromised by the experience of gender, race and class inequality. Lyn's narrative, in particular, illustrates the difficulties associated with speaking out for individuals who are members of other stigmatized and objectified minorities. Whilst some authors refer to the possibility of positively incorporating multiple identities into the sense of self (Reynolds and Pope 1991), Vernon (1999) considers the dilemmas this poses. As a result of considering the issue of race and gender in the disabled people's lives, she rejects the additive quality implied in the concept of simultaneous oppression. She argues that this theory is neglectful of the 'complex and often variable interaction between different forms of social oppression' (p.394). In effect she proposes that 'there exists an axis of oppression that constitutes the social relations of domination which shapes all our lives according to the number of privileges or penalties scored' (p.389). The experience of one stigmatized identity (in this case survivor of child sexual abuse) is often modified/ exacerbated by the existence of another marginalized identity (such as disabled person). The risk incurred in speaking out, in this instance, includes the possibility of further displacement and alienation.

The problematization of the survivor identity also marks significant progress made within the healing process. Here the shift from victim to survivor status, as can be seen in Jean's quote, eventually results in this new identity being seen as too constricting, as it denies other important aspects of the self (Phillips and Daniluk 2004). Phillips and Daniluk, in their research, evaluated the self-perceptions and identity re-construction of seven female incest survivors after a period of therapy. They found that early on in the healing process the survivor identity was integral to their ongoing ability to cope. As the process progressed, however, it became important to relinquish this identity in order to move forward in their lives.

Within our study all but one participant had undertaken counselling or therapy, which had mostly been perceived to be helpful. Some of the changes in self-perception, discussed by Phillips and Daniluk (2004), also applied to the healing process experienced by our participants. Some of these changes, however, were not seen to be solely attributable to formal therapy. They were, in some instances, positive expressions of power employed in other areas of the participant's life such as the workplace and/or education (Boone James, Husser and Gateley O'Toole 1993).

Of particular relevance, in the issues identified in the work of Phillips and Daniluk (2004), were the feelings of being more visible in the world with their internal feelings being more solidly connected with their external presentation, an issue that Jean alludes to. They also identified a sense of loss regarding the time spent recovering from sexual abuse, plus the opportunities missed, which included relationships with others. This issue undoubtedly had some relevance for participants in our study, particularly May. For other participants, the major losses identified were the 'loss of childhood' and 'loss of self'.

Phillips and Daniluk's participants spoke of other aspects of the self, particularly resilience, which had developed in childhood as a form of self-protection and which allowed them to continue functioning. They also identified a personal growth related to the process of surviving and healing from the abuse experience.

Contrary to the findings of Phillips and Daniluk (2004), where women felt that abuse had become part of their past and the therapeutic work was, in effect, completed, our research indicates the opposite. The views of participants in our study tend to be that, despite therapeutic work, or other types of input, the process of healing is an ongoing one, which supports the writings of such authors as Warner (2001). Warner suggests that there are variables in an individual's capacity to connect with the abuse narrative, proposing that survivors have 'different levels of engagement with their abuse at different times and in different situations and relationships' (p.121). Present concerns may throw up greater challenges, even if the issues presenting contain some relational substance.

DISABILITY IDENTITY: 'UNDERSTANDING THE POLITICS OF OPPRESSION'

Participants also spoke about their disability identity, which, for some, was initially subsumed by the experience of sexual abuse but later emerged, to be given differing degrees of meaning and significance. Several participants expressed a strong disability identity, which found expression in their personal politics and their involvement in the disabled people's movement:

> When you start to understand the politics of oppression and what it's about, that is so empowering and it gives you a power but also it gives you knowledge and advantage. It gives you a framework that applies to all different stuff in life including sexual abuse. And I think that's a gift. (Chloe)

> I'm actually in a place where I can work on something I really care about, that's personal to me, that I want to make an effort along with everybody else to change and I've got a whole menu of ways I can do it. You're in a place where, when it works right, and it isn't always like that, but when things are being well practised by good people, then it's good. It's about finding what skills everybody has got, and all disabled people have got something, we've all got different skills and there are so many different jobs to do. So it means that I've had chances to use all my different skills that I didn't use before. (Chloe)

> The first one I joined was the women's movement before there was the disabled people's movement, and even before then I was campaigning in my own little ways for children's rights, for them to be treated with respect, disabled children in particular. So I would volunteer to speak at conferences and put forward what was really a remarkably political case in those days. (Lizzie)

Jean talks about disability identity by raising, as she did in the last section, the issue of multiple identities and the fact that, in relation to multiple stigmatized identities, this can offer its own advantages:

> In terms of the lesbian and gay community I've always felt on the margin because of disability. As a teenager I knew that there's no way I was ever going to make the 'A' group. I was always 'spaz', I was always this gender-bending tomboy freak, and so in a sense I was able to really build an identity for myself that was outside a lot of those 'normal' things. (Jean)

Lyn's quote raises the issue of internalized oppression, which can create difficulties for some disabled people in expressing their needs and openly identifying as a disabled person:

It becomes ingrained and certainly my mother's training had been, and what she handed on to me was, it must not show, you must not do anything which draws attention to yourself. For her, when she went out, she would always put something over her arm to cover up the fact that it wasn't there. She would use a cardigan or her handbag, she had a little stump that ended here and she would always drape something around it. She would never allow herself to be photographed with the stump showing. The thing to do is to try and hide it, even if people know about it; you are succeeding if you appear not to be any different. She used to make me feel really guilty, and I'm sure she didn't do it deliberately, but she would say it was much easier for me to do that because mine didn't show. Hers showed all the time and deafness didn't show, so I had that advantage. So anything you do that is negative and makes you stand out is wrong. It's okay to stand out if it's for something good like being good at school or whatever, that was okay, but creating problems, drawing attention to yourself! (Lyn)

Nowadays I'm much more assertive. I think that the accommodations that have to be made for people with disabilities should be made, and the only reason that they seem such a pain is because people aren't used to making them. When it comes to making allowances to enable me to hear and participate at work then I'm pretty stroppy and mostly I get what I need, and I'm not particularly retiring about that. When I'm feeling tired, or in a strange place, I may be more cautious. But it's still an effort to an extent, there's still, in the background, this thing that you have no right to be asking for this, this extra effort to be made, you've got to justify it in some way. And one of the ways that I've justified it is by working hard and being productive and being a good person, being unproblematic and being a productive member of society. (Lyn)

For Josh, disability appeared less central to his identity and, whilst acknowledging others' discriminatory attitudes, he overrides these by playing down the issue of difference and questioning notions of bodily perfection:

I mean for very many years I tried to do something about it, now I've stopped trying to do something about it, and it's me and I use it. So now in my later life I give presentations, and they get the stutter as well because it's part of me, and it makes it more exciting as far as I'm concerned, so I don't let it get in the way. And I've never let my disability get in the way; other people have let my disability get in the way of me getting on. I've never allowed it to happen, I mean if I can't do something because of my disability that's fine, not everybody is good at everything, so it's other people who have held me back, and I've took no notice anyway, and I've got on in my own sweet way, and it's the only way to do it. (Josh)

Disability identity is a recurrent theme in the disability studies literature. In terms of being able to construct a positive disability identity, Shakespeare (1996b) cites a number of factors, which are prohibitive forces in the facilitation of this process. These factors may include, amongst other things, the generalized devaluation of disabled people within society, which potentially can be seen to have an adverse effect on disabled people's perception of themselves, affecting their willingness to be identified as a disabled person. This issue can be best observed in Lyn's comments relating to her own and her mother's struggles to be perceived as a non-disabled person. As described in Chapter 4, it may also include the fact that some disabled children are raised in families where they are considered a 'problem' or 'burden', and when they do eventually go out into society they can be isolated from the means to build a positive personal and collective disability identity. In addition, Swain and Cameron (1999) posit the influence of impairment-specific categorizations within society, which produce a comparative discourse of 'more or less disabled' (p.76) and which, then, erodes the potentiality of the collective.

The emergence of the disabled people's movement marked the beginning of a process whereby societal norms began to be challenged and disabled people started to be seen as a collective force (Campbell and Oliver 1996). The uniting principle embodied within the evolution of the disabled people's movement, and as present in Chloe's quotes, has been recognition of the socially oppressive forces that exclude disabled people within society and a focus on the need for change and empowerment (Watson 2002). The later extension of the social model brought about the 'affirmation model of disability'. This model describes disabled people's identity in positive terms (both personally and collectively) and as observed within disability arts (Swain and French 2000). These identities are characterized by disability pride, the problematization of the concept of normality (an issue raised by Josh), positive ownership of the impaired body, and, with reference to the work of Shakespeare, Gillespie-Sells and Davies (1996), a positive re-evaluation of the lifestyle of disabled people.

Additionally, within this culture, there has emerged a reclaiming of language, with the use of the word 'crip', for example, originally used by the non-disabled world with derogatory connotation, now being used by disabled people as a symbol of solidarity and group identification (French Gilson and Depoy 2000). In fact some authors, by building on the work of Swain and French (2000), feel that the relinquishing of the dichotomous normal–other divide may also provide insights for other marginalized minorities operating outside of the disability sphere (Galvin 2003). The actual individual process of 'coming out' and claiming a disability identity marks a declaration of belonging to a de-valued group in society and a commitment to challenge this status quo (Swain and Cameron 1999). It can take, for some, a number of years, and is complicated further by the issue of internalized oppression, an issue which will be discussed next. Clearly, Chloe's quote illustrates the acquisition of a strong individual and collective disability identity, with the recognition and confrontation of societal oppression being prevalent in the quotes of both Chloe and Lizzie.

Criticism of the early writings of disability structuralists, who viewed disability identity in fixed terms, raised concerns for a number of disabled feminists. These concerns centred round the neglect of other aspects of disability identity, particularly consideration of the experience of impairment (Crow 1996). This call for an extension of analysis later led to consideration of the psychological and emotional effect of disability on the individual's identity formation (Reeve 2002; Thomas 1999). Working along similar lines, Swain and Cameron (1999) detail the self-oppressive processes of self-punishment, denial and passing (as normal) as being the main personal strategies used by disabled people to deny their physical and emotional reality.

Reeve (2002) maintains that this internalized oppression is variously experienced and, as can be seen in Josh and Lyn's quotes, it often takes a substantial period of time to disentangle and truly understand its effects. With reference to the work of Shakespeare (1993), Reeve suggests that by raising the profile of impairment within the disabled people's movement more disabled people may feel able to claim a disability identity. Additionally, understanding and confronting the psycho-emotional effects of disablement can be equally empowering.

Both Reeve (2002) and Benjamin Darling (2003) refer to the fluidity of disability identity, with Benjamin Darling suggesting that whilst disability studies continue to produce work with differing ideological positioning (and in support of the disability movement), little is known about what are probably the majority of people who do not have access to alternative ways of conceptualizing disability. By intensive literature reviewing using a number of different sources, including both academic and autobiographical, Benjamin Darling proposes a typology of disability identities. This typology recognizes the two main oppositional constructs, which involve, first, the adherence to the cultural majority norms relating to appearance and achievement and second, as typified by Josh's quote, the minority view which questions norms and accepts diversity. This typology, however, also identifies a number of derivatives of these two positions. With reference to this conceptualization, Benjamin Darling proposes that an individual's disability identity is dependent upon a whole range of structural and interactive possibilities as opposed to any psychological determinant, and that individuals' positioning is liable to change over time, with an accompanying commitment to that one particular position.

Of particular interest in this research, Benjamin Darling (2002) cites the categories of 'normalization' and 'situational identification', with the latter category raising the wider issue of multiple identities. Benjamin Darling's normalization category includes individuals who are accepting of societal norms and have a lifestyle similar to their non-disabled peers, sometimes choosing to deny their difference. Watson (2002) offers a different perspective on this categorization, finding, in his study, that whilst some individuals did not build an identity based on impairment, neither did they accept the societal notion of the 'normal body', a theme referred to in Josh's quote. Many rejected the body as a determinant of the self, which may have been reflected in some people's desire to play down their impairment, in order to expose other aspects of their identity. Benjamin Darling's category of situational identification describes individuals who are shape shifters and who readily adapt in their interactions with others. These individuals may be reluctant or unwilling to choose between differing identities, which can make activists/affirmers less accepting. This categorization, as indicated, can also be understood in terms of multiple identities, with different identities being more salient in differing interactions.

Shakespeare (1996b) advocates acceptance of the variation in disabled people's narrative; narrative which reflects the intricacies of their lives. Recognition of multiple identities also requires an appreciation of the tensions that may arise between them, particularly when they are stigmatized identities (Appleby 1994; Vernon 1999). Authors such as Peters (2000) suggest that participation in the disability culture should be a matter of personal choice, and that commitment can still be observed, whilst not being enmeshed in the disability culture. The fact that all the participants for this study came through disability publications and websites, illustrates their involvement, in some way or another, with the disability community.

SEXUAL IDENTITY: 'TRYING IT OUT (WITH A DISABLED PERSON)'

Within this section the question of disability and sexuality will be examined, with consideration of how this has become complicated by the experience of child sexual abuse. The following quotes illustrate the intersection of sexuality, gender and impairment, and here Josh talks about how his self-consciousness, relating to his impairment, was not reflected in his ability to attract female dating partners:

> My disability didn't seem to be too much of an impediment to my ability to attract members of the opposite sex. I think that when I was younger I felt that people always noticed that I had a disability and that I looked different, or I couldn't move my arm, and that didn't help with the relationships because you just assume that they wouldn't be interested in you because you had a bad hand or you had a limp. But that actually wasn't the case because when I did have girlfriends it didn't matter. It mattered to me, but it didn't matter to them, it wasn't an issue. In the same way that it's not an issue with my wife. So it's an issue that I've had in the past, but nowadays I'm not bothered because I'm in quite a secure relationship, it's a long-term relationship, where I'm loved for all of me. (Josh)

The reality for women, however, can be somewhat different. Lizzie and May talk about their experiences of adolescence, which included an exclusion by other teenagers from the sexual scene, in Lizzie's case, and for May, it involved the neglect of a developing sexual identity:

> With regard to discovering my sexual identity in adolescence, the overwhelming thing was not feeling part of that. I only had one friend that discussed boyfriends with me. My friends excluded me from the realms of sexuality; you know, desexualizing me, or asexualizing me. Certainly when I got my first boyfriend who was a hunk, there was an absolutely overt comment from another girl, 'How on earth did you manage to land him?' I didn't see myself as a sexual being. (Lizzie)

> I know my mum ignored my developing sexuality; I realize that because I had to watch my sibling going through it. They got the chats about periods, the training bra, the support and encouragement to do things, to go places, while my development was ignored. I think I got my first bra at 15 (and even this wasn't new), I was very large and I should have had one much sooner. I also mostly had second-hand clothes. I think me being a teenager was ignored in the hope that things would stay the same in the family. (May)

These assumptions regarding an asexual identity can create limited dating opportunities for disabled women, as Lizzie describes, and can affect their own self-perceptions:

> And I really think that I am still vulnerable. I am married to someone who I love deeply, so not in the sense of needing to rush out and do anything about it, but if anybody comes on to me, well, the first reaction is always, 'I don't believe it' and then when I've made myself believe it, it's 'wow'. But looking back at it...I think that most of my relationships were with men who were already in some other relationship and they didn't mind trying it out. And then, when I wanted to take it more seriously they backed off immediately; that was most of my relationships. And I think that probably the number of times when the push came from the bloke rather than just me is quite small. (Lizzie)

Lizzie's second quote illustrates the fact that this process of asexualization can also affect other aspects of their life, including pregnancy and childbirth:

> I was in hospital for three weeks with the girls and some of it was awful really because they were so totally unprepared, you know. And I had midwives saying, 'I can't remember having a disabled mother in here before.' And they didn't even have a bath board to help you get into the bath; I had to bring that all myself. (Lizzie)

Additionally, Lizzie raises the issue of violence and the real dangers that disabled women face:

> In fact I came very close to being abused by one of my colleagues during that time, sexually. And I had to summon all my strength. This was a man who worked in a sensory team and he came to visit me. I could get up and answer the door but that was all. I was just lying on my back the whole time and he managed to touch my arm in such a way that be brushed my breasts, and that was it. I wrote to him and I absolutely don't remember what I said now but it was something to the effect of, 'I never want to see you again in my house and please don't come and visit me again.' I'm convinced that if I hadn't been strong enough by that point... Well that was only by way of being a stroppy git really. (Lizzie)

In this next selection of quotes, May, Lizzie, Lyn, Josh, Thomas and Chloe speak about the additional complicating consequences of child sexual abuse. For May, she talks about her concerns in adolescence where she was preoccupied with the possibility of becoming pregnant:

> My teenage years were spent feeling, 'Why can't I do what other people do,' and worrying about getting pregnant. I always made sure people thought I had a serious boyfriend, just in case. This usually backfired as people found out, but the alternative was much worse. (May)

Equally, Josh and Thomas talk about the problems created by a homosexual learning experience on a developing heterosexual identity:

> My problem was that my life was so dominated by the abuse, and it was male on male abuse, so that brought into focus my sexuality. I did wonder about my sexuality because it's confusing at that age anyway, and you see my learning experience had been a homosexual learning experience, but I never went down that road, I ended up in heterosexual relationships. (Josh)

Thomas, in particular, believes his stepfather's comments were located in his own sexual confusion and homophobic belief system:

> Female-wise, I didn't start developing relationships until I was like 14 or 15 and that was only through my old man constantly saying, 'You're gay, you're queer, you enjoy being abused,' which he did a lot of. I think I'd got something to prove to myself and that's why I lost my virginity at 14, I set out to prove that I wasn't gay, and I did. (Thomas)

Lyn talks about the effects of child sexual abuse, in early adulthood, on her ability to assess appropriate/inappropriate sexual behaviours in others, and identify potentially dangerous situations:

> A year after my mother died I was raped and I'm sure now that that happened, without in any sense letting the two people that did it off the hook, I'm sure it happened because in part I didn't know, I didn't understand about signals and boundaries and managing that. The two men involved were two friends of mine and it was in a situation in which I should have been able to tell that there was something not right there. I can remember feeling uneasy about the situation. They were both drunk and it was post a party, post an afternoon party. I was sober and they, I think, agreed it beforehand. They were not close friends, but there was a group of us in a way that you have at university sometimes. I would say I saw one or both of them several times a week, socially. I'd been out with one of them once but it hadn't really taken off and it was possible that this one felt jealous. But there were alarms bells ringing and I ignored them because of my life experiences. It may be too easy to blame it on that, but I didn't know how to read men in the same way that I think a lot of young women do know how to read them. (Lyn)

Josh speaks about the difficulties he had with trust in his early sexual encounters, and how this impacted on the relationship:

> One of the biggest problems that I had was trusting somebody, and if you can't trust somebody… I had this big secret and was worried they were going to find out and that was extremely difficult. I had a few girlfriends, but no sex, and that was very difficult, I tended to go for one- or two-night-stands. And it wasn't until I got to about 20 that I actually had sex with a woman and the interesting thing was…I was at a party and I'd had a few

> drinks and we were walking home across the common, and we ended up on the grass and then we had sex, but the interesting thing I noticed there, and this happened probably a couple of times afterwards when I was with other women, whilst I got the erection, had the sex, I never actually came, and that was a holding back thing. (Josh)

May also talks about her general lack of trust in members of the opposite sex, and later discusses the problems that occur in relation to disclosure:

> Relationships are a nightmare because I find it difficult to meet people, and when I do, instead of enjoying their company, I sit there terrified that I am going to do something that will give off the wrong signals and make something happen to me. I am so conscious of this that friends tell me I give men the brush off without even knowing it. I don't like having people in my house because I don't feel safe. If I have to have work done then I make sure that someone is with me, but even then I can feel myself getting jumpy. If anyone is persistent enough to want to start a relationship then I agonize over when to tell them about my past. Usually this then is met by one of two reactions: the first is that they look at me like dirt and I never see them again, the second is that they say they understand. In some ways this is worse because it means people having to deal with very difficult issues. (May)

Looking at participants' more recent sexual relationships, it can be seen from the following quotes that, for May, whilst disability may have created an increased risk of her encountering aggressive and violent men, her situation is made more difficult by the sexual abuse experience, and her family's attitude towards impairment as she was growing up. May's last quote illustrates how the sexual abuse has, additionally, affected her ability to assess objectively potentially abusive relationships, prioritize her own needs and, notwithstanding economic factors, find the impetus to leave the abusive situation:

> I think one of the biggest consequences of my abuse was being involved in a subsequent violent relationship. It started like most do with the person being really kind and caring, and I could not believe that someone actually wanted to be with me, for me. Because of some of the difficulties, which I will explain later, I had to tell them about the abuse, and then they started

to criticize me, only small things at first, but then more and more. Because I'd experienced the same criticism whilst growing up I just thought, 'Yes, it is me.' Each time I was hit or raped I was told it was my fault, and because I had grown up being told this I just thought, 'Yes, it is.' (May)

My early relationships made it hard for me to separate out what was a consequence of child abuse and what was from this relationship. However, I do feel that my parents set me up for this relationship because of the things that happened and the way I was treated whilst I was growing up. (May)

The second relationship I am still in, although it doesn't make me happy. I feel I am back in my childhood where their needs come before, or are at the expense of, mine. And although they say they love me and I am important, I don't feel it because of the things they do. I think we will probably split up before the end of the summer, despite their assurance that things will be different and they will be different. The situation has gone on for the last three years and I feel it is just a replay of my childhood and my violent relationship. (May)

May and Chloe also talk about their current difficulties in enjoying intimate sexual encounters. May refers to the consequences of 'breakthrough memories' or 'flashbacks' and Chloe speaks about her perceived promiscuity and her tendency to dissociate when involved in a sexual encounter with a man:

One of the most difficult issues is the physical side of a relationship: touching, hugging and kissing. I find it difficult because it can either cause flashbacks, or I start to feel trapped. The sexual side of a relationship is even worse because this is where men feel you are taking it out on them if things go wrong. By wrong I mean flashbacks that mean I just have to get away. I usually end up in the shower, or I end up sleeping somewhere else because I do not feel safe, neither of which reactions you hope for when you sleep with someone. One of the worst things for me is their inability to realize that this is something that is always there, whether it shows itself or not. In both of the relationships that have got this far, my partner has thought 'right, we are over the difficult bit, we have shared a bed, had sex without anything happening, so everything is okay now'; then something happens. Then they feel they have done something wrong, or believe that because I can't take it out on the people that did it, I am taking it out on them. (May)

Right now, where I'm at with sex is, if I could just switch it off so that my body never wanted to have anything to do with it again, I fucking would. If you could just take a celibacy pill…because my sex drive has done me such tremendous damage, what I've done as a consequence of having it. I'm starting to associate it with bad things. (Chloe)

Through having this conversation with my friend I could actually see that when I sleep with a man only a small piece of me goes to bed with him and the rest of me is somewhere else. But when I went to bed with Karen that large piece went to bed with her. So I'm at a very interesting point in my sexuality. I'm sort of looking at things and asking what does it all mean. The side of me with my brain attached that was with my girlfriend was the whole me, and when I actually try to put that piece in bed with the man it doesn't work. (Chloe)

Both Lizzie and Lyn offer comparative views about their particular situations. Lizzie feels that the consequences for her sexual relationships could have been more difficult if the abuse had been intrafamilial and extended over a longer period of time. In Lyn's case, she attributes the lack of problems to her choice of partner:

The inability to enjoy a sexual relationship, as experienced by some survivors, was counterbalanced by, 'Thank god I've got a sexual relationship', but if the abuse had happened over any longer a period, if it had happened in the family, things could have been very different. I just think that I have escaped with minimal damage really. (Lizzie)

Our physical relationship, our sex life, was fine and maybe if I'd been with a man it wouldn't have been fine and I would have been prompted much earlier to do something, but it was okay. (Lyn)

Lastly, May talks about the physiological repercussions of being sexually abused, which has affected both her ability to become pregnant and undergo further investigation into the problem. Similarly, Jean talks about how the sexual abuse has prevented her from being able to tend to her sexual health needs:

One of the relationships that I've had, since getting out of the violent relationship, broke down because we wanted children and it wasn't happening. We did see a doctor, they felt the problem could be a combination of the things I have gone through, but to be sure I would need tests, which I couldn't face. My partner said it didn't matter, I had been through enough, but I couldn't cope with it, I felt I was denying him the thing he wanted most. (May)

I've never been able to have a smear test. My doctor has been very good and I've talked to her about why and we still talk about it. It's still one of those things, which she checks in with me about: 'Where are you at with that?' And I still don't feel like I can do it, I really don't. And for me it's a tricky line that I walk, I need to keep my mental health well enough to keep my life going, I can't afford to go over that edge again. (Jean)

Understanding sexual identity has played a significant role in the development of sociological theory. In terms of setting the historical scene in relation to sexual identity discourse, prior to the 1960s there appeared to exist an unquestioned duality relating to masculinity and femininity, which drew its substance from biological determinism and equated masculinity with power, strength and intellectual superiority and femininity with passivity, weakness and procreation (Bohan 2002). These dualities still hold some currency within wider society today and have influenced the experiences and perceptions of participants in this study to variable degrees. Second wave feminism brought about the questioning of the social arrangements that centred round these dualities, with feminist writers, such as Butler (1990), deconstructing the meaning of sex and 'the way it is written into our bodies and into language' (Van Lenning 2004, p.41).

Authors such as Burkitt (1998), whilst acknowledging the contributions of postmodernist writers such as Butler, have attempted to ground the theorization of gender identities by focusing on the power relations that are constructed in a political process. These power relations, he argues, operate at both a macro-level, when considering the interaction between race, class and sex, for example, and at a micro-level when examining the interactions of parents and their children. Such dynamics are clearly visible in Thomas's experience where his sexuality was constructed within a working class mining community and in opposition to his stepfather's homophobic views and taunts.

Within this contextualized academic debate, little attention has been paid to the ownership and expression of sexuality in disabled people's lives, and even within Disability Studies and the disability movement the issues have been neglected for the furtherance of more pertinent concerns relating to oppression and exclusion (Shakespeare 2000). Shakespeare (2000) and Shuttleworth (2000) summarize a number of prohibitive factors, which have acted as deterrents to disabled people enjoying sexual relationships and achieving sexual intimacy. Some disabled people, it can be argued, particularly those who have grown up in segregated institutions, may have had limited access to sex education and information. As can be seen in the experiences of Lizzie, those who encountered mainstream settings have generally been excluded from the adolescent social scene where early sexual rehearsal begins. Sometimes, as can be seen in May's situation, parents can nurture an asexual identity by discouraging the development of a sex life in adolescence and adulthood. Some disabled people have had limited access to the workplace, colleges, bars and clubs, places where they may be able to meet potential partners. Some disabled people (possibly because of internalized oppression) may lack the self-esteem and confidence to talk with somebody whom they feel attracted to. Additionally, societal measures of attractiveness can effect some individuals' perceptions of their ability to establish a sexual relationship, an issue illustrated in Josh's earlier musings on the subject of his sexuality. In this sense, and using a postmodernist analysis, an asexual identity has been written into the bodies of many disabled people.

Picking up on the issue of societal ideals of masculinity, Shakespeare (1999) suggests that, for disabled men, dominant notions of masculinity, which rejects weakness and vulnerability, present a conflicting ideology, which needs to be incorporated into disabled men's psychosexual identity. For women, the stereotypical notions of femininity and impairment reinforce each other. Perhaps one of the most commonly cited pieces of research relating to the management of the masculinity–disability conundrum (and cited by Shakespeare) is that of Gerschick and Miller (1994). These authors, by employing qualitative research methodology with ten disabled men with physical impairment, identified three common management strategies. The first group included men who did not necessarily reject society's ideal, but reinterpreted it according to their own abilities.

The second group of men had internalized society's perceived ideal, despite their inability to meet it, resulting in varying degrees of inner conflict. The final group rejected the prevailing ideal of masculinity and instead focused on the potential for producing differing masculine identities. For Josh, the only male participant in this study with a visible impairment, his strategy appeared to be more consistent with a mix of approaches. The findings of Gerschick and Miller are replicated to some degree in the work of both Shakespeare (1999) and Shuttleworth (2000). Shakespeare (1999) found that many of his participants employed, as Josh may, different approaches when constructing a psychosexual identity. Shakespeare believes that the experiences of disabled men have much to offer non-disabled men in terms of deconstructing and redefining notions of masculinity in less constricting ways.

As already described, impairment can reinforce a gender stereotype for disabled women. It brings into sharp focus women's perceived inability to fulfil a number of stereotypical female roles, including that of parenthood (Hanna and Rogovsky 1991; Sheldon 2004). Howland and Rintala (2001) investigated the dating experiences of 31 disabled women with physical impairments and reported a range of negative experiences which support the argument that disabled women can often be seen in asexual and objectified terms. The authors found that disabled women were generally older when they first started to date. Dates, as described in the experiences of Lizzie, were less inclined to make the first move compared with the experience of non-disabled women. This meant that disabled women had to be more assertive in their approach. Outgoing individuals, with good interpersonal skills and extended social networks, reported that friendships were less likely to develop into romantic encounters. Disabled women reported that visible symbols of impairment (such as a wheelchair) could potentially act as barriers for would-be dates. It was also reported that dates may be less likely to approach a disabled woman because of a misguided belief that they couldn't have sex. Sometimes the prejudice of family and friends influenced a potential date from becoming involved with a disabled woman. Lizzie's reference to a sexual partner's fetishistic behaviour, i.e. trying it out with a disabled woman, also appears in the work of Howland and Rintala.

The authors reported a wide degree of variation in dating habits with some disabled women being fairly indiscriminate about their choice of partner. The fear of rejection was a significant factor. Some women denied their own needs and identity to compensate for their perceived failings, and others tolerated overly controlling partners. Sometimes, these control issues resulted in abuse of differing kinds, even rape. A number of these issues were raised by May in this study, but their causality was seen to rest in the child sexual abuse experience. Sometimes women's lack of dating experience led to abusive situations; situations that would have set alarm bells ringing in other people's mind, an issue that was raised by Lyn, but also accredited to the experience of sexual abuse. A woman's perception that a partner was interested in her for the wrong reason was sometimes borne out. Controlling and abusive men may be drawn to disabled women because of an assumption that she would tolerate any type of behaviour.

The quotes from Lizzie and May suggest that violence or the threat of violence, particularly sexual assault, is a reality in many disabled women's lives. This fact is corroborated by research findings that indicate that disabled women are at a significantly increased risk of physical violence or emotional abuse from partners or caregivers, with prevalence ranging between 39 and 85 per cent (Erwin 2000). Nosek and Howland (1998) point to research undertaken by the DisAbled Women's Network in Canada. This study illustrates that from a research sample of 245 disabled women, 40 per cent had been abused, and 12 per cent had been raped. The offenders in this study were spouses and ex-spouses (37%), followed by strangers (28%), parents (15%), service providers (10%) and dates (7%). Based on the results of a study of disabled women with physical impairments, Nosek et al. (2001) suggest that in personal relationships both non-disabled and disabled women are vulnerable to abuse. For disabled women, however, there can be additional avenues for exploitation, such as the need for help with care tasks, the reduced potential for physical resistance and escape and social isolation, which can lower emotional defences. It seems that for those disabled women, like May, who have become involved in relationships with violent and domineering men, impairment has the potential to widen the power differential. Like non-disabled women, the reasons that disabled women remain in abusive relationships are numerous and include such factors as fear of retribution, a belief that their partner will change, love, children and the lack of economic means for self-support. Impairment compounds and complicates these issues (Erwin 2000). Some of these factors are evidenced in the words of May.

Additionally, research indicates that disabled women are significantly less likely to marry than non-disabled women and disabled men (Howland and Rintala 2001). For those women who do end up in successful relationships and decide to have children, their experience, as indicated by Lizzie, can be consumed with necessity to deal with a range of other challenges. In addition to the potentially undermining attitudes of others, once in a maternity ward disabled women have to deal with a number of practical issues. Thomas (1997) asserts that disabled women, who require a degree of assistance, run the risk of receiving either unhelpful or inappropriate help or, in fact, no help at all, which was Lizzie's experience. Moreover, they are burdened with the extra responsibility of having to show that they are 'good enough mothers' (p.640). This point is also raised in the work of Grue and Tafjord Laerum (2002) where disabled mothers, later on in their parenting experience, often over-compensate in their mothering role in order to demonstrate what others refer to as an 'ideal performance'.

For disabled people, the experience of childhood sexual abuse can add another layer of difficulty to the issue of sexuality. May's quote illustrates that, for female adolescents, the normal challenges of puberty, which in some initiate a crisis of confidence, can become amplified and distorted by both the abuse experience and the contradictory and accompanying process of asexual objectification. In May's situation, she had to contend, emotionally, with both a denial of her sexuality and, at the same time, the requirement for a strategy for dealing with the possible consequences of this very real, yet denied, aspect of herself.

As far as the sexual abuse of male adolescents is concerned, Durham (2003) raises the issue that, like Thomas and Josh, individuals may have to contend with a number of concerns related to a same-sex encounter and others' perception of this. Concerns can be heightened if sexual abuse creates some sexual arousal, and can be made worse by a perpetrator espousing homophobic taunts, as was Thomas's experience. Themes relating to sexual identity confusion are prevalent in the work of Gilgun and Reiser (1990), with an example given of concerns persisting for some years. In Gill and Tutty's study (1999) of ten men sexually abused in childhood, one significant

finding included the necessity to resolve some inner conflict generated by an early masculine–victim identity.

Additionally, all the participants in Gill and Tutty's research
(1999) spoke of a compromised ability to involve themselves in
emotional relationships. The feeling was that sexual abuse had created a mistrust of others, an issue which is highlighted in both Josh
and May's quotes. The authors propose that the development of a
sexual relationship is usually determined by an ability to establish
some degree of emotional connectedness with a partner. A significant
number of the men reported having avoided sex at some point, with
others having had multiple sexual relationships. None of the men appeared to report difficulties, as Josh did, in relation to the mechanics
of sexual intercourse. Some of the men found that the concept of af-
fectionate and mutually enjoyable sex was difficult to understand. A
number of the men reported dissociative experiences during sexual
activity, by becoming, for example, an observer to the event, an issue
also described by Chloe when talking about her sexual encounters
with men.

For some of the women participants in our study, difficulties
in relation to their sexual relationships continue into adulthood, an
issue which is highlighted in the work of a number of researchers
(Fleming *et al.* 1999; Fromuth 1986; Mullen *et al.* 1994). Phillips and
Daniluk (2004) found, in their study, that problems with sexual intimacy were an ongoing consequence of child sexual abuse. Difficulties
associated with dissociation and flashbacks, as experienced by Chloe
and May, are described in other writers' work (Evans and Maines
1995). Furthermore, problems related to sexual preoccupation and involvement in risky sexual behaviour are also cited (Noll, Trinkett and
Putnam 2003). Fromuth (1986) identifies an increase in homosexual experimentation and an increased self-perception of promiscuity.
Promiscuity is an issue highlighted by Chloe, but in Fromuth's study,
it fell short of what would be considered 'deviant' sexual behaviour.

As is the experience of May, some researchers have also identified
an increased tendency for women who have been sexually abused to
later experience re-victimization in the form of physical and/or sexual
abuse (Fleming *et al.* 1999; Fromuth 1986; Herman 1992). In terms
of trying to explain why this might be the case, theories range from
pathologizing and individualizing concepts, which involve the victim's 'addiction to trauma' (Herman 1992, p.112) to more sociological

perspectives, which consider the individual's wider social positioning. By drawing on the work of others, Mullen *et al.* (1994) propose that abuse interacts with factors associated with family background (which might be disability in this case) producing a developmental disruption for the child, and creating damage to their self-worth and a limitation in the acquisition of personal agency. This is embodied in May's statement, (see above): 'I feel I am back in my childhood where their needs come before, or are set at the expense of, mine.' In fact, authors such as Fromuth (1986) suggest that family background may be a better indicator of subsequent psychological difficulty than the abuse itself.

Lyn raises another issue, which also warrants some further consideration, which is an impaired ability to 'read' dangerous social situations, potentially resulting in further abuse. This theme also appears in the work of Howland and Rintala (2001). In Howland and Rintala's research, as already described, it is accredited to a disabled women's lack of experience related to dating. For Lyn, she feels that her failure to recognize risky situations resulted from a family history of child sexual abuse, which skewed perspectives on appropriate physical and sexual boundaries. This theme also appears in the work of Herman (1992), who proposes that a woman's minimization of danger, in dangerous situations, can relate to an individual's dissociative coping mechanism.

To conclude this section, we need to pick up on the issue of the physiological implications of sexual abuse for a survivor's sexuality, as outlined in May and Jean's quotes. The physical consequences of sexual abuse have, in effect, taken second place to the consideration of the emotional impact of sexual abuse, with some tendency to view unexplained medical symptoms in terms of 'somatisization', i.e. the bodily expression of psychological pain. Commonly reported physical complaints by survivors include gynaecological problems, chronic pelvic pain and irritable bowel syndrome (Nelson 2002). Nelson advocates for an expansion of research in this area, suggesting a number of ways this can be achieved. The taking of a more detailed sexual assault history, in the medical context, could facilitate an understanding and sensitivity to survivors' reluctance to undergo those invasive procedures described by May and Jean.

CONCLUSION

As can be seen, throughout childhood, adolescence and adulthood, and through their interactions with their wider environment, participants in this study have acquired a number of collective identities, some of which have been claimed with great pride, and others which have been resisted because they are seen to be too limiting or stigmatizing. An example of such is the 'survivor identity' where the identity has signified both strength and courage, but also, by some, is seen to be too limiting or just another stigmatized label to be added to other stigmatizing labels, such as disability. The disability identity has also been dealt with in differing ways, with some individuals drawing upon its political substance, to positive affect, and others recognizing how this socially de-valued identity has impacted in terms of internalized oppression. One participant described how he dealt with his disability identity by problematizing notions of physical perfection.

Participants' sexual identity has raised some pertinent issues in relation to the interaction of impairment, gender and sexuality. Here the female form, in particular, has been ascribed an objectified asexual identity, which was reflected in parental neglect of their sexual development, their problematic dating experiences and the threat of violence later in life. The additional child sexual abuse experience has created complicating factors relating to the questioning of sexuality (primarily male participants); the need to provide cover-stories for any potential pregnancy; difficulty in identifying and avoiding risky or violent situations or relationships; problems in enjoying intimate relationships and the adverse effect that it has had on an individual's ability to tend to their sexual health needs. For many participants, and by association, the survivor identity has conferred a problematic sexual identity. In essence, it can be seen that participants in this study occupy multiple identities, many of which will be situationally determined, to positive or negative effect.

CHAPTER 9

Narratives of the Narrative

INTRODUCTION

This chapter addresses the issues of narrative and how, because of the experience of sexual abuse and the consequent necessity to protect the self-system by a process of dissociation, participants were compromised in their ability to produce an authentic narrative of the self both at the time of the abuse and later on in life. The process of storytelling, generally, requires a sense of the past (Plummer 1995) and since most participants had spent significant periods of time psychologically 'not being there' the usual developmental process concerning narration of the self had become undermined. At various points in participants' lives, when dissociative defences were less critical for survival, they were able to emotionally re-engage with the experience of child sexual abuse. This was either because an incident or circumstance triggered the recovery of a buried memory, or a life event drew the issue more solidly to the forefront of the mind. The necessity to integrate the abuse experience into a personal narrative has been a painful process of varying duration for most participants and initially created personal mayhem and, sometimes, a total emotional breakdown. Reconstructing and re-interpreting the life story was achieved using a plethora of methods, which will be expanded upon shortly. In essence, it has enabled participants to gain greater self-understanding, establish a relationship with the self and, consequently, narrate the self in more comfortable terms.

We turn first to a consideration of the current and ongoing work being undertaken by participants and, then, working backwards chronologically, examine the point at which participants actively engaged, or were forced to actively engage, with their life history in an attempt to create some improvement in their general functioning. The final section considers issues relating to the credibility of the abuse narrative, for others, particularly the recovered narrative.

NARRATIVES OF WORK IN PROGRESS

As indicated, a continuing preoccupation of participants is the reconstruction of a narrative that is both reflective of their situation in childhood and contains a 'narrative truth' as defined by themselves. Additionally, for some, the work has also included recognition of some of the major losses they have sustained through the abuse experience, particularly the 'loss of childhood' and the 'loss of self'. In some cases, reparative work has been undertaken with attempts being made to put themselves back in their own narrative. We begin with an exploration of the reconstructive process and then move on later to consider some of the losses that participants identified.

Co-constructing and rewriting the story: 'that (memory) actually makes no sense at all!'

Multiple and combined methods of narrative reconstruction have been used by participants to understand the events of childhood and facilitate the production of more reflective and empowering life history accounts. Of particular significance has been the role of psychotherapy and counselling, which has enabled difficult information to be voiced, validated and mutually re-interpreted and has, sometimes, included the constructive challenging of specific memories and the belief systems embedded within them. Additionally, the sharing of information with abused adult siblings and/or members of the immediate or extended family has offered other perspectives to the story and, by doing so, has depersonalized the experience to some degree. For one participant, documented material, in this case medical records, has provided external support and corroboration of the personal consequences of their abuse experience. In total, these avenues have enabled participants to re-build a picture of family life, re-examine their abuse experience and the behaviours of the perpetrator, and co-construct alternative interpretations of events.

The quotes that appear below, from May and Lyn, illustrate two different functions of psychotherapy for individuals who have been sexually abused. In May's situation, the simple confirmation of where blame lies has created the potential to enable her to construct a different type of meaning and corresponding narrative account, which is not shrouded in guilt and responsibility. In a similar vein, Lyn talks about how the therapeutic encounter can serve to analyze memories, locate their origins/purpose and challenge the faulty belief systems that have ensued: 'That makes no sense at all':

> One time when I visited (after I moved out) I was alone and he kissed me, like you would kiss a partner, and said, 'We haven't done that for a long time.' This made me even more nervous because I was then frightened of him visiting me in my own home as I felt the same things could happen there. At that stage I was 31 and hadn't lived at my parents' for a few years. I was so upset that I told my counsellor and she said, 'That isn't your fault, it's him,' but I still felt I must have done something wrong. (May)

> One of the most striking things for me about doing therapy and looking back over my childhood, in particular, is exposing the stories and explanations which I had been repeating to myself for many years and bringing them out into the light of day and thinking, 'That actually makes no sense at all,' but I had never questioned it as an explanation. Having to talk about it and having somebody sitting opposite me saying, 'Do you really think that?' and having to remake the story and think about where that story came from and why it was necessary, who gave it to me, or why I produced it. Those stories can be so powerful and so convincing and yet actually very wrong, either in terms of objective chronology or people's motivation. (Lyn)

Information from family members has also broadened the picture and helped facilitate a clearer understanding of family life. In particular, it has enabled the production of an extended version of the biography of the perpetrator. In this next quote Josh talks about the varying avenues, which have enabled him to piece together information, expand his own narrative and contribute to other family members' healing:

> I don't know at what point, but I know that probably my two younger brothers were also abused because one got very upset many years ago and he wouldn't discuss it, which is fine. But I

think that they were only abused once or twice at the most. But then my stepfather's own natural daughter, one of the second lot of twins, has talked openly about her abuse and I helped her a great deal with that about ten years ago. (Josh)

And I mean, this is interesting, I didn't know this at the time but it must have been one of the times when my mother was away convalescing and I reckon my oldest sister was probably about 14. And I didn't know this at the time but he was taken to court and he was sent to prison for 3–6 months for attempted rape on my eldest sister. And it wasn't something that was talked about, but she'd had to run into the toilet and climb out the window and then, after that, she went to live with some neighbours across the road so she was removed from it. And that was obviously around the time that I was being abused, but my sister never talks about that at all. (Josh)

I know he went on to abuse children in the family that he went to when he left my mum because I was told. It was the woman he left my mother for, her daughter, she was probably about 14, 15 at the time and he abused her. It came through my youngest sister, not the sister who was abused, and I think she bumped into this girl at one point and had this conversation. (Josh)

In a similar manner, Thomas has managed to co-construct a narrative via discussion with his stepbrothers and stepsisters, some of whom have been abused and others who have not. Here Thomas talks about the knowledge he has gained about his stepfather's previous family:

He'd been abusing his son and daughter from that first relationship. David, his son, who lived in Devon, told me that my stepdad had abused him. He didn't say how, he told me in the mid-1980s. David was really seriously ill with a kidney problem and my stepdad wanted to keep going down to visit him and one day when I'd gone down to see him he just snapped and said, 'I don't want him here,' and I said, 'well, why don't you want him here, why don't you want him down here?' And then he just said, 'Look, what he did to me, as a kid, should never happen to any kid' and that was it, he left it at that. My stepfather and his first wife had also adopted a child called Christine and it's a very interesting story because…and I've been told this on very good authority from a relative on my dad's first wife's side of the family, that Christine was, in fact, a product of an incestuous relationship between Jack and his daughter Anne. Christine died of meningitis when she was six. (Thomas)

By contrast, May discusses her fear of raising the issue of sexual abuse with her younger sibling who she suspects has also been abused:

> Also, there is part of me that is scared because from time to time things happen that make me wonder whether these things only happened to me. My youngest sibling has some of the same issues with men; she steers clear of them. She lacks self-confidence; always going along with what other people want even when this is unreasonable. She has a bad body self-image despite being very thin; she is always trying to lose weight. I just could not bear it if my keeping quiet meant that someone else had gone through the same. (May)

Within the next quote Jean illustrates how, in addition to her mother's information regarding her first period of hospitalization, the contribution of medical records has led to an ability to feel more confident about the content of the narrative that she is in the process of constructing:

> My mum's information has helped me with the reconstruction of my story. One other piece of the story would be medical records. I got my records from my GP and there were a few bits of information in there that helped and gave a time structure to it. I had an examination with a consultant. It was at a time when my symptoms were fairly mellow so it was just a check-up (where I would go and usually wait for about four or five hours and then have an X-ray and blood test, and then someone would come and bend my legs in painful ways and 'umm' and 'ah' and then go away and then say, come back in another two months or three months). On one of these, kind of, hospital visits I noticed that there was a note made on the records that said something like, 'This child seems unreasonably frightened by the medical examination.' So one of the consultants did notice how freaked out I was when he was examining me, although nothing was done about it. There are a few other bits of information like that in the records that helped to validate things and give a bit more structure to the story of what happened. (Jean)

It is felt, by many writers, that memory of life events are held as narrative constructs (van der Kolk and van der Hart 1991) and imparted through a process of storytelling, which provides a meaning-making function for the individual and listener. Consequently, then, it seems logical that when the narrative has been suspended and distorted by something like child sexual abuse, storytelling becomes the obvious method employed to explore the trauma memories and establish a sense of narrative coherence, which demonstrates, amongst other things, evaluative and integrated properties (Royce Baerger and McAdams 1999). The co-constructed narrative used by participants in this study, and described within this section, reflect a multi-dimensional attempt to examine memories and gather together alternative accounts from differing perspectives. Through this extended communication structure, it has been possible to facilitate the production of a more comprehensive version of the abuse-story. The re-telling of that story, which happens most typically in counselling and/or therapy, facilitates, by the continual revisiting and re-interpretation of the experience, the co-creation of a story that has resonance for the narrator (Jacobsen Wren 2003). In the long term, it enables the integration of that event into the larger narrative account of the self.

As already indicated, most of the participants had experienced counselling/therapy at some point in their recovery process, and, at the time of writing, others are still involved in this work. In terms of narrating the self within the therapeutic encounter, McLeod (1997) draws a distinction between traditional foundationalist therapeutic approaches, which utilize storytelling to access the individuals' emotional world and constructionist approaches. Here postmodernism forms the underlying philosophy and the client's process of narration constitutes the clinical currency. It may be that most participants, in this study, who accessed therapy, have experienced therapists who utilized a traditional foundationalist approach. Lyn's reference to therapeutic work, however, which calls into question the historically constructed stories that inform her current belief system, could indicate the opposite for her.

Jacobsen Wren (2003), and other authors, suggest that in therapy it is important to illicit what factors and/or belief systems act as barriers to that person's ability to process information and establish a 'narrative point of origin' for current difficulties. Simon (1998) writes that many survivors of sexual abuse are constrained by their state of 'entrapment', where a circular self-deprecating belief system operates, perpetuating and reinforcing the issue of self-blame. This state of entrapment, Simon argues, is created by the perpetrator who has given the child a conflicting and immobilizing set of messages. These messages might relate to the child not being believed, the pain that disclosure would inflict on the non-abusing parent and even the child's active part in wanting the abuse to occur. Additionally, on a wider level, Burke Draucker (1992) posits that this self-blaming belief system may be fed by negative 'societal prescriptions' relating to femininity. As discussed in the previous chapter, this state of entrapment may be reinforced and intensified for disabled children by the internalization of disabling notions of the impaired, therefore bad, body, or their complex relationship with carers.

Simon (1998) highlights the importance of positioning the therapeutic encounter within a moral context, demonstrating an unequivocal stance in relation to the abuse. Simon proposes that the moral positioning of the subject matter needs to happen fairly early on in the therapeutic encounter, with perhaps a clear message in relation to the immorality of child sexual abuse. This issue is encapsulated in the substance of May's quote: 'That isn't your fault, it's him.' For Burke Draucker (1992) and other writers, the ongoing concern of counselling/therapy rests with an imperative to challenge the self-blaming belief system of the individual and re-emphasize their status as a child in the original experience. It can also involve guiding the development of a new and more reflective belief system so facilitating, eventually, the cognitive reframing of the abuse experience. White (1993) would refer to this process as the facilitation of an 'externalizing conversation' or a 'counter-language' where the internal story no longer takes prominence for the individual. In that sense, the therapist might (in theory) be seen to be responsible for, what Crossley (2000) and others refer to as, the 'master narrative' and the facilitation of a different type of discourse, which helps extend the individual's understanding of the issue.

The therapeutic process of itself, and as indicated by Lyn, aims at the joint de-construction and re-construction of a narrative, within the context of a safe and structured environment. This involves the substitution of perhaps incompatible childhood stories for the 'correct' story (Evans and Maines 1995) that can then be told to others outside the therapeutic context. McLeod (1997) proposes that the process of deconstructing the survivor's narrative, within the therapeutic encounter, might take a number of forms including:

- The therapist incorporating the individual's story into the therapeutic approach, which then might give the story greater significance. An example of this might be the interpretation of the transference dynamic in psychodynamic encounters.

- The therapist highlighting the way the individual constructs their narrative, with perhaps encouragement to consider other ways of recounting that story.

- The therapist probing to uncover inconsistencies in the individual's narrative.

Clearly, Lyn's therapy draws from all three of McLeod's points. She is allowed to dissect her stories and consider the validity of their content and the belief systems that ensue. She is also invited to think about other, more accurate, storylines. This therapist's work appears also to be embedded within a psychodynamic framework. Here, as can be seen later, part of the narrative re-constitutive process involves the use of the transference dynamic. Regardless of the therapeutic approach, however, one successful evaluative measure of the co-constructive process is the achievement of narrative coherence where there is some connection made between internal feelings and external presentation.

The issue of the accuracy and the importance of recollection will be picked up and debated later on in this chapter but, in therapeutic terms, the overall procedure strives for the achievement of a narrative truth or what Spence (1982) refers to as 'narrative fit'. Essentially, both of these concepts describe the production of a narrative that allows the past to be viewed in a self-absolving fashion, yet is robust enough to allow for the inclusion of contradictory information (Spence 1982). For both Spence (1982) and Bruner (1990), it can be assumed that narrative truth is seen to be reflected in the individual's ability to create meaning that brings about the potential for change.

For participants in this study who had siblings and who experienced intra-familial abuse, the sharing of information between siblings and the acquisition of additional factual material from within the wider family context has been an important part of the narrative re-constructive process. In Josh's case, his own bravery and ability to 'speak out' has prompted another abused sibling to take a similar risk. The barriers to adult disclosure are well-documented and generally centre round not being believed. The first disclosure, within a sibling group, can often have variable effects. Responses can include other siblings also feeling the need to disclose their abuse as well, to a denial and re-burying of the abuse by other siblings (MacFarlane and Korbin 1983), which appears to have been the case for Josh's brothers. MacFarlane and Korbin (p.233) write that this denial may result from guilt experienced for "'allowing" the abuse through their silence', an issue raised by May. Whilst disclosure for both Thomas and Josh has been a growth-promoting experience, which has facilitated the production of an authentic narrative, for some of their siblings disclosure may be too painful at this particular moment in their life.

We believe it is worth considering briefly here the function and maintenance of family secrets from a cultural and family systems perspective. Notwithstanding the numerous barriers that sexually abused children face when contemplating disclosure, it is helpful to consider why these secrets continue to be kept within the family unit well into adulthood. Vangelisti (1994) believes that some of the function of family secrets, such as child sexual abuse, which are 'transgressions of the social and sexual "rules" of particular communities' (Crago 1997, p.103), are to guard the family from societal disapproval and prevent family breakdown. In essence, they are an extremely powerful mechanism for perpetuating an exterior illusion of familial cohesion.

Crago (1997), who maintains that secrets reproduce themselves across generations, suggests that the thinking generated by family secrets involves 'magical thinking'. There is a belief that the raising of the topic will either make the situation worse or risk personal alienation from the family. He suggests that secret-keepers feel that by keeping quiet they are safeguarding the well-being of other family members. The negative emotional repercussions for secret-keepers in their quest to remain silent, according to Karpel (1980), are generated by a fear of inadvertent disclosure and unease when particular topics are raised. Some of these dynamics have relevance for participants and their siblings in this study.

One other source that contributed to narrative re-construction, and which provided a corroborative function in one participant's process, was the use of medical records. The introduction of the *Access to Health Records Act 1990* invests doctors with an obligation to facilitate access to patients' medical records, with perhaps an ethical obligation to make sure that the patient understands what they read and are supported in the process (Brazier 1998). There are cases cited of adult victims of sexual abuse returning to view their medical notes in order to establish whether or not the medical profession had known of their sexual abuse (David 1998) but I am unaware as to whether this was the intended purpose for Jean. What the process did achieve, however, was an externally located source of substantiation, which gave credence to her recovered memories and offered a time frame for her narrative (Ross and Buehler 1994).

ACKNOWLEDGING AND RE-WORKING THE LOSS: 'MY CHILDHOOD WAS NICKED'

Part of the process of 'storying the self' has involved an acknowledgement of the parts of the personal narrative that have been eroded or, at the very least, severely tampered with. Some participants spoke of narrative loss in terms of 'loss of childhood' and others spoke about the 'loss of self'. In varying ways, and through the process of healing, a number of participants have attempted to actively reclaim some elements of their narrative, if only symbolically, and acknowledge that other aspects of their healing may be an ongoing process. For Josh his childhood 'was nicked' and for Thomas his Christmas was stolen:

> My stepfather also stole Christmas day from me since too much wine at lunchtime led to my mother having to lie down and sleep it off, leaving my stepfather to fulfil his needs. 'Happy Christmas son,' was what he said as he left the room with a smile on his face. When I think back to that afternoon that's when I know how much I lost as a child. (Thomas)

> My childhood was 'nicked', it was stolen, I was thrust into an adult world before I ever should have been; it went, it was gone from the age of five or six, so now I'm trying to make up for it. (Josh)

He stole my childhood and he stole it pretty early on. An introduction to sex and sexuality should happen naturally, it shouldn't happen at a forced pace, and I should not have been used as a rag doll. I should not have been used for someone else's pleasure at that age, and nobody should, and it took me a long time to get over it. (Josh)

Lyn speaks specifically about a particular developmental period and how the usual process of pushing familial boundaries was denied because of a need to provide structure for her parents:

Looking back on it, I had a really contained adolescence and it was easy to blame that on the disability but I don't think that was all that it was. My mother was very protective. It was very easy for it to be said that the reason that I didn't get out more, and didn't, apparently, want to get out more was because I didn't hear well, I was shy, it was difficult, and all the rest of it. I think it was more that I was the one who was providing structure in the family. I wasn't going anywhere. The fights that you have with your parents when you're 13 or 14 I had when I was 20. (Lyn)

Both Jean and Josh speak about the 'loss of self' in their personal story line and May talks about the loss of a trusting and spontaneous self:

Abuse is obviously wrong for lots and lots of different reasons but I think one of the things for me, about it, is it's like a kind of theft; a spiritual theft, and drawing myself was a way of bringing myself back. (Jean)

I see him as a sad little man who stole my identity for many years and I've got my own identity now, I'm Josh, I know what my worth is. I know what I'm good at, I know the people who love me, I know the people I love and I can actually feel those emotions now, I'm not stunted. (Josh)

More than all of this, I hate what it has taken away from me. I would love to feel proud of something I have done and feel that it is, also, good enough. I would love to feel that sex is a wonderful, important thing that people share instead of thinking, 'Please don't let anything go wrong.' I wonder what it would be like to be around people and trust them. I wonder what it would be like to have a one-night stand. I know some people might think this disgusting but everyone should be able to choose what they do with their body. I would love to feel the way that others do about their birthday. Look at clothes and buy them because they are nice rather than not buying them because I know I would be self-conscious and worry someone would use the way I was dressed as an excuse. (May)

Addressing the losses described has been achieved, or is being achieved, by a number of means including therapeutic work undertaken in a formalized therapeutic setting or personal therapeutic work happening outside this type of context. For some participants, their involvement in the research process has been another avenue for facilitating the creation of a different type of narrative and, by doing so, has also validated the self. We begin with the words of Lyn who talks about the use of transference in the psychotherapeutic encounter to re-work aspects of adolescence:

So therapy has been helpful, immensely helpful, but not in the way that I thought. I thought, 'Okay, I'll talk about it and having talked about it I'll feel better and then I'll get on with my life.' A lot of it, in that situation, is a kind of re-enactment, seeing myself behaving like an adolescent in the therapist's room and not being quite able to believe that I'm doing this, and yet still doing it, and being aware. Talking to him about the boundaries and being very clear about those, and why they are being held, meant that it had become possible to talk about my insecurities about boundaries. Because I think when you've been in a relationship with somebody older, who ought to know how to manage that, and doesn't know how to do it, you feel that you have to do it, the responsibility lies with you and that means that you dare not even explore the thought of what might happen. (Lyn)

Equally as important, some participants also spoke about therapeutic work happening in a less formalized manner, and here Josh describes his attempts to reclaim something of childhood:

And as daft as it sounds, because when I was a kid I didn't have many toys, now I buy myself toys, and so on my shelf in the bedroom I've got my Peter rabbit, I've got my rubber ducks, and I think that's really nice. My wife actually bought me the Peter rabbit many, many years ago, at the stage when I was still getting through it. I'd give him a cuddle, I'd sometimes take him to bed and that was fine. He's always on my shelf now; I don't need to do that anymore. A few years ago I saw these three yellow rubber ducks and I wanted them, and I thought 'Well I want them, so have them.' So I don't have a bath that often because I'm often in the shower because it's quicker, but occasionally I'll have one and I'll take my ducks with me, and it's okay to do that because we never had that when I was a child. I didn't have any toys, I didn't have any love, I couldn't be a kid. (Josh)

The other week I was down in a little town a few miles from here, and I needed a new wallet and I bought a new wallet, but while I was in the shop I saw this pig and it was a blue pig, a money box with pink spots on it, so I thought, 'I want that', so I bought it, and now I stick my coins in it. And it's allowing yourself to have that time back almost, and whilst I'm never going to have the time back, I think, 'Well I don't care what people think now, if they think I'm daft, if they don't like me, well that's not my problem, that's theirs.' (Josh)

Jean and Josh speak about 'grounding the self' and alternative methods of putting themselves (both as adult and child) back in the picture/narrative:

I work with mirrors a lot and when I find myself gone and I'm struggling I can bring myself back by looking at the mirror and focusing on my face and my features. So I started doing self-portraits and I still am continuing; making art is a very important part of the process for me. (Jean)

I found that picture recently (indicating the picture on the wall), it's the only picture that I've got of me at about eight, and I look at that and I think, 'Well, that kid there, he's smiling, he looks quite a happy little chap, but he was going through hell at that particular time.' So I put the picture up because he's me and I'm him, and we're both connected. (Josh)

Similarly, participant's involvement in the research process performs a comparable function:

Bearing witness is really important and being involved in research like this is a way of witnessing what happened. One of the things I have is this extreme 'manicness' going on, it's very hard to explain to somebody else but I was experiencing it a lot when I first cracked up and one of the ways of trying to handle it would be to try and occupy myself. So I had a number patience game that I would do, and I had the TV on, and I'd have music on, and I was obviously not focusing on any one of them in the way that you would if you were just doing one of those things, but I was in fact doing all three things because I needed to completely occupy my mind. One of the things I remember that particular time was that the Oscars were on and it was at the time when *Schindler's List* won a prize. One of the producers came up to speak, he was a survivor of the camps and he said, 'I remember at the camp looking into the eyes of a dying man and he said to me, witness this, witness this', and the producer said, 'I feel that I have been able to do that at long last with this film.' I was just in pieces; it spoke to me very much in that moment, in that I have to witness my experience. (Jean)

Having it (the narrative) all in one place is useful because when you have counselling you deal with separate bits at a time. I know people say that (by breaking it down) you can see how that relates to that, but I don't think that it sinks in the same as having it in front of you. (May)

In addition to the reconstructive process, detailed in the previous section, recovery from an experience such as child sexual abuse involves the acknowledgement and mourning for the losses incurred by the experience. This recognition is referred to by Herman (1992) as being part of the second stage of the recovery process and is signified by its ongoing quality. The acknowledgement of loss has, for some participants in this study, precipitated a search for methods of incorporating the loss, and its significance, into the plot structure of the narrative. As a consequence, it has enabled bringing together of fractured aspects of identity (Neimeyer and Stewart 1996) with the production of a more coherent life history account.

The losses incurred by child sexual abuse are usually psychological and unrecognized as episodes requiring grieving. Hopkins and Thompson (1984) are perhaps two of the first writers to make the link between rape/sexual assault and bereavement, and apply the widely recognized stages of loss and mourning, described by such authors as Kübler-Ross (1969), to the issue of sexual abuse. Notwithstanding individual variables, Hopkins and Thompson highlight several losses identified by survivors of child sexual abuse. These losses include the loss of trust in others, an issue prevalent in May's quote and also referred to in the previous chapter by both Josh and May. They also include the loss of freedom and an ability to do things such as wear clothes and make-up without having to be concerned about any potential negative repercussion, a point also made by May. Additionally, the authors identified the loss of what they referred to as ego identity, and we refer to as 'self'. Here, the authors describe this loss in terms of loss of security, certainty, rootedness, spontaneity, etc. Jean and Josh talk about this loss in terms of spiritual loss or 'loss of identity'.

Similarly, Bourdon and Skinner Cook (1993) researched the issue of loss with 52 female adult survivors of sexual abuse and 58 mixed gendered therapists using questionnaire methodology and background information sheets. For both survivors and therapists, the most significant losses identified were a loss of trust (also identified by Hopkins and Thompson 1984) and the loss of self-love, an issue referred to by Jean when discussing her personal recovery process. Both trust and self-love were seen to be important. The authors suggest that these losses are integral to the ability to form and maintain positive adult relationships and they may also hinder recovery. The age at which the original abuse occurred was also felt to be very significant in Bourdon and Skinner Cook's research; the earlier its occurrence, the more perceived losses were reported.

Child sexual abuse occurring early in life can interfere with early developmental processes and influence such issues as attachment and the formation of a sense of security (Clark 1993). In terms of the developmental losses identified by participants in this study, Lyn described the lack of familial circumstances that could facilitate an ability to safely engage in the typical boundary testing behaviour that signifies adolescence and which is part of the individuation process. For Josh, the loss identified was the loss of the socially constructed ideal of childhood (Scott, Jackson and Backett-Milburn 1998) that is characterized by child-like concerns and, within that ideal, the loss of an accepted sexual developmental pathway, an issue discussed by both Thomas and Josh.

In relation to this latter point, and to elaborate further, research indicates that for non-sexually abused younger children their actual sexual knowledge is very limited. They are aware of genital differences and the non-sexual function of genitals, but, according to Brilleslijper-Kater and Baartman (2000), are generally not concerned with things that do not appear in their own lives. For sexually abused children the situation is very different as they are exposed to experiences that they are developmentally ill-equipped to deal with and which can then result in re-experiencing behaviours (Deblinger *et al.* 1989) such as sexualized play and public or compulsive masturbation.

Again, therapy is one avenue for acknowledging and mourning the losses experienced in childhood. Here, the establishment of a consistent and nurturing therapeutic relationship can provide the potential for analysis of early attachments. It can provide an alternative and re-constitutive 'mirroring self-object experience' (Neuman Kulp 1991, p.64), which provides containing properties and a validation of the self. The 'acting-out' behaviour, described by Lyn, which is typical of therapy, generally operates outside the conscious awareness of the client and is symptomatic of the individual's attempt to enact complex emotion, which defy verbalization (Ganzarain and Buchele 1987). These authors write that acting-out behaviour is 'a coded message from the patient's unconscious' (p.187). Working through and understanding the messages embodied within the communication help free the client from repetition. Typically this difficult dynamic is enacted within other interpersonal relationships.

Although Lyn describes her experiences of therapy in very positive terms, it is, perhaps, worth pointing out here that some disabled people's experiences of therapy are far from positive. Corker (2003) suggests that it is possible for therapeutic value systems to be influenced by prejudicial beliefs about disabled people. She draws attention to 'root metaphors' and oppositional constructs of therapy (normal/pathological, sane/insane, etc.) that can potentially be incorporated into therapists' thinking. Swain, Griffiths and Heyman (2003) propose that there is a danger that individualizing approaches in the counselling setting can preclude the social context of disability and the very real obstacles that disabled people face in relation to their inclusion in society. Corker (2003) points to practitioner reflexivity as a way to address some of these issues.

Of course, as indicated by participants in this study, there are other avenues available for mourning the losses aside from therapy/counselling, which also enable the individual to place the 'self' back in the narrative. Josh, for example, although recognizing that what was stolen in childhood is irreplaceable, has referred to the symbolic re-claiming of childhood. This has been reflected in his purchase of toys, which have been used in difficult times as a source of comfort, and the relocation of a childhood photograph in a prime

position within his home, so indicating the retrieval and ownership of his childhood identity. Additionally, Jean's use of mirrors and
her artwork are examples of self-affirming methods and ways of re-
establishing the self within the personal narrative. Writing is also a well-
recognized therapeutic tool used in the recovery process of survivors
(Green Lister 2002). Both Thomas and Jean have used poetry as part
of their recovery process and as a means of emphasizing their presence in the abuse experience. Thomas has also produced an extended
and detailed autobiographical account of his earlier years. Etherington
(2000) refers to the function of writing for survivors, which might
include its cathartic affect; its potential to deepen understanding and
its ability to articulate difficult and painful experiences.

By drawing on the work of Frank (1995), Etherington (2000)
posits the existence of three types of narrative: the restitution narrative, the chaos narrative and the quest narrative. The restitution narrative has as its central theme the return to how things were before the
event. The chaos narrative reflects the suspension of the individual
in their current dilemma (an issue which will be picked up on in the
next section of this chapter). The quest narrative can contain a sense
of reflection and a motivation to bring about social change by exposing truths and informing others. Clearly, many research participants,
including those in the present study, undertake the co-construction
of a narrative within the context of the research process with the intention of producing a quest narrative. With reference to the work of
Herman (1992), Robson (2001) discusses the 'narrative cure' which is
comparable to the emergence of the quest narrative in the survivor's
recovery process. This type of narrative is often a form of testimony
and has both a personal healing and political function. As Jean describes, it is a form of 'bearing witness' to a societal atrocity, but it
also acts as documented confirmation of the experience and validation of the self, an issue which may also have some validity for May.

Swatton and O'Callaghan (1999) offer another dimension to
the function of the healing narrative that may be applicable to the
research context. In their research, the issue of mirroring is raised,
where the narrative is described as a mirror, which can be used to reflect upon the self. Swatton and O'Callaghan also employ the concept
of the evoked companion (Stern 1985), feeling that the narrative can
provide a prototype, which can be used to 'evaluate and inform the

subsequent life experience' (p.426). Again, these functions may have some significance for May and Jean.

In concluding this section, it is worth returning to the writings of Herman (1992) who emphasizes the importance of the mourning process. She suggests that survivors may try to resist the mourning process, for fear of becoming locked into a never-ending cycle of grief. It is possible, instead, for survivors to become involved in fantasies of revenge or forgiveness. She proposes that, despite the necessary work involved in the mourning process, eventually, over time, the abuse narrative will no longer occupy such a prime position. The participants in this study can be seen to be at different stages in this mourning process.

NARRATIVE CHAOS:
'SUDDENLY I KNEW, I JUST KNEW'

This section looks at the process of narrative chaos, where, in later life, and when dissociative processes became less vital for survival, the individual's circumstances dictated a necessity to re-engage with, and make sense of, the abuse experience. The consequence of this process resulted in narrative chaos or what Frank (1995) describes as narrative wreckage, whereby incoming information had a destabilizing impact on the self and further suspended an ability to narrate the self in coherent terms.

The process of being forced to engage with the abuse narrative has been a significant feature of most participants' stories, triggered by a number of factors, variable in their nature and sometimes accompanied by detrimental consequences. Two participants, who had repressed or forgot the sexual abuse experience, had no conscious awareness of the experience in early adulthood. Retrieval of the memory later in life helped these individuals to gain a retrospective meaning-making function to their personal narrative. Two other participants who had continuous recall had involvement with small children, either as a mother or as a babysitter, which created a situation whereby their dissociative defences became ineffective and raw emotion relating to their violation and became exposed for the first time. For one participant, a sibling's partial disclosure forced the individual to divulge his own abuse to his partner, with the recovery of further abuse memories that up until that point had not been present.

Most of these participants at the time had a safe enough environment to risk the further exploration of the abuse narrative. At the time of writing, one participant continued to experience intrusive images and sensation, so signifying their unrelenting involvement in the process of working through the abuse memories and their continuing state of narrative chaos. As with many of the participants, there is an acknowledgement of gaps in their narrative. One person realized that further recovery may have the potential to bring about additional disruption in their life. We begin, however, with the words of Lizzie who describes the recovery of repressed memory in counselling following an incident of physical assault whilst living in India and 'suddenly just knew':

> In terms of recovering the memory of sexual abuse, I went back to live in India for a couple of years in the mid-1980s and whilst I was there I was attacked during a robbery at the place where I was living. And it was when I got back and I started co-counselling about the attack. It just...I can't explain it except that I think that I knew that one of the things that my abuser did in hospital...because he didn't only sexually abuse me, most of them don't, do they? I think one of the things he used to do was hit kids on the head, because if you do that you don't leave a mark, the mark is hidden by the hair, so I think he hit me on the head. There are other reasons that I think that, but in this attack I was hit on the head with something a bit like a scimitar; a curved blade that is either used for cutting crops or attacking people. So it was counselling on that and suddenly I just knew, I just knew I'd been abused in hospital. You've got to take into account by that time I was 37 and I had already been co-counselling for 15 years. (Lizzie)

> But what it means is that I had done quite a lot of preparatory work to make it possible that when the trigger was sufficiently similar it was safe for the memory to come back. I could handle it by then. (Lizzie)

> Through counselling, what emerged over the years were snapshots, which I'm sure other women would describe, i.e. that if the abuse happened when you are very young, in fact pre-verbal, you can't describe it, no that's not true; you can end up describing it but your memory is not words, your memory

is photographs or body memories frozen in time. So gradually I would uncover little bits and little bits more and little bits more. (Lizzie)

Lizzie describes the relief gained by retrieving the memory and being able to produce a more coherent narrative:

Each time I put together another piece of the jigsaw it was a relief, but I don't really feel like I have completed the jigsaw actually. I probably haven't, but each time another piece slotted in it was a huge relief because I knew life had to be better having slotted that in, than without it. (Lizzie)

For Jean, there had been a number of triggers that precipitated the recovery of the repressed memory. These included her mother deciding to share what she knew about Jean's first period of hospitalization; her daughter reaching the age when Jean was abused; the presence of a supportive partner and network of supportive friends, and Jean deciding to stop smoking cannabis following an illness episode:

Something happened when I was about 26, when I went to visit my parents, my mum had decided that it was time to tell me and she sat me down for the first time and she told me the whole story of what happened in hospital, in detail, from her point of view. The information that she had was shocking and upsetting even though it didn't include all the information I later retrieved as repressed memory. (Jean)

When my daughter was around the age when the abuse started to happen to me in the hospital, around 18 months, things started to really go downhill for me and I was really struggling. I don't think that was a coincidence. I was still smoking and really wanted to stop. I got myself therapy. I'd got that far, I'd got a therapist set up and I'd had an initial meeting and a first session with her. Then it hit Christmas time and I got very ill. (Jean)

And then, when I was just beginning to come out of that (chicken pox) with the help of antibiotics, I decided that I was just going to stop smoking. Looking back on it I think, 'Well, that was interesting that I did that,' I just completely stopped and within five days I was just completely gone; completely in an altered state. (Jean)

Here Jean talks about the process of memory recovery and the form that the memory took:

I'd shaved my head and I wasn't eating at all. I think that the time was just right really for it to all erupt, and suddenly I was in this world of feelings and sensations and these bodily experiences, it was very intense. I had some friends who knew enough about the process of repressed memory to be able to help me. So the second therapy session that I went to, I was led to the door in this very frail state. Luckily my therapist was great and handled it really well. (Jean)

So I was in this altered state for a while. I was weak, I was doing that kind of process that people do, you know, trying to understand the physical sensations and the dreams. I'd been having dreams for a long time that I didn't understand, so it was that process of putting it all together. (Jean)

There is a difference between repressed memory and recall memory, and some of what happened I have in recall memory and a lot of it is repressed memory, and to me the nature of the memories is quite different. There is a lot of evidence to suggest that we process the memories in different ways. So for repressed memory, as well as the visual images of tiles and things, there were also smells and the feel of things, like cold metal. I got cold metal, she had a cross on, a big flat cross, and there were times when the nun was abusing me where it was banging into my face and I got that sensation of a cold flat metal thing against my face. And sounds, but not words or phrases in the same way as later on. I think the recall memory and the repressed memory is different, the repressed memory is always a lot more 'trippy' and like an altered state, which would make sense. A lot of my recall memory is quite visual too. (Jean)

Additionally, she comments on the role that therapy played in the recovery process:

The therapy that I was doing was called 'process orientated psychology', which is very interesting because it is very client focused, it's all about the process. So the therapist really worked with me and what I was doing, I wasn't getting the memories in therapy, it was mostly happening at other times, and therapy was helping me with the tools to understand what was happening and to start to put together the picture of what had happened in the past and how to deal with it now. (Jean)

In these next quotes Jean talks about the costs and benefits for her of recovering and actively engaging with the recovered material:

> But there's a cost for that, and I think that for some people those costs are too great. Overwhelming is an incredible understatement, nobody dies from feelings but you can die from the consequences of feelings. I did get very close to suicide when things were very bad in that first year, when I was feeling those intense feelings of fear and pain and self-hate: the hate that the nun put on me, and the hate of those medics who were able to objectify a person to the extent that they can justify murder. (Jean)

> My relationship did not survive, unfortunately, which is the case for a lot of people that go into crisis around child abuse. It is very rare that the relationship will survive it. It was very hard for my partner because she wasn't skilled, or knowledgeable, or confident with emotional issues. (Jean)

> The process of uncovering the repressed memory is a process of survival in itself. I think that many people do carry on their lives without recovering the memory and that's maybe okay for those people. But I realized that I needed to live my life, I wanted to have feelings and I didn't want to live this dispassionate, disconnected kind of life. That is happening for me, and again it's slow, but I'm getting there and I do cry now, I am able to do it, and I am much more in touch with my feelings. (Jean)

Lynn and Chloe speak about how at some point the anaesthetizing effect of dissociation began to wear off for them and difficult emotions began to surface. This created a breakdown in their mental health (suicidal ideation in Lyn's case and psychosis in Chloe's) and an accompanying narrative turmoil. In both instances the trigger appears to be the exposure to young children and below both women elaborate further on this point:

> A good part of it was that my boss, whom I'm a good friend with, has two daughters, and he's very affectionate to them. I'm quite sure that there is nothing sinister behind that but I couldn't read it right. When I saw it I didn't know what was happening. I'd get very upset; I'd know that I was behaving irrationally. I'd have to make an excuse to leave the room. There was an occasion when I babysat for them, at that time they were about five and eight, and the five-year-old came to

say goodnight to him and sat on his lap, she sort of squirmed around and her night dress rode up and she wasn't wearing any knickers, and he wasn't at all embarrassed about this. He had his hands around her chest and she was sort of leaning backwards and tickling his chin and she was obviously completely relaxed and happy with him in a way that I never was with my dad and I just couldn't bear it, I wanted to pick her up and take her away or just abandon her to him. I just didn't want to watch it, what I thought was going to happen, even although rationally I knew it wasn't going to happen. His wife was around too, and the other girl was there, and he would have never done it in front of me. But then part of me felt, 'Well my dad did it in front of other people.' (Lyn)

Iqra started to become a toddler, become a little person. And I think it was something to do with her just getting just that bit older and becoming a little person. And again at that age they start...already you start to see early sexual behaviours that I didn't want to acknowledge were there. But they do start having their early sexual behaviours that again, as a responsible adult, you just encourage them...'If you want to do that, do it when you're in the bath on your own.' And that's the sort of stuff that I think was going on with me, those sorts of things. I think there is probably an age connection, she was probably a similar age to when maybe my memories are coming from; the ones where I don't really know what happened. So I'm looking at her and I'm also thinking, she's just brilliant and someone's going to come and want her because, look at her, who wouldn't, I mean she's fantastic, she's the best kid in the world. And again because she's disabled, so I know she's more vulnerable and I think that's what started going on and I didn't want to leave her with people. (Chloe)

As a consequence of these triggered emotions, Lyn describes the process of getting to the point of needing to seek help:

So it got to the stage where there were too many things that I couldn't think about. I was spending my entire life lurching from topic to topic because everything became too dangerous, everything reminded me. There seemed to be constant references in the newspapers, I couldn't look at a man with a child in the street. (Lyn)

There was a constant feeling of not being able to not feel it anymore. I was apparently doing all right, I was still functioning at work, nobody was saying to me, 'God, what's wrong with you,' so clearly I was still hacking it, and yet inside I felt awful. At its peak I was going 15-minute stretches of not thinking about killing myself. I was thinking, 'If I can get through the next 15 minutes without thinking about it, and then the next,' and this was all, without really consciously relating it to anything that had gone previously, I just felt dreadful. (Lyn)

What once had been deadness was no longer deadness, the anaesthesia was wearing off and there was a kind of despair that it was wearing off, and I had no idea how bad it would get. I'd been thinking, 'I can't live like this, but supposing I woke up tomorrow and it actually felt twice as bad.' It was like living with a physical pain and trying to gauge at what point you take the Aspirin or something stronger. But there didn't seem to be anything I could take, and all the strategies that I had had for coping with it were no longer working and I didn't have any others. (Lyn)

Thomas's acknowledgement of his abuse followed his sister's disclosure and also led to an emotional breakdown which was accompanied by flashbacks and the retrieval of repressed memories from early childhood:

The flashbacks started about six months after it all came out. I started to have really bad night terrors and I wet the bed a few times. I'd wake up as though I couldn't breathe, you know, like a panic attack. Obviously I'd be having it in my sleep and I'd wake up and I couldn't breathe. (Thomas)

During the day there were strange little things like, we'd go out somewhere and I'd see something and it would just be like someone playing a videotape backwards, I'd feel scrambling in my head, and I'd try and adjust my eyes and next minute I'd be either back in my living room at 39 West View, or in the bathroom. And my stepdad would be there and I could smell his aftershave, his body odour, and things like that, and I'd just feel like I was going to black out. When this happened we would just have to go home. (Thomas)

I think that that initial disclosure to Sharon, and her acceptance and support, provided a sense of safety that allowed the memories to start flooding back. Whilst I always knew I had been abused, the early memories were out of reach. Bit by bit the pieces of the jigsaw started fitting into place. It was like... I went walking one day in Pleasley and came across a dry-stone wall. The image started to play on my mind, and gradually over time, I started to recover the memory of the camping trip in Matlock, which hadn't been there up until that point. (Thomas)

In May's situation, the narrative disorganization continues with intrusive thoughts and memories frequently breaking through into consciousness creating a situation where the abuse experience still feels very much part of the present:

I'm not sure if this happens because there is so much to cope with. It must be very difficult having to deal with someone who keeps 'dropping out', as I call it, something which happens because of my abuse. I cope by just blanking it out, and then coming back when it is over. It has the reverse effect these days; anything can make me 'drop out', a word, a touch, a smell, but rather than taking me away from the way I feel, I seem to get locked into a re-run of something that happened. It must be frightening for people around me because I'm just not there; it is like being unconscious. Flashbacks cause a similar thing; it's like being there, and it's all happening again. Flashbacks can cause me to be very violent, it is like this feeling of anger or hatred of myself comes over me and I just have to get it out. I usually end up trashing a room or self-harming. When I come back to myself I feel horrible because I feel like they have controlled me again. I also cannot believe what I have done sometimes; I am scared that one day I will hurt someone. I also feel dirty and disgusting, which means I have to get in the shower for ages. I go from really hot water or stone cold, without knowing, because I am obsessed with washing. I find that things that are on TV, or other things that I can't quite figure out, can cause flashbacks or mood swings. (May)

These last two quotes from Josh and Chloe acknowledge the incomplete nature of their narrative, with Chloe recognizing that further retrieval also has the potential to create narrative chaos:

These memories have always been with me but there's a lot more I don't remember. (Josh)

I know that I've got memories to come, that haven't come yet, and I want them to, I want to have them. Not that I particularly wish to remember it, you know, it's not like it's enjoyable, but you want to know what's happened. Because people do get flashbacks, they get them suddenly often, as well. (Chloe)

Participants in this study demonstrated varying degrees of repression of the abuse memory ranging from complete amnesia, as detailed by Jean and Lizzie, to partial and continuous recall, as described by Lyn, Chloe, May, Thomas and Josh. This finding is consistent with the research of others who see the process of remembering and forgetting as a continuum of experience (Fivush and Edwards 2004). Research illustrates that delayed recall of sexual trauma in childhood is not an uncommon phenomenon. Elliott and Briere (1995) found, in their non-clinical sample, that 42 per cent of participants spoke of some degree of forgetting, whilst 20 per cent described a time when they had a complete loss of memory of the sexual abuse. Andrews *et al.* (2000), by comparison, whose research involved the narratives of therapists of child sexual abuse survivors, reported total amnesia in just over half of their clinical sample. Some of these individuals described prior unconscious clues, as referred to by Jean, such as distressing dreams, etc. Or, similar to the way that Jean recounts, people in the individual's network sharing knowledge relevant to their abuse, but with the individual concerned having no conscious awareness of it.

Researchers such as Briere and Conte (1993) have found that forgetting is associated with violent abuse (physical injury, multiple perpetrators, fears concerning what would happen if disclosure is made), early onset of abuse and a longer duration. Chu *et al.* (1999) also confirm this relationship between early onset and higher incidence of amnesia, as in Lizzie and Jean's accounts. Williams (1995) found that, in her study of women whose abuse was documented at the time of its occurrence, the age of onset of the abuse and a poor level of support gained from the mothers, increased the likelihood of forgetting and then later recovering memories of abuse.

For the participants in the study of Andrews *et al.* (2000), the triggers for abuse recall were variable. Prior to therapy they included some form of physical contact or danger to the individual (13%), as described in Lizzie's situation, a change in medication or substance use (4%), as described by Jean, or the information sharing of another

(7%), as detailed by Thomas. Similar to research that describes the possible impact of pregnancy on the surfacing of abuse memories (Briere 1989), Andrews *et al.* found that for 17 per cent of their sample the trigger involved their children, either in terms of particular events, or their child reaching the same developmental stage that they were when they were sexually abused. This issue was also relevant for Jean.

For both Chloe and Lyn, who had partial or continuous recall memory, their involvement with children, both their own and others, triggered the recovery of a painful emotional state that had previously been repressed by dissociation, and which also created internal instability and consequent narrative chaos. Of particular significance for Chloe was the fact that, like herself, her daughter also had an impairment, which potentially increased her vulnerability. The recovery of memories of child sexual abuse in therapy has been the subject of continued controversial academic debate, which will be covered in more detail in the next section, but for the participants in the study conducted by Andrews *et al.* (2000), therapy acted as a trigger for memory recovery in 37 per cent of the sample. For some, therapy provided the exploratory questioning mechanism or comment that facilitated memory recall. For others, recall resulted from the use of a therapeutic technique. This might have included things as such as hypnosis or guided imagery. For Jean, however, the role that therapy played in relation to the recovery of her repressed memory seemed to fit neither of these categories.

Research also indicates that individuals who have abuse recall, from a prior state of amnesia, can show an increased demonstration of distressing symptoms, particularly in the early years of memory retrieval. These symptoms include such things as flashbacks that can take the form of intrusive images or sensations (Elliott and Briere 1995; Evans and Maines 1995), this latter point being clearly visible in Jean and May's narrative. Similar to some of Thomas's recollections, participants in the study of Andrews *et al.* (2000) described these flashback experiences as either full or partial re-living experiences, with the majority of the participants (60%) experiencing 'all or part of the event in the present, with bodily and other vivid sensations and intense affect' (p.19). In fact Evans and Maines (1995, p.313) describe this state as the individual being 'temporarily locked in the past', an issue powerfully detailed by May. As in May's case, these re-living experiences can also be accompanied by emotion such as disgust, which for May involves a need to obsessively wash (Andrews *et al.* 2000). Elliott and Briere (1995) imply that these symptoms may decrease with time, but that this increase in symptoms connected with new access to repressed material in the early stages of the recovery process could represent emotions associated with the original trauma. These authors contend that, although distressing at the time, exposure to sensory information, in the form of flashbacks, could have some therapeutic benefit by gradually desensitizing the individual to the recovered material.

Andrews *et al.* (2000) found that in the majority of cases in their study the memory recalled took the form of episodes, as opposed to being recalled as autobiographical detail, and often the memories were fragmented. This finding is consistent with research that suggests that trauma information may be laid down in the memory differently to other non-traumatic events (van der Kolk and Fisler 1995). With reference to the work of other authors, van der Kolk an Fisler propose that trauma material is arranged in the memory on several levels; sensori-motor and affective. Accordingly, it appears in later recall in the form of sensory fragments of the original abuse experience. These might include such things as visual imagery, auditory and olfactory stimulation, bodily sensation, and overwhelming emotion, all of which Jean, Lizzie, Thomas and May describe. Frequently this type of memory presents with a minimal verbal component (van der Kolk and Fisler 1995). This issue is raised in a quote of Lizzie's and particularly applies to abuse events experienced by pre-verbal children.

As indicated by Andrews *et al.* (2000), not all abuse recall takes the form of specific episodes and some memories are recovered in an autobiographical format. This occurrence also gives support for more physiologically orientated models, and the existence of 'dual representation theory' (Brewin, Dalgleish and Joseph (1996). Brewin and Andrews (1998) contend that separate cognitive processing pathways potentially give way to both autobiographical recall without reliving experiences, and a sensory response. They write that one is 'explicit and deliberately accessible (verbally accessible memory) and one automatically triggered by situational cues' (p.966). Other writers, such as Sivers, Schooler and Freyd (2002), propose that there are, in fact, three pathways responsible for the processing and retrieval of trauma related material.

From a narrative perspective, recovered memory, and the breakdown of emotional defences that have previously protected that individual, can create intense anxiety with the result that the abuse memory can no longer be accommodated or 'transformed into a neutral narrative' (Uehara *et al.* 2001, p.33). In fact, it creates what Frank (1995) refers to as narrative chaos or narrative wreckage. Here, the regular functions of an individual's narrative, such as the production of coherence, meaning-making and self-evaluation (Tuval-Mashiach *et al.* 2004) become de-stabilized.

Frank (1995), who writes principally in relation to the illness narrative, believes that people operating in narrative chaos are individuals suspended in crisis. Their narrative is characterized by its contradictory sense of immediacy, yet stuckness. Frank writes that 'the body is imprisoned in the frustrated needs of the moment' (p.98). The ability to reflect is denied, and the ability to articulate may not be possible. In fact, Frank describes this type of narrative as the most embodied form of discourse. Any attempt by others to push the person through the crisis compounds the difficulty and typically, as Jean recounts, relationships surrounding the chaos narrative may break down. May's latter quote is highly illustrative of what Frank refers to as 'chaos embodied', where there is an experience of (emotional) pain and a need for dissociation. Whilst in this state May describes herself as being potentially dangerous, self-injuring and unrecognizable.

As previously indicated, and as present within Thomas's quote, healing stems from the ability to allow others to hear the individual's pain and perhaps, on a secondary level, at least, experience their fear and loss (Uehara *et al.* 2001). Verbalization of the trauma and the processing of the memories, as described by Jean, is a painful and costly exercise. Farrants (1998) proposes that defences such as dissociation (which might include forgetting) may be more preferable, in some cases, to exposing the trauma. The advantages are, however, specified by Jean and Lizzie and include an ability to live an emotionally integrated life, with the production of a more comfortable narrative. Similarly for individuals such as Chloe and Josh, who know there are gaps in their narrative, the eventual retrieval of this information, despite the risk of causing more chaos, may provide the same function in terms of narrative coherence. Even when recall material is largely sensory (as in Jean and Lizzie's situation) research, including this work, indicates that over time it is possible for that individual to construct a more integrated narrative account.

On a political and sociological level, and with reference to the work of other writers, it can be seen how the chaos narrative, in its telling, epitomizes how the abuse narrative can cross from the 'public space to traumatize inner space' (Uehara *et al.* 2001, p.34) and then back again in the survivor's attempt to bear witness to the experience in its later re-telling. As the participants' narratives demonstrate, it can cross back yet again, a third time, so bringing about a more fine-tuned level of narrative coherence.

NARRATIVE RELIABILITY: 'I'VE GOT NOTHING FAINTLY RESEMBLING PROOF'

Within this section we turn to the participants' views on the historical truth embedded within their emergent sexual abuse narrative, its believability for others and the rumination they are prone to themselves. The two participants who had been abused in early childhood, and who had then become amnesic for these memories, although very clear about the validity of the recovered information, experienced variable reactions from others about these recollections. In Jean's case, she predicts that she would receive a similar degree of scepticism should she inform outside agencies. Other participants spoke about the perceived plausibility of their life story, in general, or discussed family dynamics and impairment related issues that have had the potential to undermine it. Lizzie and Jean talk about the problems for others of believing recovered memory from such a young age, and providing anything 'faintly resembling proof':

> So the main abuse happened between 14–18 months and one of my worries has always been that people would not believe me because I was so young and I've got nothing faintly resembling proof, but when I realized it, it made sense of so many things about me. (Lizzie)

> Repressed memory is hard to explain to other people and I know it sounds very odd; 'These awful things happened and you forgot and now you've suddenly remembered!' It sounds ridiculous. (Jean)

I am doubtful I will be believed particularly around the eutha-
nasia stuff. I know that people don't want to believe that it happens, and also with me being so young when it happened; I
know that the repressed memory is not valid in the same way
as recall memory. (Jean)

In this next selection of quotes, Lizzie and Jean talk about the reactions of their parents to their disclosure of recovered memory:

It was difficult that it was my dad who was counselling me (because I taught my dad co-counselling) at the moment that I
first uncovered the abuse. And he found it very difficult to believe, which is extremely understandable. So that was unhelpful
but not devastating because he didn't rubbish it, he wouldn't
do that. But I knew he was wrong, you know, I knew he was
wrong. It was such an absolute moment of knowing, it wasn't a
kind of maybe; it was an absolute moment of knowing. (Lizzie)

My mum couldn't cope with it really and of course she would
never poo poo it, but I don't think she really wanted to think
about it. She really didn't want to accept that it was proba-
ble rather than improbable. So she never stopped being very
loving and very supportive of me, but I never took the issue to
her. And also because I could see how awful it would be for
a mother to discover at any point, even 30 odd years on, no
wonder she wanted to say, 'No I don't think so.' (Lizzie)

When I cracked up I decided to tell her and they came up, Mum
and my stepdad came up and stayed for a few days. She helped
with some bits of information. I think she had been expecting
me to crack up. I've not told her all of it, it's difficult because
she sometimes says things and does things that are very in-
sensitive. I think that's part of her process, she's carrying a lot
of trauma, she's still very affected by it, and she doesn't have
all the information. I did talk to her specifically about the anal
abuse; I haven't yet talked to her about the water stuff or the
ritualistic nature of the nun's abusive behaviours. I did talk to
them about the murder and, to be honest with you, I'm not
quite sure whether they believe me or not. But I was quite
clear with myself when I told them, that I didn't need them to
validate this in any way. I don't need that because I know it happened. I'm a hundred per cent sure about it. From the moment
I had it I was just a hundred per cent, and the detail of it has

never faltered, I've never felt doubtful about it. I've had more doubts about the other stuff than I have about that. (Jean)

Jean discusses her feelings about how the authorities, including the legal profession, would respond to the recovered material:

> Passing the information on to the authorities was never a feasible option because it was so long ago, and also because I know I'd be greeted with a lot of scepticism from people. I've always felt that it's pointless to go to the authorities with this, there's probably nothing they can do now. (Jean)

> I've never had an expectation that I'm going to ever get any kind of legal justice with this. (Jean)

Lyn, who had continuous recall of her sexual abuse experience, talks about the feared, and potentially rejecting, responses of others to her life history account:

> I discovered when I started telling people about this sort of life history that I found myself thinking this life story is beginning to look implausible because it's so awful. It took something like two or three years for me to risk telling somebody and wait for them to vomit on the floor or sort of send me out of the room, which is what I thought would happen because it was just so awful. (Lyn)

Chloe describes her parents' dismissive attitude toward the validity of her narrative, in general, and how this has impacted upon her self-confidence and, perhaps, her sister's ability to stand by her own previous abuse allegations made against her father. Later Chloe talks about the impairment-related difficulty that she encounters with memory that can potentially lead to suggestibility:

> For half my life I've been told I'm a liar with a result that I don't even believe my own feelings three quarters of the time. I've been brought up as the one who makes it dramatic, I've been brought up as the one who doesn't really know what she's talking about. (Chloe)

> So my sister I know could quite happily sit there and say 'no I was lying' (about previous abuse allegations concerning her father) and even believe it, even if it had really happened. She would sit there and say it and think it was true, because they can actually make you think that things that you have actually

done, that you were actually there when they happened, are not what they were. They can actually somehow do that to you, I don't know how, but you know, a combination of fear and lies. (Chloe)

I do take things literally and I don't remember things well afterwards. So if something happened to me, and someone kept telling me that something else had really happened, I would start to believe that, because that's what's in front of me now, that's real, and what happened before is a bit not really there. (Chloe)

By contrast, Chloe describes her experience with the police when she made a statement regarding her extra-familial abuse. She later refers to her credibility as a witness in court:

At the end of the day they've treated it as a complaint, as an incident, as a crime. They just believed me, and you think nobody is going to believe you. It's a thing that you have been told, it's so deep in your head; people won't believe you. (Chloe)

But I'd never be a good witness in court, if they found this little ring of people, I would never be a witness in court, I just don't remember enough things. (Chloe)

In addition to the ambivalent and contradictory views held by society in relation to the issue of child sexual abuse, the credibility of the child sexual abuse narrative, particularly those that involve recovered memory, is enmeshed within the recovered memory/false memory debate that surfaced in the US in the late 1980s/early 1990s. This debate has a historical legacy, which dates back to the close of the 1800s when Freud 're-evaluated' his writings on child sexual abuse. This resulted, instead, in his emphasis on theories of childhood sexual fantasy associated with the oedipal stage of a child's development (Masson 1984). The re-emergence of the recovered memory/false memory debate in more recent times has signified, for feminists in particular, a societal 'backlash' against the increased incidence of child sexual abuse in the media and the number of cases in the US, involving recovered memory, that were reaching litigation. It culminated, following a well-publicized case of recovered memory, in the establishment of the False Memory Syndrome Foundation (Mollon 1996). There followed a generalized distrust of therapists, so imbuing the subject of recovered memory with an air of suspicion, which has consequently influenced many survivors' concerns about the believability of their abuse narrative for others. This debate cannot fail to have impacted upon and underpinned, to some degree, the concerns relating to narrative plausibility/believability expressed by participants in this study. It may also have influenced the views of parents hearing their adult child's initial disclosure of child sexual abuse involving recovered material.

The emergence of the recovered memory/false memory debate was accompanied by the writings of a number of key memory researchers, who have been seen to add some academic weight to the false memory argument (Lindsay and Read 1994; Loftus 1993). Neither of these papers deny the existence of child sexual abuse nor, in the case of Lindsay and Read (1994), deny the fact that memory can be later recovered during a process of non-suggestive therapy, but both researchers voice specific areas of concern. Lindsay and Read, for example, are sceptical of memories recovered using certain therapeutic techniques (hypnosis, guided imagery, interpretation of dreams, interpretation of physical symptoms). They are also sceptical about memory recall that has been influenced by the use of self-help literature such as *The Courage to Heal* (Bass and Davis 1988). This book, which has had a significant influence on some survivors' narrative, suggests that if certain symptoms are present, and despite the lack of memory, sexual abuse is likely. Lindsay and Read propose that such literature 'inadvertently run a substantial risk of leading some readers to create illusionary memories or beliefs of childhood sexual abuse' (p.295).

Loftus (1993) cites a study conducted by herself, which is seen to add support to the concept of false memory by demonstrating that error in memory re-call is a common, and that non-existent, non-traumatic memories can be introduced into the minds of individuals. Without going into precise detail of this 'lost in the shopping mall' research, this type of research might be criticized as being indicative of that which creates 'false beliefs about memory, rather than false memory per se' (Sivers, Schooler and Freyd 2002, p.183). Consequently, this type of research can be considered misleading and, for feminists, a badly-timed diversion from their consciousness raising imperative. With reference to the work of others, Loftus (1993) is unconvinced about memories, such as those of Lizzie and Jean, where recollections are retrieved from earlier than age of three or four. In discussing the issue of memory, Loftus refers to the constructionist nature of memory and the influence of other sources when constructing what might be a false memory.

Lindsay and Read (1994) describe the following factors as relevant to memory distortions:

- Long delays between the proposed event and remembering.

- Childhood memories are susceptible to misleading suggestions.

- The authority of the source of suggestion.

- The perceived plausibility of the suggestion.

- The repetition of suggestion.

- Mental rehearsal of the event.

- Recovery therapies.

Furthermore, these authors may be considered to be dismissive of the emotional pain that accompanies the recovery of the abuse memories, suggesting instead that the distress reported by individuals around the time of recovery (and as described by some participants in this study), might be symptomatic of the process of 'coming to believe' that event, despite whether it did occur or not. Another argument that Lindsay and Read (1994) use to discredit recovered memory (particularly recall happening within therapy) is the significant numbers of subsequent retractors. This issue is problematic and potentially a 'red herring' in the sense that, under normal circumstances, there are an array of other factors that might predict a retraction, including the influence of other family members.

The issue raised by Jean, in relation to the credibility of the recovered memory with regard to police and the legal system, can carry some of the same elements of scepticism described above. More commonly, situations involving recovered memory of child sexual abuse have reached the courtroom in the US, where cases have been brought either by the survivor against the perpetrator, or by a retracting survivor or third party (perpetrator) against a therapist (Gothard and Cohen Ivker 2000). The role of the court is to establish historical truth, which is unlike the narrative truth described in previous sections and achieved through the healing process. Historical truth or recollections of the past, according to Spence (1982), may be marked by their disconnected nature and visual quality. Consequently, a court might deem less reliable narrative which appears to have been 'worked over' in therapy. Whitfield (2001) describes some of the strategies used by a perpetrator's defence lawyer, within the courtroom situation, to elevate their position in the eyes of the jurors and discredit the testimony of the survivor. Before elaborating further on these strategies it is worth noting that many of these tactics can be applicable to the prosecution of historical cases where the complainant has continuous or partial recall. They may also be relevant for the general public when assessing the overall validity of a narrative involving child sexual abuse, a factor that Lyn alludes to when talking about the general plausibility of her narrative for others.

Research indicates that often a defence lawyer/defendant will submit factors relating to his (her) general character, such as being a church-goer or a trusted community figure, in order to increase their credibility (Whitfield 2001). Whitfield suggests that they will present themselves as victim to the 'implanters of false memories,' i.e. the therapists, the media, the books. The testimony of the survivor, by contrast, will be undermined by attempts to call into question their mental health. Whitfield rightly argues that, quite often, emotional destabilization accompanies recovered memories (as can be observed in participants' quotes in the previous section of this chapter), which can then be used to this effect. The victim's narrative may also be criticized for being unable to offer corroborative evidence, such as eyewitness testimony or physical signs; a factor which clinicians appreciate is seldom apparent.

Expert witness testimony is commonly taken from individuals that are associated with the False Memory Syndrome Foundation. Whitfield (2001) suggests that these witnesses, who are generally not clinicians, offer their own versions of published research. They might demonstrate limited understanding of the psychological processes that serve to protect a survivor's integrity. Whitfield also describes how incidents that could be perceived to be quite extreme, such as satanic and ritualistic abuse, are used as comparative substance to add an air of depreciation to the subject of recovered memory. The reality of the situation is that research data illustrate that satanic and ritualistic abuse are, clearly, an actuality for some children, and that amidst this incomprehensible adult behaviour children can develop dissociative behaviours to cope with these extreme abuses (Scott, 1998), which may also include amnesia. For women like Jean, whose sexual abuse is consistent with ritualistic practices, and who witnessed events that some would consider to be extreme (but that others, particularly disabled people, would know to be highly likely) her experience sits within a societal discourse of disbelief, which exceeds an individual's own tendency for narrative scrutiny.

Whitfield (2001) proposes that attempts to redefine dissociative amnesia as a 'memory problem' and the appearance of a false memory defence signifies one of the most powerful attempts to deny the presence of child sexual abuse in society. The push towards pathologization is further reflected in the addition of the word 'syndrome' to the phenomenon of false memory. It is yet another ploy designed to undermine the voices of women struggling to establish their narrative truth (Saraga and Macleod 1997). Feminism, as already indicated, identifies this discourse as another form of counterattack against women and their attempts to threaten the power structure of the nuclear family. Symptomatic of this concern, according to Gaarder (2000), has been the systematic depreciation of anything female, but more notably the survivors, the therapists, the mothers and feminism itself.

Chloe raises, in her quotes, the subject of believability, both in terms of the issues created by her impairment and her general experiences of being parented. This meant that when she did encounter supportive questioning by the police, with regard to her experience of extra-familial abuse, she found it difficult to reconcile their approach with her own personal experiences. Notwithstanding the many obstacles faced by particular groups of disabled women when making a police statement (Keilty and Connelly, 2001), the result for Chloe, when faced with a positive police interview experience, was disbelief that these professionals took her abuse allegations seriously.

CONCLUSION

For children, generally, research indicates that the beginning of an ability to produce narrative that reflects an understanding of the self occurs between the ages of two to four years (Jenkins 2004). A trauma experience, such as child sexual abuse, seriously undermines the child's ability to use the usual function of narrative to process the experience (Neimeyer and Stewart 1996) as it is not within the realms of their developmental capabilities. This is illustrated in the first quote from Josh, with the second highlighting the consequence of 'narrative blockage' for the development of the child's larger narrative:

> The first time it happened I just couldn't collate it, I just couldn't work out what was happening, I had no experience of that, I had no knowledge of it, all that blood, all that damage, and I think you switch off, it's too much. (Josh)

> I went to school but I don't remember much about school, I don't know much about those early years because for the simple reason that there was so much trauma going on in other places. When I look back, I can see that I wasn't so concerned about my disability because I was so wrapped up in the abuse, whereas if I hadn't have had the abuse then my focus might have been solely on the disability. (Josh)

Within this chapter it becomes apparent that when the usual defence mechanisms (dissociation) become less necessary and when external triggers are prevalent, the unprocessed sexual abuse narrative emerges, usually creating narrative chaos (Frank 1995), but generally requiring some attention in terms of its integration into the coherent whole. The 'wearing down' of dissociative defences, for some, resulted in the retrieval of other previously buried memories. For two participants, who had developed dissociative amnesia in childhood, although being aware that something was amiss, the piecing together of recovered, fragmentary sensory episodes created a narrative that contributed significantly to understanding previous thoughts, feelings and events. One participant raised an issue relevant to the interaction of impairment and abuse, which arose from dysfunctional family interactions and led to her own inability to recognize and validate her narrative truth.

The later and ongoing work undertaken by participants has included the reconstruction of the abuse narrative. Essentially, this has been achieved via involvement in therapeutic conversations, discussions with members of the nuclear and extended family and their consultation of medical records, which have provided an additional validating source. As well as an ability to construct a different and more empowering story, healing has also involved, for some, the acknowledgement of the losses inherent within their narrative. The desired end result for participants, which has been achieved by different participants to varying degrees, is the attainment of a coherent narrative that joins together previously dissociated material. From a position of being unable to, truly, make sense of past experiences and behaviours, narrative reconstruction has conferred an ability to reflect upon and evaluate the experience of abuse. As is apparent, the emphasis within this chapter has been on the participants' production of an abuse narrative, with disability taking secondary importance.

Finally, the analysis of 'narratives of the narrative' is underpinned by a 'politics of hope'. The context elaborated in these stories speaks to a shared foundation for a politics of hope. Barton (2001) writes:

> Hope is essential in the struggle for change. It involves a recognition of the unacceptable nature of present conditions and relations... It arises from within a social context characterized by unacceptable inequalities and discrimination. It is of paramount importance that hope is grounded in an informed understanding of the social conditions and relations of the past... (pp.3–4)

The process of narrative production, the telling of stories of abuse, can itself promote healing and encourage the development of an authentic sense of self. As we have seen, however, this process is neither easy nor linear.

Towards a
Non-Abusive Society

INTRODUCTION

This may be a difficult book to read and was certainly a difficult book to write. We return to our starting point. Love, intimacy, attachment connect us to each other and ourselves and, for many, define humanity. Abuse, sexual abuse, is the violation and distortion of connectedness with others and our selves, and defines inhumanity. As Doyle (2006) says, 'Working with abused children requires emotional resilience' (p.88). The major objective of this book was to give voice to the experiences of individuals who have been silenced by the experience of child sexual abuse, in the first instance, and then once again by societal discourse, which relegates the experiences and opinions of disabled people. Through the clear articulation of their ever-evolving personal narratives, the participants have extended our existing knowledge of this subject area and have offered unique perspectives, which require society's focused attention.

The participants, five of whom were women and two men, all told reconstructed stories of abuse based on a continuum of remembering (Fivush and Edwards 2004), with all of them feeling that the recovery process continues to this day. Different individuals identified themselves as being at different points in the healing process which can best be observed in the struggles that some individuals have with the limitations offered by the survivor identity and others have in dealing with the ongoing problem of breakthrough reliving experiences. For one participant, it was painful to even acknowledge that there was, indeed, some linkage between disability and child sexual abuse. One of the key features of these accounts is that, although they had all clearly suffered at the hands of perpetrators of sexual abuse, they had on the whole 'suffered in silence'. Theses narratives show how assiduously children will hide the abusive situation at home and how difficult it is for them to disclose any maltreatment. The accounts also show the violation generated through the experience of abuse. The depth of their suffering as children is clear.

There are two sections to this concluding chapter. The first attempts to weave together the complex relationship between disability and sexual abuse. Despite the fact that each participant's circumstances differed in a variety of ways, we endeavour to highlight the key pressure points where disability and sexual abuse interacted and difficulties were exaggerated. This will be achieved by drawing out the specificities of the relationship for each of the individuals concerned, the violation of childhood and the distortions evident in self-blaming, disassociations, denial, isolation and confusion. This section of the conclusion includes both current adult perceptions of childhood experiences and the problems that the experiences are seen to create later, with regard to identity formation and narrative production. The second section of the conclusion sets out some of the key possible repercussions of this research for current policy and practice within education, social and health care provision.

DISABILITY AND CHILD SEXUAL ABUSE: 'THE DOUBLE WHAMMY'

Each of the narratives in this text is powerful in its own right. They are distinct accounts, however some commonalities do emerge. Doyle (2006) documents five accounts of victims of childhood sexual abuse. She draws on Erikson's (1965) theory of stages of development to analyze the distortions of development in these accounts. She states:

> The alternative progression results in the acquisition of a sense of basic mistrust, shame/doubt, guilt, inferiority, role confusion, isolation, stagnation and despair. (p.57)

It is clear, as summarized below, that such psychological factors reso-
nate through the participants' narrative in this text. It is clear too,
however, that such psychological factors do not capture the full story,
if indeed it is possible to capture it in full. 'The double whammy',
the complex interaction of disability and childhood sexual abuse,
is ingrained in these narratives, further distorting the distortion of
development, and crossing the divide between the psychological, or
personal, and the political, or social. Furthermore, these are the narratives of adult survivors of childhood abuse. They ring with resilience. These stories do reflect on psychological effects for the victim,
but also the questioning and challenging of the violence perpetrated
on victims; questions of why. As is evident in the following examples
from the participants' narratives, self-blaming can be the key to the
generation of distorted development.

Several of the women perceived themselves, as children, to be a
'problem' or a 'burden' to their families. Jean saw this problematic
identity reflected in the visible pain her mother experienced when
dealing with a child whose body conflicted with an idealized norm
and who required medical interventions. May saw, and was told by
her mother, that her 'problem status' had contributed to the breakdown of her parents' relationship early on in May's life. She also
felt that it was probably responsible for her subsequent institutionalization in a residential school. For Lyn, her parents' difficulties in
accepting their child's impairment manifested itself in their encouraging her to hide her hearing aid, in the same way that her mother
disguised the fact that she had a missing limb. The imperative was
to underplay any sense of difference and Lyn described feeling guilty
and apologetic, within her family, a large percentage of the time.

The sense of indebtedness created in May by her family, who
later sought her return from residential education, was one of the factors that precluded her ability to disclose her subsequent sexual abuse
by her stepfather. In Lyn's situation, she believed that her de-valued
position within her family led to a personal belief that she deserved
to be sexually abused and that this was something that she could
do well, by comparison to a non-disabled peer who was also being
abused but, unlike Lyn, was failing to function in the school setting.
Josh, who did not talk about feeling particularly de-valued in his
family in relation to his disability status, believes that, because of his
need for personal assistance with intimate care tasks, his impairment

provided the necessary opportunities for sexual and physical abuse to occur. This was a view also shared by May who required physiotherapy from family members. Later, Josh's impairment fulfilled the criteria for his placement in a residential school. This was used as a method of dealing with his mother and doctor's suspicions of sexual abuse and was felt, by Josh, to have deprived him of an appropriate level of education. Additionally, this placement also exposed him to further sexual abuse by an older child resident. As a child, a relationship was probably being formed, in his mind, between impairment, punishment and child abuse. Additionally, May made linkage between institutionalization and an inability to disclose child sexual abuse and medical objectifying procedures and the creation of the potential for later sexual victimization.

Thomas, who had learning difficulties, believed that his stepfather singled him out for sexual abuse because he was perceived to be unable to offer the same level of resistance as his stepbrothers and stepsisters. Some of these siblings, he later found out, were also being abused. For Thomas, and as is to be expected, the sexual abuse exacerbated his learning difficulties. Chloe felt that her family circumstances illustrated how the pressures associated with an undiagnosed and unsupported impairment can easily lead to a significant deterioration in the parent–child relationship. In her case, she contended that this was responsible for her emotional availability, her need to seek out adult stimulation outside the home environment and her subsequent involvement in a paedophile ring. Chloe also argued that her impairment and associated difficulties with memory could have singled her out as a suitable target for paedophiles. Similarly, Lyn felt that her difficulties with communication could have provided a similar function for the extra-familial abuse that she also experienced by a family friend.

Both Lizzie and Jean had recovered their memories of child sexual abuse from a previous state of dissociative amnesia. Prior to the recovery of their memories, both spoke of a significant degree of emotional turmoil within their lives, with Lizzie attributing some of these emotional difficulties to the effects of disablism both within the school setting, where she was excluded by her peers, and subsequently within her work environment. Both Lizzie and Jean felt that the recovered memory helped them to make sense of previous life experiences and, for Jean, it provide the impetus for trying to achieve some degree of connectedness within her emotional world. Lizzie, who spoke of witnessing other non-disabled children also being abused on the same hospital ward, felt that she was not singled out specifically because of her impairment, but, rather, because of her availability. Jean, on the other hand, felt the opposite and believed that some of her abuser's 'purging' type behaviours were symptomatic of what disability represented for the clergy within the Catholic Church. For other members of staff, she believed that their abusive behaviour and, in one instance, their life-taking actions were associated with the low value that they attached to disabled children's lives.

For all of the participants, identity formation and identity enactment had been a complex and confusing matter. Similar to the methods used by non-disabled children, they all employed a series of dissociative behaviours to deal with the feelings generated by the abuse experience, either at the time that it was happening or after the event. These behaviours are understandable expressions of pain and confusion to a dangerous family environment (Summit 1983; Young 1992). Jean's views draw particular attention to one key dynamic that may be operating for some sexually abused disabled children. Already having to contend with the notion of a 'bad body' created by the experience of disability, their feelings are compounded by the sexual abuse experience. The abuse experience aggravates their negative perceptions of their body and its worth, and further compromises their emotional and psychological well-being.

Despite this, inherently, disadvantaged starting position all participants continue to successfully 'carve out' a series of identities, many of which are seen to have an empowering influence on their lives. For both Lizzie and Chloe, their personal and political beliefs offer validating perspectives that counter any tendency to individualize the issue of child sexual abuse. For Chloe, in particular, the understanding gained from the social model of disability and the associated concept of oppression has been readily applied, with positive effect, to her experiences of abuse. Some participants, such as Thomas, wholeheartedly embrace the survivor identity, feeling that it offers an accurate description of the challenges he has faced and the achievements that have been made. Lyn, on the other hand, feels that certain identities can be conflicting in nature, with the societal discourse that surrounds the issue of impairment creating some opposition to the acquisition of yet another stigmatized identity, i.e. the survivor identity.

Forging intimate sexual relationships has been problematic for both male and female participants. Some heterosexual females described the difficulties they encountered when trying to pursue a relationship, in the first instance, or the risk they faced of meeting abusive men. For May, in adolescence, she describes how her experience of asexual objectification conflicted with the reality of having to provide cover stories for any potential pregnancy. In adulthood, she experienced a series of violent partners, but this factor is felt to be an emotional consequence of child sexual abuse and her inability to prioritize her own needs. Furthermore, disability has the potential to complicate the matter further and widen power differentials. In relation to heterosexual men, the main issue was centred on the resolution of a homosexual experience with a heterosexual identity. For many of the participants, recovery has also involved the creation of a narrative identity and an ability to produce narrative of the self, which demonstrated a capacity to reflect upon and evaluate their experience (Royce Baerger and McAdams 1999).

The social model of disability is, for us, central to understanding the relationship between disability and sexual abuse. The social model, which by the reorganization of language (Swain and French 2000) and the highlighting of oppressive forces in society that work against us (Barnes 1996), reconstructs the meaning attached to disability in western society. The participants' narratives illustrate the range of ways in which disabled children are invalidated by societal attitudes and practices. This invalidating discourse has been shown to create dysfunctional organizational cultures and practices that work, often in an insidious fashion, to marginalize or negate disabled children's emotional well-being, so placing them in situations of unacceptable risk. Clearly, extended periods of hospitalization and residential education are examples of such practices, where the parent–child bond is compromised and there is the possibility of encountering paedophiles.

Equally, the accounts illustrate how devaluing societal discourse can impact on family life, influencing the attitudes and behaviour of some parents, so creating, for that child, feelings of insecurity and indebtedness. These feelings can then manifest themselves in the disabled child's inability to 'speak out' about the abuse experience.

They can also precipitate a need for others to indiscriminately seek out adult attention outside the home, placing them at risk of extra-familial abuse. The social model reframes the traditional perspective on this subject by rejecting an individualizing approach that links causality to the perceived shortcomings created by impairment and posits, instead, a perspective that reformulates the issue in terms of the broader social context of invalidation and indifference to disabled children's welfare (Calderbank 2000).

Using a narrative methodology, this project has prioritized personal experience and has highlighted the ways in which disability, impairment and child sexual abuse have interacted and shaped the lives of the participants concerned. As a result of the combined impact of these entities, it has paid particular attention to the embodiment and expression of emotional pain for these individuals. The methodological approach therefore accords with the writings of disabled feminists who argue that 'the personal is political' (Morris 1992) and has demonstrated, through the deconstruction of participants' narrative, that the political dimensions of the story inevitably reveal themselves. The research adds to the small, but growing, body of work written by disabled people about the experiences and opinions of other disabled people.

The accounts problematize the victim–survivor dichotomy that pervades child protection literature, by demonstrating that these identities have the potential to become limiting and oppressive categorizations. The participants in this study were clearly survivors, but tended to oscillate between these categories depending on the triggers prevalent in their immediate environment. It was possible for them, using this limiting discourse, to be 'survivors' one day and 'not quite survivors' the next. This debate highlights the possible limiting number of identities available to individuals who have lived through this type of experience.

The accounts also draw attention to the complications implicit in being a disabled survivor of child sexual abuse. As illustrated, the usual difficulties of formulating an identity and constructing a narrative are aggravated by the experience of disability. Much of the general child abuse research takes the form of prevalence studies, which use a quantitative methodology and the complexities of individual experiences are less frequently described. This text attempts to extend the parameters of feminist debate and the theorization of the body by positing disabled women/young people as individuals who can experience both asexual objectification and sexual violation simultaneously, potentially reinforcing a 'bad body' identity and a sense of further psychological disruption.

IMPLICATIONS FOR POLICY AND PRACTICE

We have not specifically directed this text towards people who work with children, adults who have been sexually abused, or adults who work with disabled children. We hope it will reach a wide audience. We approached the book believing that these stories of sexual abuse by disabled people touch upon us all. They reach deeply into what it means to be human, into our understandings of humanity and the society in which we live. We have prioritized these narratives and they are the core of the book.

Nevertheless, engaging with the complex narratives of disabled survivors offers a lucid appraisal of the consequences for the individual concerned and the liberation of the voices of a previously silenced and de-valued sector of society. The narratives also offer a solid base for challenging current policy and practice, mirroring some of the previously expressed concerns of disability writers (Morris 1999; Shakespeare 1996a). They add weight to the argument that disabled children's family circumstances and care requirements can place them at an increased risk of abuse. This issue, undoubtedly, requires more focused attention by those invested with the responsibility to monitor and promote disabled children's well-being. This is broad, including investigative processes and procedures, therapeutic work, child protection work, work with individual abused children, work with adult survivors and work with families. This would require another book. Here we can only offer a few starting points generated by these narratives and the research process itself.

The first rings through the participants' narratives: the process of developing storytelling in a context in which the story is believed and valued. In this project a narrative approach provided the necessary flexibility to capture the depth and richness of these individuals' life stories. These stories have required a re-evaluation and reconstruction of the abuse memories and the relinquishing of any possible residual feelings of blame and responsibility. Some participants' healing has involved a re-working of the losses that they perceive were incurred by the experience of child sexual abuse. Some of these restorative stories also involved a formal therapeutic relationship and others describe the nurturing of their neglected 'child self' by, for instance, the purchase of children's toys; a developmental period which was eclipsed by abuse. Jean and Josh spoke of their loss of identity or their loss of self, with both being involved in reparative work involving such things as self-portraits, the use of mirrors, repositioning of childhood photographs and their involvement in the narrative research process. A number of participants are actively involved in re-writing their experiences in story format or poetry.

The process of being able to tell or write this reconfigured narrative has been precipitated, for most participants, by circumstances that have permitted or, sometimes, forced their engagement with a previously dissociated lifestyle and an incoherent narrative. This re-engagement process created, for many, extremes of emotional destabilization and a degree of narrative suspension (Frank 1995).

Some of the participants' stories include tales of problematic relationships with their birth families, where sexual abuse created tensions and conflicts. Thomas's mother, for instance, has chosen to dismiss her adult child's abuse narrative and idealize, instead, her deceased partner and former paedophile. May's mother, who was aware of the abuse at the time of its occurrence, continues to deny her daughter's reality creating, for May, a continuing sense of worthlessness and a fear of confronting her sister in case May's childhood silence facilitated her sister's abuse. Other participants' mothers have pledged their support, and siblings have responded by either sharing their abuse stories or burying the secret even further. This range of family reactions, however, has not deterred participants from continuing to vocalize their narratives with some degree of determination.

In the accounts in this text, the two experiences of recovered memory required a necessity to consider the recovered memory/false memory debate. This issue of 'truth' required a distinction to be made between narrative truth, which is formulated within a therapeutic context, and historical truth, which carries some factual and legalistic connotation. These two individuals reconstructed their abuse narratives from fragmented sensory episodes and, despite the varying reactions of close family members to their disclosures, Lizzie and Jean's clarity about the validity of these memories have never faltered. This is a factor which may have some relevance to the general societal invalidation of recovered memory and may, or may not, have some relevance to the abuse narratives of disabled women who have to state their case louder, clearer and with more voracity than others. Nevertheless, where the overlap between disability and narrative disclosure becomes more apparent is in the difficulties that Chloe experienced in believing and validating her own experience and memories of sexual abuse.

Narrative, or narrative therapy, is a key strategy promoted within contemporary social work theory and practice (Peace 2002). As McDonald (2006) states:

> It largely involves creating real alliances between practitioners and 'clients' (both temporary and permanent) in which alternative stories can be told and in which alternative strategies can be both imagined and developed. (p.182)

Such alliances provide relationships which are the context for developing accounts of sexual abuse, with all the embarrassment, fear, anger and emotional sensitivity this can entail; relationships characterized by trust, unconditional acceptance, empathy and genuineness. Inherent within the above notion of narrative, though not specifically a key theme of these accounts, is the importance of interpersonal communication.

The availability of effective support for families of disabled children, with both diagnosed and undiagnosed impairments, is obviously of crucial importance. A review of relevant literature also suggests that parents may have to fight for the services they need for their children (Duncan 2003), which inevitably means that the services which children receive may be dependent on how articulate and willing or able to fight their parents are, and unavailable to the families of the participants in this project. Support from individual members of staff and professionals can make a difference in the lives of disabled children and young people and their families (Audit Commission 2003). However, mothers in Read's study (2000) stated that contact with services was some of the most difficult and stressful experiences that they had. The inherent danger for the families in the study is that the private lives of families with disabled children and young people become more public as they are subject to the scrutiny of professionals and service providers (Runswick Cole 2007).

Watson, Abbott and Townsley (2007) highlight the need for professionals to listen to each individual child who has unique needs. Kennedy (2002) examines communication problems, not all of which are readily anticipated, such as the difficulties she encountered when her own sign language was different from that used by a deaf child she was supporting. In relation to child protection matters, she recommends a communication assessment at the outset as well as the use of facilitators, and the co-working of disability and child protection workers. This inevitably requires time and flexibility on the part of the professional, and it should be noted that constraints of 'the system' such as lack of resources can be as frustrating for professionals as it is for parents.

Read and Clements (2001) provide a succinct and pertinent summary:

> Across almost two decades, a wide range of literature and official reports records considerable levels of unmet need and substantial parental dissatisfaction with many services. Further, it has been shown that parents have to be extremely active and persistent in order to gain access to what they regard as appropriate information and provision. (p.35)

Dominelli (2009), along with many others, notes that disabled children have been, and continue to be, abused, including sexual abuse, by so-called 'carers' in organizations of all kinds, including residential establishments. She tells us that, 'Institutional abuse occurs when an organization does not discharge its duty of care appropriately or as a deliberate act of exploitation' (p.43). The periodic scandals provide ample evidence of serious abuse by 'carers' such as the sexual abuse scandal in Clwyd (Waterhouse 2000). There is evidence, too, as we have seen, in the narratives in this project.

As far as hospital settings are concerned, the main issue raised relates to the culture of the organization. An improvement in existing systems is indicated which facilitates the identification and management of unhealthy cultures that exhibit objectifying characteristics. For many of these issues, relevant to both local authorities and health settings, the problems can begin to be addressed by disability training, founded in a social model approach, which demands a degree of reflexivity and a challenging of personal belief systems. Disability equality training must remain central to challenging institutional disablism across all institutional settings, such as the need for disability training in mainstream schools which genuinely promotes an inclusive ideology.

Finally, a good starting point rests with those professionals who both assist in the birth of a disabled child and then support parenting back in the home environment. Similar to Thomas (1998), we would argue that much could be achieved here by challenging the 'tragedy model' of disability and promoting a more positive and empowering model of parenting for disabled children.

A FINAL WORD

We recognize, of course, that we have only touched upon the surface of the implications of the sexual abuse of disabled children for policy and practice. To bring the book to a close, however, we must return to the words of our participants which we have attempted to prioritize throughout. We began this Conclusion chapter by pointing to the arduous experiences for us as authors and possibly you as readers of the violation of children, childhood and selves, the affront to humanity that such accounts entail, and the resilience required for survival.

Central, however, has been the experiences of the participants in opening up and documenting these gruelling accounts and their personal strengths and resilience in doing so. We have selected three quotes (used in previous chapters) to provide the most basic overview of the picture painted by these accounts, moving from the experiences of stolen childhood to the reaffirmation of self through narrating such violating experiences:

> My childhood was 'nicked', it was stolen, I was thrust into an adult world before I ever should have been, it went, it was gone from the age of five or six, so now I'm trying to make up for it. (Josh)

> The process of uncovering the repressed memory is a process of survival in itself. I think that many people do carry on their lives without recovering the memory and that's maybe okay for those people. But I realized that I needed to live my life, I wanted to have feelings and I didn't want to live this dispassionate, disconnected kind of life. That is happening for me, and

again it's slow, but I'm getting there and I do cry now, I am able to do it, and I am much more in touch with my feelings. (Jean)

Having it (the narrative) all in one place is useful because when you have counselling you deal with separate bits at a time. I know people say that (by breaking it down) you can see how that relates to that, but I don't think that it sinks in the same as having it in front of you. (May)

We can only hope that these accounts will empower disabled people to disclose and recount experiences of their violation. We also hope that they will empower those who would support the developments of such narratives and the creation of a society in which the double whammy is part of the history of man's inhumanity to man.

References

Ablon, J. (1990) 'Ambiguity and difference: families with dwarf children.' *Social Science and Medicine 30*, 8, 879–887.

Aldridge, M. and Wood, J. (1999) 'Interviewing child witnesses with disabilities: a survey of police officers in England and Wales. *Police Journal January*, 33–42.

Andrews, B., Brewin, C., Ochera, J., Morton, J. *et al.* (2000) 'The timing, triggers and qualities of recovered memories in therapy.' *British Journal of Clinical Psychology 39*, 11–26.

Appleby, Y. (1994) 'Out in the margins.' *Disability and Society 9*, 1, 19–31.

Araji, S. and Finkelhor, D. (1986) 'Abusers: a review of the literature.' In D. Finkelhor, S. Araji, L. Baron, A. Browne, S. Doyle Peters and G. Wyatt (eds) *A Sourcebook on Child Sexual Abuse*. Newbury Park, CA: Sage Publications.

Armstrong, L. (2000) 'What happened when women said incest.' In C. Itzin (ed.) *Home Truths about Child Sexual Abuse: Influencing Policy and Practice, a Reader*. London: Routledge.

Atkinson, R. (1998) *The Life Story Interview*. London: Sage Publications.

Audit Commission (2003) *Services for Disabled Children: A Review of Services for Disabled Children and their Families*. London: Audit Commission Public Sector Briefing.

Avery, D. (1999) 'Talking tragedy: identity issues in the parental story of disability.' In M. Corker and S. French (eds) *Disability Discourse*. Buckingham: Open University.

Bacon, H. (2003) 'Attachment, trauma and child sexual abuse: an exploration.' In S. Richardson and H. Bacon (eds) *Creative Responses to Child Sexual Abuse: Challenges and Dilemmas*. London: Jessica Kingsley Publishers.

Bacon, H. and Richardson, S. (2001) 'Attachment theory and child abuse: an overview of the literature for practitioners.' *Child Abuse Review 10*, 377–397.

Baginsky, M. (2003) 'Newly qualified teachers and child protection.' *Child Abuse Review 12*, 119–127.

Bagley, C. and Thurston, W.E. (1996) *Understanding and Preventing Child Sexual Abuse: Male Victims, Adolescents, Adult Outcomes and Offender Treatment*. Aldershot: Arena.

Baker, C. (2002) *Female Survivors of Sexual Abuse*. Hove: Brunner-Routledge.

Barker-Callo, S. (2001) 'Adult reports of child and adult attributions of blame for childhood sexual abuse: predicting adult adjustment and suicidal behaviours in females.' *Child Abuse and Neglect 25*, 1329–1341.

Barnes, C. (1992) *Disabling Imagery and the Media: An Exploration of the Principles for Media Representations of Disabled People*. The British Council of Organisations of Disabled People. Derby: Ryburn Publishing.

Barnes, C. (1996) 'Theories of disability and the origins of the oppression of disabled people in western society.' In L. Barton (ed.) *Disability and Society: Emerging Issues and Insights*. Essex: Addison Wesley Longman.

Barnes, C. (2001) '"Emancipatory" disability research: Project or process?' Public lecture at City Chambers, Glasgow, 24 October 2001. Available at www.leeds.ac.uk/disability-studies/archiveuk/Barnes/glasgow%20lecture.pdf, accessed 15 September 2009.

Barnes, C. (2003) 'What a difference a decade makes: reflections on doing "emancipatory" disability research.' *Disability and Society 18*, 1, 3–17.

Barton, L. (2001) 'Disability, struggle and the politics of hope.' In L. Barton (ed.) *Disability, Politics and the Struggle for Change*. London: David Fulton.

Bass, E. and Davis, L. (1988) *The Courage to Heal*. New York: Harper and Row.

BBC News (2004) 'Huntley case: Key mistakes made.' Available at http://news.bbc.co.uk/1/hi/uk/3826355.stm, accessed 2 October 2008.

Beckett, R., Beech, A., Fisher, D. and Fordham, A. (1994) *Community-based Treatment for Sex Offenders: An Evaluation of Seven Treatment Programmes*. London: Home Office Publications Unit.

Beech, A., Fisher, D. and Beckett, R. (1998) *Step 3: An Evaluation of the Prison Sex Offender Treatment Programme*. London: Home Office Publications Unit.

Begum, N. (1996) 'General practitioners' role in shaping disabled women's lives.' In C. Barnes and G. Mercer (eds) *Exploring the Divide: Illness and Disability*. Leeds: The Disability Press.

Bell, P. (2003) '"I'm a good mother really!" Gendered parenting roles and responses to the disclosure of incest.' *Children and Society 17*, 126–136.

Benjamin Darling, R. (2003) 'Towards a model of changing disability identities: a proposed typology and research agenda.' *Disability and Society 18*, 7, 881–895.

Berliner, L. and Elliot, D (2002) 'Sexual abuse of children.' In J. Myers, L. Berliner, J. Briere, C. Terry Hendrix, C. Jenny and T. Reid (eds) *The APSAC Handbook on Child Maltreatment*. Thousand Oaks, CA: Sage Publications.

Bernard, C. (2001) *Constructing Lived Experiences: Representations of Black Mothers in Child Sexual Abuse Discourse*. Aldershot: Ashgate Publishing.

Blumstein, P. (2001) 'The production of selves in personal relationships.' In A. Branaman (ed.) *Self and Society*. Oxford: Blackwell Publishers.

Bohan, J. (2002) 'Sex differences and/in the self: classic themes, feminist variations, postmodern challenges.' *Psychology of Women Quarterly 26*, 74–88.

Bolen, R. (2002) 'Child sexual abuse and attachment theory: are we rushing headlong into another controversy?' *Journal of Child Sexual Abuse 11*, 1, 95–124.

Bolen, R. and Scannapieco, M. (1999) 'The prevalence of child sexual abuse: a corrective analysis.' *Social Services Review 73*, 3, 281–313.

Bolen, R., Russell, D. and Scannapieco, M. (2000) 'Child sexual abuse prevalence a review and re-analysis of relevant studies.' In C. Itzen (ed.) *Home Truths about Child Sexual Abuse: Influencing Policy and Practice: A Reader*. London: Routledge.

Boney-McCoy, S. and Finkelhor, D. (1995) 'Prior victimisation: a risk factor for child sexual abuse and for PTSD-related symptomatology among sexually abused youth.' *Child Abuse and Neglect 19*, 12, 1401–1421.

Boone James, J., Liem, J. and Gateley O'Toole, J. (1993) 'In search of resilience in adult survivors of childhood sexual abuse – linking outlets for power motivation to psychological health.' In R. Josselson and A. Lieblich (eds) *The Narrative Study of Lives*. London: Sage Publications.

Booth, T. and Booth, W. (1997) 'Making connections: a narrative study of adult children of parents with learning difficulties.' In C. Barnes and G. Mercer (eds) *Doing Disability Research*. Leeds: The Disability Press.

Bourdon, L. and Skinner Cook, A. (1993) 'Losses associated with sexual abuse: therapist and client perceptions.' *Journal of Child Sexual Abuse 2*, 4, 69–82

Bower, G. and Sivers, H. (1998) 'Cognitive impact of traumatic events.' *Development and Psychopathology 10*, 4, 625–653.

Bowlby, J. (1969) *Attachment and Loss. Volume 1: Attachment*. New York: Basic Books.

Bowlby, J. (1973) *Attachment and Loss. Volume 2: Separation, Anxiety and Anger*. New York: Basic Books.

Bowlby, J. (1979) *The Making and Breaking of Affectional Bonds*. London: Tavistock.

Bowlby, J. (1980) *Attachment and Loss. Volume 3: Loss, Sadness and Depression*. New York: Basic Books.

Bowlby, J. (1982) 'Attachment and loss: retrospect and prospect.' *The American Journal of Orthopsychiatry 52*, 664–678.

Brazier, M. (1998) 'Wider public interest may come before issues of confidentiality' *British Medical Journal 316*, 3 January, 57.

Brewin, C. and Andrews, B. (1998) 'Recovered memories of trauma: phenomenology and cognitive mechanisms.' *Clinical Psychology Review 18,* 8, 949–970.

Brewin, C., Dalgleish, T. and Joseph, S. (1996) 'A dual representation theory of posttraumatic stress disorder.' *Psychological Review 103,* 4, 670–686.

Bricher, G. (2000) 'Disabled people, health professionals and the social model of disability: can there be a research relationship?' *Disability and Society 15,* 5, 781–793.

Briere, J. (1989) *Therapy for Adults Molested as Children: Beyond Survival.* New York: Springer Publishing.

Briere, J. and Conte, J. (1993) 'Self-reported amnesia for abuse in adults molested as children.' *Journal of Traumatic Stress 6,* 1, 21–31.

Brilleslijper-Kater, S. and Baartman, H. (2000) 'What do young children know about sex? Research on the sexual knowledge of children between the ages of 2 and 6 years.' *Child Abuse Review 9,* 166–182.

Brown, H. (1999) 'Vulnerable to abuse.' In J. Swain and S. French (eds) *Therapy and Learning Difficulties: Advocacy Participation and Partnership.* Oxford: Butterworth-Heinemann.

Brown, H., Stein, J. and Turk, V. (1995) 'The sexual abuse of adults with learning disabilities: report of a second two-year incidence survey.' *Mental Handicap Research 8,* 1, 3–24.

Browne, A. and Finkelhor, D. (1986) *A Sourcebook on Child Sexual Abuse.* London: Sage Publications.

Brownlow, C. and O'Dell, L. (2002) 'Ethical issues for qualitative research in on-line communities.' *Disability and Society 17,* 6, 685–694.

Bruner, J. (1990) *Acts of Meaning.* London: Harvard University Press.

Bruzy, S., Ault, A. and Segal, E. (1997) 'Conducting qualitative interviews with women survivors of trauma.' *AFFILIA 12,* 1, 76–83.

Burke, P. (2008) *Disability and Impairment: Working with Children and Families.* London: Jessica Kingsley Publishers.

Burke Draucker, C. (1992) *Counselling Survivors of Childhood Sexual Abuse.* London: Sage Publications.

Burkitt, I. (1998) 'Sexuality and gender identity: from a discursive to a relational analysis.' *Sociological Review 46,* 3, 483–503.

Butler, J. (1990) *Gender Trouble. Feminism and the Subversion of Identity.* London: Routledge.

Calderbank, R. (2000) 'Abuse and disabled people.' *Disability and Society 15,* 3, 521–534.

Campbell J. and Oliver, M. (1996) *Disability Politics: Understanding Our Past Changing Our Future.* London: Routledge.

Case, S. (2000) 'Refocusing on the parents: what are the social issues of concern for parents of disabled children?' *Disability and Society 15,* 2, 271–292.

Castor-Lewis, C. (1988) 'On doing research with adult incest survivors: some initial thoughts and considerations.' *Women and Therapy 7,* 7, 73–80.

Cawson, P., Wattam, C., Brooker, S. and Kelly, G. (2000) *Child Maltreatment in the United Kingdom: A Study of the Prevalence of Child Abuse and Neglect.* London: National Society for the Prevention of Cruelty to Children.

Children Act (1989) London: HMSO.

Chu, J., Frey, L., Ganzel, B. and Matthews, J. (1999) 'Memories of childhood abuse: dissociation, amnesia and corroboration.' *American Journal of Psychiatry 156,* 5, 749–755.

Clark, K. (1993) 'Seasons of light/seasons of darkness: the effects of burying and remembering traumatic sexual abuse on the self.' *Clinical Social Work Journal 21,* 1, 25–43.

Clark, L. (2003) 'Disabling comedy: only when we laugh.' University of Leeds Centre for Disability Studies Research Archive. Available at www.leeds.ac.uk/disability-studies/archiveuk/Clark,%20Laurence/clarke%20on%20comedy.pdf, accessed 15 September 2009.

Closs, A. (1998) 'Quality of life of children and young people with serious medical conditions.' In C. Robinson and K. Stalker (eds) *Growing up with Disability.* London: Jessica Kingsley Publishers.

Cooke, P. and Standen, P. (2002) 'Abuse and disabled children: hidden needs?' *Child Abuse Review 11,* 1–18.

Corker, M. (2003) 'Developing anti-disabling counselling practice.' In C. Lago and B. Smith (eds) *Anti-discriminatory Counselling Practice.* London: Sage Publications.

Cotterill, P. and Letherby, G. (1993) 'Weaving stories: personal autobiographies in feminist research.' *Sociology 27,* 1, 67–79.

Courtois, C. (1999) *Recollections of Sexual Abuse: Treatment Principles and Guidelines.* New York: W. W. Norton.

Crago, H. (1997) 'The "not to be opened" letter: family secrets, hidden knowledge and violated prohibitions.' *ANZJ Family Therapy 18,* 2, 99–108.

Craig, L., Browne, K. and Beech, A. (2008) *Assessing Risk in Sex Offenders.* Chichester: John Wiley and Sons.

Crisp, R. (2000) 'A qualitative study of the perceptions of individuals with disabilities concerning health and rehabilitation professionals.' *Disability and Society 15,* 2, 355–367.

Crosse, S. (1993) 'Incidence and prevalence.' In J. Plucker, K. Keeney and J. Atallo (eds) *Responding to Sexual Abuse of Children with Disabilities: Prevention, Investigation and Treatment. A Think Tank.* Huntsville: The National Resource Centre.

Crossley, M. (2000) *Introducing Narrative Psychology: Self, Trauma and the Construction of Meaning.* Buckingham: Open University Press.

Crow, L. (1996) 'Including all of our lives: renewing the social model of disability.' In C. Barnes and G. Mercer (eds) *Exploring the Divide: Illness and Disability.* Leeds: The Disability Press.

Crowley, S. (2000) *The Search for Autonomous Intimacy: Sexual Abuse and Young Women's Identity Development.* New York: Peter Lang.

Cunningham, C., Morgan, P. and McGucken, R. (1984) 'Down's syndrome: is dissatisfaction with diagnosis inevitable?' *Developmental Medicine and Child Neurology 26,* 33–39.

David, T. (1998) 'Child sexual abuse: when a doctor's duty to report abuse conflicts with a duty of confidentiality to the victim.' *British Medical Journal, 316,* 3 January, 55.

Davis, J. (2004) 'Disability and childhood: deconstructing the stereotypes.' In J. Swain, S. French, C. Barnes and C. Thomas (eds) *Disabling Barriers – Enabling Environments.* 2nd edition. London: Sage Publications.

Davis, J. and Watson, N. (2001) 'Where are the children's experiences? Analysing social and cultural exclusion in "special" and "mainstream" schools.' *Disability and Society 16,* 5, 671–687.

Deblinger, E., McLeer, S., Atkins, M., Ralphe, D. and Foa, E. (1989) 'Post-traumatic stress in sexually abused, physically abused and nonabused children.' *Child Abuse and Neglect 13,* 403–408.

Department of Health (1999) *Working Together to Safeguard Children: A Guide for Inter-agency Working to Safeguard and Promote the Welfare of Children.* London: HMSO.

Dhawan, S. and Marshall, W. (1996) 'Sexual abuse histories of sexual offenders.' *Sexual Abuse: A Journal of Research and Treatment 8,* 7–15.

Disch, E. (2001) 'Research as clinical practice: creating a positive research experience for survivors of sexual abuse by professionals.' *Sociological Practice: A Journal of Clinical and Applied Sociology 3,* 3, 221–239.

Dominelli, L. (2009) *Introducing Social Work.* Cambridge: Polity Press.

Dorries, B. and Haller, B. (2001) 'The news of inclusive education: a narrative analysis.' *Disability and Society 16,* 6, 871–891.

Douglas, M. (1966) *Purity and Danger: An Analysis of Concepts of Pollution and Taboo.* London: Routledge and Keegan Paul.

Doyle, C. (2006) *Working with Abused Children.* 3rd edition. Houndmills: Palgrave Macmillan.

Doyle Peters, S. Wyatt, G. and Finkelhor, D. (1986) 'Prevalence.' In D. Finkelhor, S. Araji, L. Baron, A. Browne, S. Doyle Peters and G. Wyatt (eds) *Sourcebook on Child Sexual Abuse.* Newbury Park, CA: Sage Publications.

Drake, R. (1996) 'A critique of the role of the traditional charities.' In L. Barton (ed.) *Disability and Society: Emerging Issues and Insight.* Essex: Addison Wesley Longman.

Duncan, N. (2003) 'Awkward customers? Parents and provisions for special educational needs.' *Disability and Society 18,* 3, 341–356,

Durham, A. (2003) *Young Men Surviving Child Sexual Abuse: Research Stories and Lessons for Therapeutic Practice.* Hoboken, NJ: John Wiley and Sons.

Eder, R. (1994) 'Comments on children's self-narratives.' In U. Neisser and R. Fivush (eds) *The Remembering Self.* Cambridge: Cambridge University Press.

Elliott, D. and Briere, J. (1995) 'Posttraumatic stress associated with delayed recall of sexual abuse: a general population study.' *Journal of Traumatic Stress 8,* 4, 629–647.

Elliott, M. (1993) 'What survivors tell us – an overview.' In M. Elliott (ed.) *Female Sexual Abuse of Children.* New York: The Guilford Press.

Elliott, M., Browne, K. and Kilcoyne, J. (1995) 'Child sexual abuse prevention: what offenders tell us.' *Child Abuse and Neglect 19,* 579–594.

Erikson, E. H. (1965) *Childhood and Society.* 2nd edition. Harmondsworth: Penguin.

Erooga, M. (2002) *Characteristics of Adult Sex Offenders.* NSPCC Inform: Adult Sex Offenders. Available at www.nspcc.org.uk/inform/research/briefings/adultsexoffenders_wda48227.html, accessed on 18/12/08.

Erwin, P. (2000) Intimate and caregiver violence against women with disabilities. Commissioned by: Battered Woman's Justice Project–Criminal Justice Office. Irvine, CA: Department of Criminology, Law and Society.

Etherington, K. (2000) *Narrative Approaches to Working with Adult Male Survivors of Child Sexual Abuse: The Clients', the Counsellor's and the Researcher's Story.* London: Jessica Kingsley Publishers.

Evans, W. and Maines, D. (1995) 'Narrative structures and the analysis of incest.' *Symbolic Interaction 18,* 3, 303–322.

Faller, K. (1990) *Understanding Child Sexual Maltreatment.* Beverley Hills, CA: Sage.

Farrants, J. (1998) 'The "false memory" debate: a critical review of the research on recovered memories of child sexual abuse.' *Counselling Psychology Quarterly 11,* 3, 229–238.

Feiring, C., Tasca, L. and Lewis, M. (1999) 'Age and gender differences in children and adolescents' adaptation to sexual abuse.' *Child Abuse and Neglect 23,* 2, 115–128.

Fergusson, D. and Mullen, P. (1999) *Childhood Sexual Abuse: An Evidence Based Perspective, Volume 40. Developmental Clinical Psychology and Psychiatry.* London: Sage.

Finkelhor, D. (1984) *Child Sexual Abuse: New Theory and Research.* New York: The Free Press.

Finkelhor, D and Russell, D. (1984) 'Women as perpetrators.' In D. Finkelhor (ed.) *Child Sexual Abuse: New Theory and Research.* New York: Free Press.

Firth, H., Balogh, R., Berney, T., Bretherton, K. Graham, S. and Whibley, S. (2001) 'Psychopathology of sexual abuse in young people with intellectual disabilities.' *Journal of Intellectual Disabilities 45,* 3, 194.

Fisher, D. (1994) 'Adult sex offenders: who are they? Why and how do they do it?' In T. Morrison, M. Erooga and R. Beckett (eds) *Sexual Offending against Children: Assessment and Treatment of Male Abusers.* London: Routledge.

Fivush, R. (1994) 'Constructing narrative, emotion, and self in parent–child conversations about the past.' In U. Neisser and R. Fivush (eds) *The Remembering Self: Construction and Accuracy in the Self-Narrative.* New York: Cambridge University Press.

Fivush, R. and Edwards, V. (2004) 'Remembering and forgetting childhood sexual abuse.' *Journal of Child Sexual Abuse 13,* 2, 1–19.

Fleming, J., Mullen, P., Sibthorpe, B. and Banner, G (1999) 'The long-term impact of childhood sexual abuse in Australian women.' *Child Abuse and Neglect 23,* 2, 145–159.

Flick, U. (1998) *An Introduction to Qualitative Research.* London: Sage Publications.

Flynn, M. (1987) 'Independent living arrangements for adults who are mentally handicapped.' In N. Malin (ed.) *Researching Community Care.* London: Croom Helm.

Frank, A. (1995) *The Wounded Storyteller: Body, Illness and Ethics.* Chicago: The University of Chicago Press.

Fraser, S. (1987) *My Father's House: A Memoir of Incest and Healing.* London: Virago Press Ltd.

Freedman, J. and Combs, G. (1996) 'The narrative metaphor and social constructionism: a postmodern world view.' In J. Freedman and G. Combs (eds) *Narrative Therapy: The Social Construction of Preferred Realities.* New York: W. W Norton.

Freedman, J. and Coombs, G. (1996) *Narrative Therapy: The Social Construction of Preferred Realities.* New York: W. W. Norton.

Freeman, M. (1999) 'Children are unbeatable.' *Children and Society 13,* 130–141.

Freeman, M. (2000) 'The future of children's rights.' *Children and Society 14,* 277–293..

French, S. (1994) 'Disabled people and professional practice.' In S. French (ed.) *On Equal Terms – Working With Disabled People.* Oxford: Butterworth-Heinemann.

French, S. (1996a) 'The attitudes of health professionals towards disabled people.' In G. Hales (ed.) *Beyond Disability*. London: Sage Publications Ltd.

French, S. (1996b) 'Out of sight, out of mind: the experience and effects of a "special residential school."' In J. Morris (ed.) *Encounters with Strangers: Feminism and Disability*. London: The Women's Press.

French, S and Swain, J. (2000) 'Institutional abuse: memories of a "special" school for visually impaired girls – a personal account.' In J. Bornat, R. Perks, P. Thompson and J. Walmsley (eds) *Oral History Health and Welfare*. London: Routledge.

French, S. (2004) 'Reflecting on ethical decision-making in therapy practice.' In J. Swain, J. Clark, K. Parry, S. French, and F. Reynolds (eds) *Enabling Relationships in Health and Social Care: A Guide for Therapists*. Oxford: Butterworth-Heinemann.

French, S. (ed.) (2006) *An Oral History of the Education of Visually Impaired People: Telling Stories of Inclusive Futures*. New York: The Edwin Mellen Press.

French Gilson, S. and Depoy, E. (2000) 'Multiculturalism and disability: a critical perspective.' *Disability and Society 15*, 2, 207–218.

Fromuth, M.E. (1986) 'The relationship of childhood sexual abuse with later psychological and sexual adjustment in a sample of college women.' *Child Abuse and Neglect 10*, 5–15.

Gaarder, E. (2000) 'Gender politics: the focus on women in the memory debates.' *Journal on Child Sexual Abuse 9*, 1, 91–106.

Gallagher, B. (1998) *Grappling with Smoke, Investigating and Managing Organised Child Sexual Abuse: A Good Practice Guide*. London: NSPCC.

Galvin, R. (2003) 'The paradox of disability culture: the need to combine versus the imperative to let go.' *Disability and Society 18*, 5, 675–690.

Ganzarain, R. and Buchele, B. (1987) 'Acting out during group psychotherapy for incest.' *International Journal of Group Psychotherapy 37*, 2, 185–200.

Garth, B. and Aroni, R. (2003) 'I value what you say: seeking the perspectives of children with disability, not just their parents.' *Disability and Society 18*, 5, 561–576.

Gelinas, D. (1983) 'The persisting negative effects of incest.' *Psychiatry 46*, 312–332.

Gerschick, T. and Miller, A. (1994) 'Coming to terms: masculinity and physical disability.' *Masculinities 2*, 1, 262–275.

Gilgun, J. (1994) 'Avengers, conquerors, playmates and lovers: roles played by child sexual abuse perpetrators.' *Families in Society: The Journal of Contemporary Human Services 75*, 467–480.

Gilgun, J. and Reiser, E. (1990) 'The development of sexual identity among men sexually abused as children.' *Families in Society: The Journal of Contemporary Human Services 71*, 515–523.

Gill, M. and Tutty, L. (1999) 'Male survivors of childhood sexual abuse: A qualitative study and issues for clinical consideration.' *Journal of Child Sexual Abuse 7*, 3, 19–33.

Glaser, D. (2002) 'Emotional abuse and neglect (psychological maltreatment): a conceptual framework.' *Child Abuse and Neglect 26*, 697–714.

Glaser, D. and Frosh, S. (1988) *Child Sexual Abuse*. Basingstoke: Macmillan Education.

Glaser, M., Kolvin, I., Campbell, D., Glaser, A., Leitch, I. and Farrelly, S. (2001) 'Cycles of child sexual abuse: links between being a victim and becoming a perpetrator.' *British Journal of Psychiatry 179*, 482–494.

Glasgow, D., Horne, L., Calam, R. and Cox, A. (1994) 'Evidence, incidence, gender and age in sexual abuse of children perpetrated by children: towards a developmental analysis of child sexual abuse.' *Child Abuse Review 3*, 196–210.

Goffman, E. (1961) *Asylums*. New York: Anchor Books.

Goffman, E. (1963) *Stigma: Notes on the Management of Spoiled Identities*. Englewood Cliffs, NJ: Prentice-Hall.

Goodley, D. (2000) *Self-advocacy in the Lives of People with Learning Difficulties*. Buckingham: Open University Press.

Gothard, S. and Cohen Ivker, N. (2000) 'The evolving law of alleged delayed memories of childhood sexual abuse.' *Child Maltreatment 5*, 2, 176–189.

Gottlieb, B. (1980) 'Incest: therapeutic interventions in a unique form of sexual abuse.' In C. Warner (ed.) *Rape and Sexual Assault*. German-town, Maryland: Aspen.

Green, S. (2003) 'What do you mean what's wrong with her? Stigma and the lives of families of children with disabilities.' *Sociology Online* April 2003.

Green Lister, P. (2002) 'Retrieving and constructing memory: the use of creative writing by women survivors of sexual abuse.' In C. Horrocks, K. Milnes, B. Roberts and D. Robinson (eds) *Narrative, Memory and Life Transitions.* Huddersfield: University of Huddersfield Press..

Grewal, I., Joy, S., Lewis, J., Swales, K. *et al.* (2002) *Disabled for Life? Attitudes Towards, and Experiences of, Disability in Britain.* London: National Centre for Social Research on behalf of the Department of Work and Pensions.

Groth, A., Hobson, W. and Garry, T. (1982) 'The child sexual molester: clinical observations.' In J. Conte, and D. Shore (eds) *Social Work and Child Sexual Abuse.* New York: Howarth Press.

Grue, L. and Tafjord Laerum, K. (2002) '"Doing motherhood": some experiences of mothers with physical disabilities.' *Disability and Society, 17,* 6, 671–683.

Hamer, M. (2002) *Incest: A New Perspective.* Cambridge: Polity Press.

Hanna, W. and Rogovsky, B. (1991) 'Women with disabilities: two handicaps plus.' *Disability, Handicap and Society 6,* 1, 49–63.

Harding, S. (1987) 'Introduction: is there a feminist methodology?' In S. Harding (ed.) *Feminism and Methodology.* Milton Keynes: Open University Press.

Harrison, P., Fulkerson, J. and Beebe, T. (1997) 'Multiple substance abuse among adolescent physical and sexual abuse victims.' *Child Abuse and Neglect 21,* 6, 529–539.

Hart, J. (1991) 'From property to person status: historical perspectives on children's rights.' *American Psychologist 46,* 53–59.

Hartt, J. and Waller, G. (2002) 'Child abuse, dissociation, and core beliefs in bulimic disorders.' *Child Abuse and Neglect 26,* 923–938.

Haugaard, J. (2000) 'The challenge of defining child sexual abuse.' *American Psychologist 55,* 9, 53–59.

Health Care Commission (2006) *Joint Investigation into the Provision of Services for People with Learning Disabilities at Cornwall Partnership NHS Trust.* London: Commission for Healthcare Audit and Inspection.

Heatherton, T. and Baumeister, R. (1991) 'Binge eating as an escape from self-awareness.' *Psychological Bulletin 110,* 86–108.

Herman, J. (1992) *Trauma and Recovery: From Domestic Abuse to Political Terror.* London: Pandora.

Higgins, M. (2006) *An Exploration of the Lives of Disabled People Sexually Abused in Childhood: The Double Whammy Effect.* Unpublished PhD Thesis.

Home Office (2002) *Achieving Best Evidence in Criminal Proceedings: Guidance for Vulnerable or Intimidated Witnesses, Including Children.* A Consultation Paper. London: HMSO.

Home Office (2005) *Public Protection Arrangements Working to Defend Communities.* Home Office press release. Available at http://press.homeoffice.gov.uk/press-releases/public-protection-working?version=1, accessed 15 September 2009.

Home Office and Department of Health (1992) *Memorandum of Good Practice on Video Interviewing with Child Witnesses for Criminal Proceedings.* London: The Stationary Office.

Hooper, C.-A. (1992) *Mothers Surviving Child Sexual Abuse.* London: Routledge.

Hooper, C.-A. and Humphreys, S. (1998) 'Women whose children have been sexually abused: reflections on a debate.' *British Journal of Social Work 28,* 565–580.

Hopkins, J. and Thompson, E. (1984) 'Loss and mourning in victims of rape and sexual assault.' In J. Hopkins (ed.) *Perspectives on Rape and Sexual Assault.* London: Harper and Row.

Hornby, G. (1992) 'A review of fathers' accounts of their experiences of parenting children with disabilities.' *Disability, Handicap and Society 7,* 4, 363–374.

Howland, C. and Rintala, D. (2001) 'Dating behaviors of woman with physical disabilities.' *Sexuality and Disability 19,* 1, 41–69.

Hughes, B. and Furgusson, R. (2000) *Ordering Lives: Family, Work and Welfare.* London: Routledge.

Hunt, P. (1981) 'Settling accounts with the parasite people: a critique of "a life apart" by E.J. Miller and G.V. Gwynne.' *Disability Challenge 1,* 37–50.

Itzin, C. (2000) 'Child sexual abuse and the radical feminist endeavour: an overview.' In C. Itzin (ed.) *Home Truths About Child Sexual Abuse: Influencing Policy and Practice: A Reader.* London: Routledge.

Jacobsen Wren, L. (2003) 'Trauma: conscious and unconscious meaning.' *Clinical Social Work Journal 31,* 2, 123–137.

Jaudes, P. and Diamond, L. (1983) 'The handicapped child and child abuse.' In *Child Abuse and Neglect 9*, 341–347.

Jenkins, R. (2004) *Social Identity*. London: Routledge.

Jennings, K. (1993) 'Female child molesters: a review of the literature.' In M. Elliot (ed.) *Female Sexual Abuse of Children*. New York: The Guilford Press.

Johnson, D., Pike, J. and Chard, K. (2001) 'Factors predicting PTSD, depression and dissociative severity in female treatment-seeking childhood sexual abuse survivors.' *Child Abuse and Neglect 25*, 179–198.

Karpel, M. (1980) 'Family secrets: (i.) Conceptual and ethical issues in the relational context; (ii.) Ethical and practical considerations in therapeutic management.' *Family Process 19*, September, 295–306.

Keilty, J. and Connelly, G. (2001) 'Making a statement: an exploratory study of the barriers facing women with an intellectual disability when making a statement about sexual assault to the police.' *Disability and Society 16*, 2, 273–291.

Kelly, L., Regan, L. and Burton, S. (1991) *An Exploratory Study of the Prevalence of Sexual Abuse in a Sample of 16-21 Year Olds*. Child Abuse Studies Unit. London: PNL.

Kennedy, M. (1989) 'The abuse of deaf children.' *Child Abuse Review 3*, 1, 3–6.

Kennedy, M. (1996) 'Sexual abuse and disabled children.' In J. Morris (ed.) *Encounters with Strangers, Feminism and Disability, the Major Issues Confronting Feminism Today*. London: The Women's Press.

Kennedy, M. (2000) 'Disability and child abuse.' In K. Wilson and A. James (eds) *The Child Protection Handbook*. 2nd edition. Edinburgh: Harcourt..

Kenny, K. (2001) 'Child abuse reporting: teachers perceived deterrents.' In *Child Abuse and Neglect 25*, 81–92.

Kitzinger, C. and Wilkinson, S. (1996) 'Theorizing representing the other.' In Wilkinson, S. and Kitzinger, C. (eds) *Representing the Other*. London: Sage Publications.

Kliewer, C. and Drake, S. (1998) 'Disability, eugenics and the current ideology of segregation: a modern moral tale.' *Disability and Society 13*, 1, 95–111.

Knutson, J. and Sullivan, P. (1993) 'Communication disorders as risk factors in abuse.' *Topics in Language Disorders 13*, 1–14.

Koch, T. (2000) 'Life quality versus the quality of life: assumptions underlying prospective quality of life instruments in health care planning.' *Social Science and Medicine 51*, 3, 419–427.

Kübler-Ross, E. (1969) *On Death and Dying: What the Dying Have to Teach Doctors, Nurses, Clergy and Their Own Families*. New York: Macmillan.

Kuhse, H. and Singer, P. (1985) *Should the Baby Live? The Problems of Handicapped Infants*. London: Oxford University Press.

Kvam, M. (2004) 'Sexual abuse of deaf children. A retrospective analysis of the prevalence and characteristics of childhood sexual abuse among deaf adults in Norway.' *Child Abuse and Neglect 28*, 241–251.

Lancaster, E. and Lumb, J. (1999) 'Bridging the gap: feminist theory and practice reality in work with the perpetrators of child sexual abuse.' *Child and Family Social Work 4*, 119–129.

Leder, D. (1990) *The Absent Body*. Chicago: Chicago University Press.

Lee, P. (2002) 'The pro-life argument from substantial identity.' *Bioethics 18*, 3, 249–263.

Lee, R. (1993) 'Asking sensitive questions: interviewing.' In R. Lee (ed.) *Doing Research on Sensitive Topics*. London: Sage.

Linde, C. (1993) *The Creation of Coherence in Life Stories: An Overview*. New York: Oxford University Press.

Lindsay, S. and Read, D. (1994) 'Psychotherapy and memories of childhood sexual abuse: a cognitive perspective.' *Applied Cognitive Psychology 8*, 281–338.

Loewenstein, R. (1991) 'An office mental status examination for complex chronic dissociative symptoms and multiple personality disorder.' *Psychiatric Clinics of North America 14*, 3, 567–604.

Loftus, E. (1993) 'The reality of repressed memories.' *American Psychologist 48*, 5, 518–537.

London, K., Bruck, M., Ceci, S. and Shuman, D. (2005) 'Disclosure of child sexual abuse: what does the research tell us about the ways that children tell?' *Psychology, Public Policy and Law 11*, 1, 194–226.

Love, A., Cooke, P. and Taylor, P. (2003) 'The criminal justice system and disabled children.' In *It Doesn't Happen to Disabled Children: Child Protection and Disabled Children*. Report of the National Working Group on Child Protection and Disability. London: NSPCC.

Lupton, D. (1994) *Medicine as Culture: Illness, Disease and the Body in Western Society*. London: Sage.

Macfarlane, A. (1994) 'Watershed.' In L. Keith (ed.) *Mustn't Grumble: Writing by Disabled Women*. London: The Women's Press.

MacFarlane, K. and Korbin, J. (1983) 'Confronting the incest secret long after the fact: a family study of multiple victimization with strategies for intervention.' *Child Abuse and Neglect 7*, 225–243.

MacFie, J., Cicchetti, D. and Toth, S. (2001) 'Dissociation in maltreated versus non-maltreated preschool-aged children.' *Child Abuse and Neglect 25*, 1253–1267.

MacKay, R. (2003) 'Tell them who I was: the social construction of aphasia.' *Disability and Society 18*, 6, 811–826.

Maine, D.R. (1993) 'Narrative's moment and sociology's phenomenon: towards a narrative sociology.' *Sociological Quarterly 34*, 1, 17–37.

Malloy, H. and Vasil, L. (2002) 'The social construction of Asperger's syndrome: the pathologising of difference?' *Disability and Society 17*, 659–669.

Mann, C. and Stewart, F. (2000) *Internet Communication and Qualitative Research: A Handbook for Researching Online*. London: Sage Publications Ltd.

Marchant, R. and Page, M. (2003) 'Child protection practice with disabled children.' In *It Doesn't Happen to Disabled Children: Child Protection and Disabled Children*. Report of the National Working Group on Child Protection and Disability. London: NSPCC.

Marks, D. (1999a) *Disability: Controversial Debates and Psychosocial Perspectives*. London: Routledge.

Marks, D. (1999b) 'Dimensions of oppression: theorising the embodied subject.' *Disability and Society 14*, 5, 611–626.

Marshall, P. (1997) *The Prevalence of Convictions for Sexual Offences*. Home Office Research Findings No. 55, RDS. London: Home Office.

Marshall, W. and Marshall, L. (2000) 'The origins of sexual offending.' *Trauma, Violence and Abuse 1*, 3, 250–263.

Marshall, W. and Mazzucco, A. (1995) 'Self-esteem and parental attachment in child molesters.' *Sexual Abuse: A Journal of Research and Treatment 7*, 279–285.

Marshall, W., Serran, G. and Cortoni, F. (2000) 'Childhood attachments, sexual abuse, and their relationship to adult coping in child molesters.' *Sexual Abuse: A Journal of Research and Treatment 12*, 17–26.

Martin, J.P. (1984) *Hospitals in Trouble*. Oxford: Basil Blackwell.

Masson, H. and Erooga, M. (1999) *Children and Young People who Sexually Abuse Others*. London: Routledge.

Masson, J. (1984) *The Assault on Truth: Freud's Suppression of the Seduction Theory*. New York: Harper Perennial.

Mayer, A. (1983) *Incest: A Treatment Manual for Therapy with Victims, Spouses and Offenders*. Holmes Beach, FL: Learning Publications.

McAdams, D. (1993) *The Stories We Live By: Personal Myths and the Making of the Self*. New York: The Guilford Press.

McCarron, A.L., Ridgeway, S. and Williams, A. (2004) 'The truth and lie story: developing a tool for assessing child witnesses' ability to differentiate between truth and lies.' *Child Abuse Review 13*, 43–50.

McDonald, C. (2006) *Challenging Social Work: The Context of Practice*. Houndmills: Palgrave Macmillan.

McLeod, J. (1997) *Narrative and Psychotherapy*. London: Sage Publications.

McLeod, M. and Saraga, E. (1988) 'Challenging the orthodoxy: towards a feminist theory and practice.' *Feminist Review 28*, 16–55.

McNulty, C. and Wardle, J. (1994) 'Adult disclosure of sexual abuse; a primary cause of psychological distress.' *Child Abuse and Neglect 18*, 7, 549–555.

Middleton, L. (1992) *Children First: Working with Children and Disability*. Birmingham: Venture Press.

Middleton, L. (1999) *Disabled Children: Challenging Social Exclusion*. Oxford: Blackwell Science.

Miller, A. (1984) *Thou Shalt Not Be Aware: Society's Betrayal of the Child*. London: Pluto Press.

Miller, D., McCluskey-Fawcett, K. and Irving, L. (1993) 'The relationship between childhood sexual abuse and subsequent onset of bulimia nervosa.' *Child Abuse and Neglect 17*, 305–314.

Mollon, P. (1996) 'Incest, false accusations of incest and false denials of incest. Discerning the truth in the debate about recovered memory.' *Journal of Mental Health 5*, 2, 167–172.

Moran, P., Vuchinich, S. and Hall, N. (2004) 'Associations between types of maltreatment and substance use during adolescence.' *Child Abuse and Neglect 28*, 565–574.

Morris, J. (1991) *Pride Against Prejudice: Transforming Attitudes to Disability.* London: Women's Press.

Morris, J. (1992) 'Personal and political: a feminist perspective on researching physical disability.' *Disability, Handicap and Society 7*, 2, 157–166.

Morris, J. (1999) 'Disabled children, child protection systems and the Children Act.' *Child Abuse Review 8*, 91–108.

Morris, J., Abbott, D. and Ward, L. (2002) 'At home or away? An exploration of policy and practice in the placement of disabled children at residential schools.' *Children and Society 16*, 3–16.

Mulder, R., Beautrais, A., Joyce, P. and Fergusson, D. (1998) 'Relationship between dissociation, childhood sexual abuse, childhood physical abuse, and mental illness in a general population sample.' *American Journal of Psychiatry 155*, 806–811.

Mullen, P., Martin, J., Anderson, J., Romans, S. and Herbison, G. (1994) 'The effect of child sexual abuse on social, interpersonal and sexual function in adult life.' *British Journal of Psychiatry 165*, 35–47.

Muris, P. and Maas, A. (2004) 'Strengths and difficulties as correlates of attachment style in institutionalised and non-institutionalised children with below average intellectual abilities.' *Child Psychiatry and Human Development 34*, 317–328.

Murray, P. and Penman, J. (1996) *Let Our Children Be: A Collection of Stories.* Sheffield: Parents With Attitude.

Naples, N. (2003) 'Deconstructing and locating survivor discourse: dynamics of narrative, empowerment and resistance for survivors of childhood sexual abuse.' *Signs: Journal of Woman in Culture and Society 28*, 4, 1151–1185.

Neimeyer, R. and Stewart, A. (1996) 'Trauma, healing and the narrative emplotment of loss.' *Families in Society: Journal of Contemporary Human Services, June*, 360–375.

Nelson, S. (2002) 'Physical symptoms in sexually abused women: somatisation or undetected injury?' *Child Abuse and Neglect 11*, 51–64.

Neuman Kulp, E. (1991) 'Grieving the loss of narcissistic entitlement: a case study.' *Journal of College Student Psychotherapy 5*, 4, 45–65.

Newman, E., Kaloupek, D., Keane, T. and Folstein, S. (1997) 'Ethical issues in trauma research: the evolution of an empirical model for decision-making.' In G. Kantor and J. Jasinski (eds) *Out of the Darkness: Contemporary Perspectives on Family Violence.* Thousand Oaks, CA: Sage Publications.

Newman, E., Walker, E.A. and Gefland, A. (1999) 'Assessing the ethical costs and benefits of trauma-focused research.' *General Hospital Psychiatry 21*, 187–196.

Niederberger, J. (2002) 'The perpetrators strategy as a crucial variable: a representative study of sexual abuse of girls and its sequelae in Switzerland.' *Child Abuse and Neglect 26*, 1, 55–71.

Noll, J., Trinkett, P. and Putnam, F. (2003) 'A prospective investigation of the impact of childhood sexual abuse on the development of sexuality.' *Journal of Consulting and Clinical Psychology 71*, 3, 575–586.

Nosek, M. and Howland, C. (1998) *Abuse and Women with Disabilities.* Available at http://new.vawnet.org/category/Main_Doc.php?docid=369, accessed 15 September 2009.

Nosek, M., Clubb Foley, C., Hughes, R. and Howland, C. (2001) 'Vulnerabilities for abuse among women with disabilities.' *Sexuality and Disability 19*, 3, 177–189.

NSPCC (2006) *The NSPCC's Response to the Home Office Child Sexual Offenders Review.* Available at www.nspcc.org.uk/Inform/policyandpublicaffairs/Consultations/2006/child_sex_offender_review_wdf48619.pdf, accessed 15 September 2009.

O'Toole, R., Webster, S., O'Toole, A. and Lucal B. (1999) 'Teachers' recognition and reporting of child abuse: a factorial survey – improving system response to mandate reports.' *Child Abuse and Neglect 23*, 11, 1083–1101.

Oakley, A. (1981) 'Interviewing women: a contradiction in terms.' In H. Robert (ed.) *Doing Feminist Research.* London: Routledge and Keegan Paul.

Oates, K. and Cohen Donnelly, A. (2000) *Classic Papers in Child Abuse.* Thousand Oaks, CA: Sage Publications Inc.

Ochs, E. and Capps, L. (1996) 'Narrating the self.' *Annual Review of Anthropology 25*, 19–43.

Oliver, M. (1992) 'Changing the social relations of research production.' *Disability, Handicap and Society* 7, 2, 101–114.

Oliver, M. (1997): 'Emancipatory research: realistic goal or impossible dream?' In C. Barnes and G. Mercer (eds) *Doing Disability Research*. Leeds: The Disability Press.

Oliver, M. (1998) 'Theories of disability in health practice and research.' *British Medical Journal, 317,* 1446–1449.

Oppenheimer, L. (2002) 'Self or selves? Dissociative identity disorder and complexity of the self-system.' *Theory and Psychology 12,* 1, 97–128.

Orbach, S. (1993) *Hunger Strike: The Classic Account of the Social and Cultural Phenomenon Underlying Anorexia and Other Eating Problems.* London: Penguin Books.

Oswin, M. (1971) *The Empty Hours: A Study of the Week-end Life of Handicapped Children in Institutions.* London: The Penguin Press.

Peace, B. (2002) 'Rethinking empowerment: a postmodern reappraisal for emancipatory practice.' *British Journal of Social Work, 32,* 135–47.

Peters, S. (2000) 'Is there a disability culture? A syncretisation of three possible world views.' *Disability and Society 15,* 4, 583–601.

Phillips, A. and Daniluk, J. (2004) 'Beyond "survivor": how childhood sexual abuse informs the identity of adult women at the end of the therapeutic process.' *Journal of Counselling and Development 82,* 2, 177–184.

Plummer, K. (1995) *Telling Sexual Stories; Power, Change and Social Worlds.* London: Routledge.

Plummer, K. (2001) *Documents of Life: An Invitation to Critical Humanism.* London: Sage Publications.

Polkinghorne, D.E. (1988) *Narrative Knowing and the Human Sciences.* Albany: State University of New York Press.

Priestley, M. (1997) 'Whose research? A personal audit.' In C. Barnes and G. Mercer (eds) *Doing Disability Research.* Leeds: The Disability Press.

Priestley, M. (1999) *Disability Politics and Community Care.* London: Jessica Kingsley Publishers.

Prior, V., Glaser, D. and Lynch, M. (1997) 'Responding to child sexual abuse: the criminal justice system.' *Child Abuse Review 6,* 128–140.

Provus McElroy, L. (1992) 'Early indicators of pathological dissociation in sexually abused children.' *Child Abuse and Neglect 16,* 833–846.

Putnam, F. (1997) *Dissociation in Children and Adolescents: A Developmental Perspective.* New York: Guilford Press.

Quarmby, K. (2008) *Getting Away with Murder: Disabled People's Experiences of Hate Crime in the UK.* London: Scope.

Rabiee, P., Sloper, P. and Beresford, B. (2005) 'Doing research with children and young people who do not use speech for communication.' Available at http://eprints.whiterose.ac.uk/1628/1/speech.pdf, accessed 15 September 2009.

Read, J. (2000) *Disability, the Family and Society: Listening to Mothers.* Buckingham: Open University Press.

Read, J. and Clements, L. (2001) *Disabled Children and the Law: Research and Good Practice.* London: Jessica Kingsley Publishers.

Reavey, P. (2003) 'When past meets present to produce a sexual "other": examining professional and everyday narratives of child sexual abuse and sexuality.' In P. Reavey and S. Warner (eds) *New Feminist Stories of Child Sexual Abuse: Sexual Scripts and Dangerous Dialogues.* London: Routledge.

Reavey, P. and Gough, B. (2000) 'Dis/locating blame: survivors' constructions of self and sexual abuse.' *Sexualities 3,* 3, 325–346.

Reavey, P. and Warner, S. (2003) *New Feminist Stories of Child Sexual Abuse: Sexual Scripts and Dangerous Dialogues.* London: Routledge.

Reeve, D. (2002) 'Negotiating psycho-emotional dimensions of disability and their influence on identity constructions.' *Disability and Society 17,* 5, 493–508.

Reynolds, A. and Pope, R. (1991) 'The complexities of diversity: exploring multiple oppressions.' *Journal of Counselling and Development 70,* 174–180.

Ribbens, J. (1989) 'Interviewing – an unnatural situation?' *Women Studies International Forum 12,* 6, 579–592.

Robertson, J. (1952) *A Two-year Old Goes to Hospital (film).* Ipswich: Concord Films Council.

Robson, K. (2001) 'Curative fictions: the "narrative cure" in Judith Herman's trauma and recovery and Chantal Chawaf's le manteau noir.' *Cultural Values 5,* 1, 115–130.

Roelofs, K., Keijsers, G., Hoogduin, K., Naring, G. and Moene, F. (2002) 'Childhood abuse in patients with conversion disorder.' *American Journal of Psychiatry 159,* 11, 1908–1913.

Roets, G. and Van Hove, G. (2003) 'The story of Belle, Minnie, Louise and the Sovjets: throwing light on the dark side of an institution.' *Disability and Society 18,* 5, 599–624.

Rosenthal, G. (1993) 'Reconstruction of life stories: principles of selection in generating stories for narrative biographical interviews.' In R. Josselson and A. Lieblich (eds) *The Narrative Study of Lives.* Newbury Park, CA: Sage Publications.

Ross, M. and Buehler, R. (1994) 'Creative remembering.' In U. Neisser and R. Fivush (eds) *The Remembering Self: Construction and Accuracy in the Self-Narrative.* New York: Cambridge University Press.

Royce Baerger, D. and McAdams, D. (1999) 'Life story coherence and its relation to psychological well-being.' *Narrative Inquiry 9,* 1, 69–96.

Runswick-Cole, K. (2007) '"The Tribunal was the most stressful thing: more stressful than my son's diagnosis or behaviour": the experiences of families who go to the Special Educational Needs and Disability Tribunal.' *Disability and Society, 22* 3, 315–328.

Russell, D. (1986) *The Secret Trauma: Incest in the Lives of Girls and Women.* New York: Basic Books.

Russell, D. and Bolen, R. (2000) *The Epidemic of Rape and Sexual Abuse in the United States.* Thousand Oaks, CA: Sage.

Rutter, M. (1972) *Maternal Deprivation Reassessed.* Harmondsworth: Penguin.

Salaman, G. (1979) *Work Organisations, Resistance and Control.* London: Routledge and Kegan Paul.

Saraga, E. and MacLeod, M. (1997) 'False memory syndrome: theory or defence against reality.' *Feminism and Psychology 7,* 1, 46–51.

Scott, S. (1998) 'Here be dragons: researching the unbelievable, hearing the unthinkable. A feminist sociologist in uncharted territory.' *Sociological Research Online 3,* 3.

Scott, S. (2001) 'Surviving selves: feminism and contemporary discourses of child sexual abuse.' *Feminist Theory 2,* 3, 349–361.

Scott, S., Jackson, S. and Backett-Milburn, K. (1998) 'Swings and roundabouts: risk, anxiety and the everyday worlds of children.' *Sociology 32,* 4, 689–705.

Sgroi, S. and Sargent, N. (1993) 'Impact and treatment issues for victims of childhood sexual abuse by female perpetrators.' In M. Elliot (ed) *Female Sexual Abuse of Children.* New York: Guilford Press.

Shakespeare, T. (1993) 'Disabled people's self-organisation: a new social movement?' *Disability, Handicap and Society 8,* 249–264.

Shakespeare, T. (1996a) 'Power and prejudice: issues of gender, sexuality and disability.' In L. Barton (ed.) *Disability and Society: Emerging Issues and Insights.* Essex: Addison Wesley Longman.

Shakespeare, T. (1996b) 'Disability, identity and difference.' In C. Barnes and G. Mercer (eds) *Exploring the Divide: Illness and Disability.* Leeds: The Disability Press.

Shakespeare, T. (1997) 'Cultural representation of disabled people: dustbins for disavowal?' In L. Barton (ed.) *Disability Studies: Past, Present and Future.* Leeds: The Disability Press.

Shakespeare, T. (1998) 'Choices and rights: eugenics, genetics and disability equality.' *Disability and Society 13,* 5, 665–681.

Shakespeare, T. (1999) 'The sexual politics of disabled masculinity.' *Sexuality and Masculinity 17,* 1, 53–64.

Shakespeare, T. (2000) 'Disabled sexuality: towards rights and recognition.' *Sexuality and Disability 18,* 3, 159–166.

Shakespeare, T., Gillespie-Sells, K. and Davies, D. (1996) *The Sexual Politics of Disability.* London: Cassell.

Shaw, L. (1998) 'Children's experiences of school.' In C. Robinson and K. Stalker (eds) *Growing up with Disability.* London: Jessica Kingsley Publishers.

Sheldon, A. (2004) 'Women and disability.' In J. Swain, S. French, C. Barnes and C. Thomas (eds) *Disabling Barriers – Enabling Environment.* London: Sage Publications.

Shuttleworth, R. (2000) 'The search for sexual intimacy for men with cerebral palsy.' *Sexuality and Disability 18,* 4, 263–282.

Simon, D. (1998) *Guiding Recovery from Child Sexual Abuse: Horizons of Hope.* London: Jessica Kingsley Publishers.

Sin, C. H. (2005) 'Seeking informed consent: reflections on research practice.' *Sociology 39,* 2, 277–294.

Sinason, V. (undated) Untitled paper. London: Tavistock and Portman Clinics Special Committee.

Singer, P. (1993) *Practical Ethics.* Cambridge: Cambridge University Press.

Sivers, H., Schooler, J. and Freyd, J. (2002) 'Recovered memories.' *Encyclopedia of the Human Brain 4,* 169–184.

Smallbone, S. and McCabe, B. (2003) 'Childhood attachment, childhood sexual abuse, and onset of masturbation among adult sex offenders.' In *Sexual Abuse: A Journal of Research and Treatment 15,* 1, 1–9.

Snell, S. and Rosen, K. (1997) 'Parents of special needs children: mastering the job of parenting.' *Contemporary Family Therapy 19, 3,* 425–442.

Sobsey, D. (1994) *Violence and Abuse in the Lives of People With Disabilities: The End of Silent Acceptance?* Baltimore: Paul H. Brookes.

Sobsey, D. and Doe, T. (1991) 'Patterns of sexual abuse and assault.' *Sexuality and Disability 9,* 3, 243–259.

Sobsey, D., and Mansell, S. (1994) 'Sexual abuse patterns of children with disabilities.' *International Journal of Children's Rights 2,* 96–100.

Sobsey, D. Randall, W. and Parrila, R.K. (1997) 'Gender differences in abused children with and without disabilities.' *Child Abuse and Neglect 21,* 8, 707–720.

Solomon, J. (1992) 'Child sexual abuse by family members: a feminist perspective.' *Sex Roles 27,* 9/10, 473–485.

Spatz Widom, C. and Ashley Ames, M. (1994) 'Criminal consequences of childhood sexual victimization.' *Child Abuse and Neglect 18,* 4, 303–318.

Spence, D. (1982) *Narrative Truth and Historical Truth, Meaning and Interpretation in Psychoanalysis.* London: W. W. Norton.

Stanley, L. (1990) 'Feminist praxis and the academic mode of research production.' In L. Stanley (ed.) *Feminist Praxis: Research, Theory and Epistemology in Feminist Sociology.* London: Routledge.

Stanley, L. and Wise, S. (1990) 'Method, methodology and epistemology in feminist research processes.' In L. Stanley (ed.) *Feminist Praxis: Research, Theory and Epistemology in Feminist Sociology.* London: Routledge.

Stanley, L. and Wise, S. (1983) *Breaking Out: Consciousness and Feminist Research.* London: Routledge and Keegan Paul.

Statham, J. and Read, J. (1998) 'The pre-school years.' In C. Robinson and K. Stalker (eds) *Growing Up With Disability.* London: Jessica Kingsley Publishers.

Stern, D. (1985) *The Interpersonal World of the Infant: A View from Psychoanalysis and Developmental Psychology.* New York: Basic Books.

Stuart-Green, L. and Stone, J. (1996) 'The sexual abuse of children with visual impairments.' *The British Journal of Visual Impairment 14,* 2, 59–61.

Sullivan, P. and Beech, A. (2002) 'Professional perpetrators: sex offenders who use their employment to target and sexually abuse the children with whom they work.' *Child Abuse Review 11,* 153–167.

Sullivan, P. and Knutson, J. (1998) 'The association between child maltreatment and disabilities in a hospital-based epidemiological study.' *Child Abuse and Neglect 22,* 4, 271–288.

Sullivan, P. and Knutson, J. (2000) 'Maltreatment and disabilities: a population based epidemiological study.' *Child Abuse and Neglect 24,* 10, 1257–1273.

Sullivan, P., Vernon, M.C. and Scanlan, J. (1987) 'Sexual abuse of deaf youth.' *American Annals of the Deaf,* October, 256–262.

Summit, D. (1983) 'The child sexual abuse accommodation syndrome.' In K. Oates and A. Cohn-Donnelly (eds) *Classic Papers in Child Abuse.* London: Sage Publications.

Sutherland, A. (1981) *Disabled We Stand.* London: Souvenir Press.

Swain, J. and Cameron, C. (1999) 'Unless otherwise stated: discourses of labelling and identity in coming out.' In M. Corker and S. French (eds) *Disability Discourse.* Buckingham: Open University Press.

Swain, J. and French, S. (2000) 'Towards an affirmation model of disability.' *Disability and Society 15,* 4, 569–582.

Swain, J. and French, S. (2008) 'There but for fortune.' In J. Swain and S. French (eds) *Disability on Equal Terms: Understanding and Valuing Difference in Health and Social Care.* London: Sage Publications.

Swain, J. and Gillman, M. (2000) 'Narrative approaches to research.' In S. French, F. Reynolds and J. Swain (eds) *Practical Research: A Guide for Therapists 2nd Edition.* Oxford: Butterworth-Heinemann.

Swain, J., Griffiths, C. and Heyman, B. (2003) 'Towards a social model approach to counselling disabled clients.' *British Journal of Guidance and Counselling 31,* 1, 137–152.

Swain, J., Heyman, B. and Gillman, M. (1998) 'Public research, private concerns: ethical issues in the use of open-ended interviews with people who have learning difficulties.' *Disability and Society 13,* 2, 21–36.

Swanston, H., Parkinson, P., O'Toole, B., Plunkett, A. *et al.* (2003) 'Juvenile crime, aggression and delinquency after sexual abuse.' *British Journal of Criminology 13,* 729–749.

Swatton, S. and O'Callaghan, J. (1999) 'The experience of "healing stories" in the life narrative: a grounded theory.' *Counselling Psychology Quarterly 12,* 4, 413–429.

Terr, L. (1991) 'Childhood traumas: an outline and overview.' *American Journal of Psychiatry 148,* 1, 10–20.

Thomas, C. (1997) 'The baby and the bathwater: disabled women and motherhood in social context.' *Sociology of Health and Illness 19,* 5, 622–643.

Thomas, C. (1998) 'Parents and family, disabled women's stories about their childhood experiences.' In C. Robinson and K. Stalker (eds) *Growing Up with Disability.* London: Jessica Kingsley Publishers.

Thomas, C. (1999) *Female Forms: Experiencing and Understanding Disability.* Buckingham: Open University Press.

Thomas, C. (2004) 'How is disability understood? An examination of sociological approaches.' *Disability and Society 19,* 6, 569–583.

Thomas P., Gradwell, L. and Markham N. (1997) 'Defining impairment within the social model of disability.' *Greater Manchester Coalition of Disabled People, July.* Available at www.leeds.ac.uk/disability-studies/archiveuk/thomas%20pam/Defining%20Impairment%20within%20the%20Social%20Model%20of%20Disability.pdf, accessed 15 September 2009.

Thompson, B. (1995) 'Ethical dimensions in trauma research.' *American Sociologist 26,* 2, 54–69.

Thompson, N. (2003) *Promoting Equality, Challenging Discrimination and Oppression.* Basingstoke: Palgrave Macmillan.

Tominson, A. (1995) 'Update on child sexual abuse.' *Issues in Child Abuse Prevention 5, Summer.* Available at www.aifs.gov.au/nch/pubs/issues/issues5/issues5.html, accessed 15 September 2009.

Triangle/NSPCC (2001) *Two Way Street.* London: NSPCC.

Turrell, S. and Armsworth, M. (2000) 'Differentiating incest survivors who self-mutilate.' *Child Abuse and Neglect 24,* 2, 237–249.

Tuval-Mashiach, R., Freedman, S., Bargai, N., Boker, R., Hadar, H. and Shalev, A. (2004) 'Coping with trauma: narrative and cognitive perspectives.' *Psychiatry 67,* 3.

Uehara, E., Farris, M., Morelli, P. and Ishisaka, A. (2001) '"Eloquent chaos" in the oral discourse of killing fields survivors: an exploration of atrocity and narrativization.' *Culture, Medicine and Psychiatry 25,* 29–61.

van der Kolk, B. and Fisler, R. (1995) 'Dissociation and the fragmentary nature of traumatic memories: overview and exploratory study.' *Journal of Traumatic Stress 8,* 4, 505–525.

van der Kolk, B. and van der Hart, O. (1991) 'The intrusive past: the flexibility of memory and the engraving of trauma.' *American Imago 48,* 4, 425–454.

van der Kolk, B., van der Hart, O. and Marmar, C. (1996) 'Dissociation and information processing in posttraumatic stress disorder.' In B. van der Kolk, A. McFarlane and L. Weisaeth (eds) *Traumatic Stress: The Effects of Overwhelming Experience on Mind, Body and Society.* New York: Guilford Press.

Van Lenning, A. (2004) 'The body as crowbar, transcending or stretching sex?' *Feminist Theory 5,* 1, 25–47.

Vangelisti, A. (1994) 'Family secrets: forms, functions and correlates.' *Journal of Social and Personal Relationships 11,* 113–135.

Vernon, A. (1997) 'Reflexivity: the dilemmas of researching from the inside.' In C. Barnes and G. Mercer (eds) *Doing Disability Research.* Leeds: The Disability Press.

Vernon, A. (1999) 'The dialectics of multiple identities and the disabled people's movement.' *Disability and Society 14,* 3, 385–398.

Walby, S. (1990) *Theorising Patriarchy.* Cambridge: Basil Blackwell.

Walmsley, J. (1993) 'Explaining.' In P. Shakespeare, D. Atkinson and S. French (eds) *Reflecting Research Practice Issues in Health and Social Welfare*. Buckingham: Open University Press.

Walmsley, J. (1998) 'Life history interviews with people with learning disabilities.' In R. Perks and A. Thompson (eds) *The Oral History Reader*. London: Routledge.

Walmsley, J. (2001) 'Normalisation, emancipatory research and inclusive research in learning disability.' *Disability and Society 16*, 2, 187–205.

Ward, E. (1984) *Father Daughter Rape*. London: Women's Press.

Wardhaugh, J. and Wilding, P. (1993) 'Towards an explanation of the corruption of care.' *Critical Social Policy 13*, 4–31.

Warner, S. (2001) 'Disrupting identity through visible therapy: a feminist post-structuralist approach to working with women who have experienced child sexual abuse.' *Feminist Review 68*, Summer, 115–139.

Waterhouse, R. (2000) *Lost in Care: Report on Child Abuse in North Wales*. London: The Stationary Office.

Watson, D., Abbott, D. and Townsley, R. (2007) 'Listen to me, too! Lessons from involving children with complex health care needs in research about multi-agency services.' *Child: Care, Health and Development 33*, 1, 90–95.

Watson, N. (2002) 'Well, I know that this is going to sound very strange to you, but I don't see myself as a disabled person: identity and disability.' *Disability and Society 17*, 5, 509–527.

Wendell, S. (1996) *The Rejected Body: Feminist Philosophical Reflections on Disability*. London: Routledge.

Westcott, H. (1993) *Abuse of Children and Adults with Disabilities*. London: NSPCC.

Westcott, H. and Cross, M. (1996) *This Far and No Further: Towards Ending the Abuse of Disabled Children*. Birmingham: Venture Press.

Westcott, H. and Jones, D. (1999) 'Annotation: the abuse of disabled children.' *Journal of Child Psychology and Psychiatry 40*, 4, 497–506.

Westcott, H. and Kyman, S. (2004) 'The application of a "story-telling" framework to investigate interviews for suspected child sexual abuse.' *Legal and Criminal Psychology 9*, 37–56.

White, M. (1993) 'Deconstruction and therapy.' In S. Gilligan and R. Price (eds) *Therapeutic Conversations*. New York: W. W. Norton.

Whitfield, C. (2001) 'The "false memory" defence: using disinformation and junk science in and out of court.' *Journal of Child Sexual Abuse 9*, 3, 53–75.

Wilde, A. (2004) 'Disabling masculinity: the isolation of a captive audience.' *Disability and Society 19*, 4, 355–370.

Williams, A. and Morris, J. (2003) 'Child protection and disabled children at residential special schools.' The Report of the National Working Group on Child Protection and Disability: *It Doesn't Happen to Disabled Children: Child Protection and Disabled Children*. London: NSPCC.

Williams, C. (1993) 'Vulnerable victims? A current awareness of the victimisation of people with learning difficulties.' *Disability, Handicap and Society 8*, 2, 161–172.

Williams, L. (1995) 'Recovered memories of abuse in women with documented child sexual victimisation histories.' *Journal of Traumatic Stress 8*, 4, 649–673.

Wolf, S.C. (1985) 'A multifactor model of deviant sexuality.' *Victimology 10*, 359–374.

Wolfensberger, W. (1994) 'The growing threat to the lives of handicapped people in the context of modernistic values.' *Disability and Society 9*, 3, 395–413.

Wyre, R. (2000) 'Paedophile characteristics and patterns of behaviour; developing and using a typology.' In C. Itzin (ed.) *Home Truths about Child Sexual Abuse: Influencing Policy and Practice: A Reader*. London: Routledge.

Young, L. (1992) 'Sexual abuse and the problem of embodiment.' *Child Abuse and Neglect 16*, 89–100.

Ystgaard, M., Hestetun, I., Loeb, M. and Mehlum, L. (2004) 'Is there a specific relationship between childhood sexual and physical abuse and repeated suicidal behaviour?' *Child Abuse and Neglect 28*, 863–875.

Zavirsek, D. (2002) 'Pictures and silences: memories of sexual abuse of disabled people.' *International Journal of Social Work 11*, 270–285.

Zimrin, H. (1986) 'A profile of survival.' *Child Abuse and Neglect 10*, 339–349.

Subject Index

Author Index